DECEIVED BY REASON

DECEIVED BY REASON

Our Categorical Attitude and the Nature of Things

A Historical Review and Critique
of Metaphysical Realism-Rationalism

Caroll Thomas Jacobs, Ph.D.

First Printing: January 2018

ISBN 978-0-9991187-2-6 paperback

Available as a paperback, online

ACKNOWLEDGEMENTS

In gratitude to the philosophers at Columbia University who gave me a solid foundation in the discipline. My thanks also to Stephanie Edgerton and Henry Perkinson at New York University for inculcating a critical and falsifiable attitude toward what we learn, teach, and accept as truth and knowledge.

A special thanks to Ruta Sevo without whom this work would not have seen the light.

TABLE OF CONTENTS

PART I   How a Categorical Approach
to the Cosmos Created Major
Unsolved Problems in Philosophy
and the Sciences

Introduction

Our rational approach to the cosmos was created by the first philosophers, the Pre-Socratic Phusikoi, in ancient Greece. In their work we find the beginnings of theoretical scientific thinking reflecting on what the world was made up of and the transformations it undergoes. The Phusikoi were searching for natural causes and reasoned explanations. Their focus was on physical substances, earth, air, fire, water observed in the processes and cycles of nature. Later thinkers added entities, which we are unable to apprehend through our senses; non-physical or "metaphysical" entities and powers, which they felt, were required, by thought and language, to make our experience of things in the natural world fully intelligible. Philosophy became increasingly sophisticated, especially in the works of Plato and Aristotle, both of whom in their different ways supplied whatever metaphysical factors (forms, essences, The Good, in Plato's case, one or more Unmoved Movers in Aristotle's). This was a reasoned and therefore logical way of understanding. Combining sensed actualities with metaphysical entities became the preferred, or standard, mode of understanding. It was honed to a fine art. It is known in philosophy as Metaphysical Realism-Rationalism.

Metaphysical Rationalism is alive and well today

through the efforts of philosophers, scientists, and especially mathematicians, over the centuries. However, all is not well under the umbrella of this dominant way of understanding for our philosophic and scientific heritage is one of unsolved problems surrounding the actualities of nature. Are the non-sensed or "real" factors part of the character or "natures" of the actual things generated by nature?

The unsolved problems emerged and were known quite early in the history of philosophy. I have selected three major ones, which will be subjected to critical analysis. These are the one-many problem, the problem caused by Plato's distinction and separation of reality (and its "real" or "ideal" entities) from actuality (and its actual entities), and the problem of the universals of language (i.e. what common nouns, for example, refer to). These early problems center on the imagined need and acceptance of metaphysics. As a result actual things in the experience of ordinary people became embraced by categories. An entangled mix of actual and real entities was the result. I will show why the categories and entanglements were thought necessary, what realists gained in creating real entities and realities, and how all this has affected our knowledge of things in our actual world while creating fictions and illusory worlds. When the metaphysical realities have been removed (and this is the central thread of the work) Metaphysical Rationalism's ways will be fully exposed and understood. Discovering that the natures of things have been falsified and that the universe is not what we have been taught to believe, the scope of Rationalism will need re-thinking. Since the structure of scientific theories depends on a rational approach involving valid "concepts" (which cannot be supplied) it will also require adjustments. It is not my aim to pursue either of those possibilities here. This work will focus only on those unsolved problems, which relate to our categorical attitude and the actual nature of things.

Chapter 1 From the Big Bang Came the Actualities of the Natural World

Astronomers, cosmologists, and particle physicists have been working for some time now, building a mathematical model of our cosmos from its explosive beginning to its probable end. The story they want to tell is from bang to return crunch or, more probably, dispersion of the cosmic stuff in the great void. Their aim is a theory that will comprehend all the entities and forces constituting nature and its physical processes.

Early fractions of the second after the creative bang have been comprehended in some detail. What some of the earlier cosmic stuff was and what it later became in the grip of newly evolving forces. Unexpectedly, however, more than 90% of what is out there (the so-called dark energy and matter) has not yet been identified.

Of the relatively stable materials known, the two lightest are the gases, hydrogen and helium, the stuff of stars. The nuclear furnaces of stars generate the heavier atoms, those depicted on the periodic table hanging in chemistry classrooms. Of the 118 reported, 92 elements are naturally occurring. The atoms of these elements are placed in families, showing relationships. It is their multitudinous combinations that add diversity to the universe and give us the great variety of things, living and non-living, we are aware of on earth.

The nuclei of atoms, the protons and neutrons, are composed of quarks. There are a host of other particles resulting from atom smashing. More smashing has occurred in the search for a unified theory over the last 20 years when in 1993 one scientist wrote:

> The world of elementary particles is getting to be a populous place. In the three families are the quarks (six of them, in three colors each), and the electron and its two heavier siblings, the muon and the tauon, each of which comes with a neutrino. That makes twenty-four particles, arranged into three families of eight. Outside the families are the lone photon and the eight gluons, along with one or more particles for the weak interaction another ten particles at least." (Lindley, 1993, p. 122)

My aim in giving the foregoing account is to prepare for our discussion of how human minds deal with what there is in the cosmos. What there is, is of fundamental importance to the sciences, for all such constitutes the universe which scientists want to understand. What there is are actualities and these actualities are determined to be so by observation and experiment. Those unimaginably small vibrating strings which have been proposed as the ultimate components of what there is, are not known actualities. Theory may or may not posit them down the road. Some say that by means of strings, sense can be made of all actualities, all the known forces, all the matter and energy. As mathematically generated hypothetical entities, strings are useful in

8

stretching our understanding (just as the notion of atoms was useful before atoms were discovered). However, we are reminded by Nobel physicist Sheldon Glashow that there is a distinction between a science such as physics and the inquiries we call philosophy. Physical theory is required to be tied to actualities and not float free of them no matter how satisfying the theory or how beautiful the mathematics.

The first philosophers, in the 6th century B.C.E., were interested in what there is and are celebrated for their inquiries. Back then, of course, philosophers were not scientists and did not hold to the important distinction Glashow makes between physics and philosophy. As a result, philosophy came to contain a host of non-actualities, which were thought necessary to make the world intelligible. These "meta-physical entities" are often claimed to be part of what there is, in one way or another. Scientists, among others, found some of them to be obstacles in their search for truths about the nature of the universe. It is my belief that such "entities" are also harmful to our intellectual health and that we ought to be rid of them. Others believe that we cannot formulate good scientific theories without them.

Philosophical proponents of metaphysical entities argue that while such entities may not be actual, they are real. We can apprehend them; we are told, by means of intuition (Plato's way) or visually (Aristotle's way).

A large stumbling block for the reader is the confusion caused by the words "real," "reality," and "real" (as in real entities). In this work (as in philosophy) those are metaphysical terms which in transiting from philosophy to common usage have undergone a reversal in meanings. Real, for Plato, is something not actual while his view of Reality transcends actuality, as heaven for believers transcends the earthly. Nor is real a higher kind of actuality.

As will become clear in this work, real and reality are metaphysical expressions (introduced early in the history of philosophy) with no validated reference to any actual entities or states. I will sometimes use m-real and m-reality for metaphysical entities and states to distinguish them from the modern but ambiguous use of real and reality and realism, which can and usually does refer to actual things and states. Ambiguity is endemic to the use of the terms real, reality, and realism in philosophy and contemporary writing and speech. My critical remarks concerning metaphysics and metaphysical entities and states will, of course, be explained and justified. I need to make a further point to aid our discussion down the road. Those who believe in the existence of metaphysical entities are called realists (i.e., m-realists). Those who do not believe metaphysical entities have existence of any sort are called nominalists. Traditional nominalism, however, does not put an end to m-realism as I will try to do because it has been unable to successfully put an end to belief in real or metaphysical entities. Unfortunately, while nominalism is an honorable position, by leaving the door open to realists it allows them to flourish. Realists and nominalists have been arguing with one another for centuries.

It is my aim to critique the claims of m-realists. On the way, we will focus on the categorical attitude, the actual natures of things, and the question of validity concerning the formation of concepts, categories, classes, and kinds. The critique will impact rationalism (i.e. the logic of inference), and also suggest the need to re-structure the theoretical modes of the sciences.

The intent of this work is admittedly broad. Realism of the metaphysical sort is in bed not only with philosophers, but scientists and mathematicians as well. It is an old truth that theologians are married to metaphysical realism (aka Metaphysics or, henceforth, M-R). She was the queen of the sciences in the Middle Ages. Metaphysics does not occupy so exalted a role these days. My analyses and critique will encompass only those parts of philosophy and science relevant in the history of metaphysical realism. Mathematics is also involved, so I will briefly pause to consider Zeno and his paradoxes and indicate the problems, which emerge when systems of pure mathematics are considered a part of the physical world.

Viewing the cosmos theoretically/mathematically is to view it in terms of concepts and entities which are not part of the cosmos; namely, by means of numbers, figures and universals. All of these are m-real entities, but the claim need not be made that they somehow exist. One may remain a nominalist. Empirical data from Millikan's experiments on the charge of the electron, for example, indicate that electrons are not too different, one from another, not that each is "identical" or "the same." They become identical or the same by a priori legislation and fiddling with the numbers and generalizing over the particular ones examined. Because the logic of the mathematical treatment of classes of physical, chemical and biological entities requires each of them to be identical (in some respect) or (over-all) the same, a mathematical reality (of oneness, sameness, or identity) covers up their ontological actuality and individuality.

Thus is born m-realism, the doctrine that there are

real entities and relations and that such entities and relations, called abstract, truly represent actual entities, relations, and processes. As a doctrine, m-realism is embedded in rationalism, the reasoning involved in inductive and deductive logic which uses real entities and relations in constructing models and theories and laws of the natural world.

Our current view of the cosmos is an achievement of the few who have been constructing it over the last twenty-five hundred years. The development of rationalism, which is the way of the sciences, began with the early Greeks. Along with rationalism came m-realism and, therefore, the problems which, because they were not solved, have worried philosophers and scientists for these two and a half millennia.

This work is both an attempt to understand the structure and function of m-realism-rationalism and its critique. It is also an attempt to view whatever there is in the world as it actually is and can and does become. It aims to solve those major philosophic problems we inherited when m-realism-rationalism became the dominant mode of thinking about ourselves and the world.

To be successful, the critique must do the following: first, it must point to the "nature" (or character) of actual things. That is, it must clearly explain whether or not actual things can be categorized. Secondly, it must show that our categorical attitude falsifies the actual natures of whatever things there are. In regard to the functioning of the categorical attitude, I must show that mistakes follow from three notions, which have been used to "unify" particulars (i.e., reduce their diversity) from the very beginning of philosophy. The three notions are identity, similarity or resemblance, and commonality.

It may sound strange, even arrogant, but the world is different in significant ways from what philosophers, mathematicians, theoretical scientists, and even ordinary folk imagine or construct and call the real world. What were the turns in philosophic thinking, which created m-realism, and what motivates its protection even today? As with so much else in philosophy, it began in ancient Greece.

Chapter 2 The First Major Philosophic Problem: One over Many

The Pre-Socratic Phusikoi

Between 600 and 400 B.C., the nature philosophers of Ionia and the Greek colonies of Italy and Sicily began the inquiries that we call philosophy and science. They were the first to give up mythological and religious explanations for the world in which they lived. Physical explanations about the world, its origin, current content, and processes, centered on one or more substances and the transformations or combinations which produced all the variety they observed.

These rational speculations vied with myths generated in and around Greece. The myths pointed to the belief, says Guthrie, that the world "arose from a primitive state of unity and the cosmogonic process was one of separation or division." (Edwards, 1972, p. 442).

The earlier myth-makers more often than not imagined the major components of the cosmos (e.g. earth, sky, water) as somehow human and requiring the motive force of one god or another to separate heaven and earth, or to stir the undefined mass of watery cloud or the primeval waters, and bring forth the great variety of living things.

Whether we begin with the anthropomorphic images of myth or imaginative rational explanation, diversity is viewed as something requiring explanation, and it is usually thought of as coming from a prior unity or oneness. For the earliest, and even for modern, scientists, thinking about the world as a totality is in terms of one and many, unity and separation. For the Greek nature philosophers, the Phusikoi, the "all" is usually "one" (the water of Thales, the undifferentiated of Anaximander, the air of Anaximenes, the fire of Heraclitus), but then it divides or separates into or generates diversity. For later philosophers such as Empedocles, the diverse (earth, air, fire, water) is already present and simply cycled and transformed into a multitude of things. For Leucippus and Democritus, the diverse atoms in the void combine and separate, producing the variety we observe. Heraclitus, a pre-Socratic, thought the diverse would return to the oneness that is fire and then generate the diverse again and again in eternal cycles.

If thinking about the Cosmos, then and now, is in terms of the pattern: first there was unity, then comes diversity, then we would like to know what exactly was the stuff that was "unified" and what made it one. Was there one indivisible force holding everything together (i.e., forceful unification of a multitude)? Such would still not be a one. How was unity brought about for it to be the beginning of the later diversity? We must rely on particle physicists who have gone cosmological in order to gain some insight about the what and how of the original stuff. Meanwhile, however, we can ask another question: how are we to understand the diversity that comes after the breakdown of the primordial unity. That is, how diverse is diversity? Is every bit that was

16

in, or comes out of, the alleged primordial unity *other and different* (non-identical, non-same) from every other or are the bits gathered into sub-unifications and therefore, as pluralities, somehow the same or identical? Lastly, if some plurality of these simple or complex bits of diversity is the same or unities, actually or in our view of them, whence comes their sameness or unity?

When we finish reading the fragments of the pre-Socratics we are left wondering. For either the primordial unity is not explained (as with Thales, Anaximander, Anaximenes, Heraclitus) or (as with Parmenides, whom we will focus on in greater detail later) it is explained, but in a way, that is unacceptable; that is, from Parmenides' eternal, unchanging, unified "one" we can get no actual, changing world.

We, on the front edge of the 21st century, are also left wondering when we try to imagine the unification within the Big, which occurred in something relatively quite small, just before it Banged. Primordial unification (whether of stuff or forces) that was total or complete is not just a mystery, it is a candidate for nonsense; if whatever there was absolutely unified, then why would it bang, generating diversity? Perhaps the Bang demonstrates that no unification (absolute steady state) was, or is, possible. Unity may be a temporary and apparent state of any number of cosmological banging balls, each of which is diverse, hence involving energies, forces, and entities which, in actuality, cannot be unified. The universe just may not generate anything other than diversity. Perhaps the only actuality which is not diverse is the void, or nothingness. Not being anything, nothingness cannot be unified nor can it give rise to anything. Perhaps the urge to

17

unify the cosmos, or natural parts of it, is quite mistaken, misdirected, having its source in a psychological aim normally directed toward the self or the social or the political or the religious.

The notions of oneness and unity with respect to the diverse contents of the cosmos became the first horn of the one-many problem in the history of philosophy and science. It is the horn which attracts m-realists, rationalists, idealists and accounts for about half of philosophy. The other horn of the one-many problem, the problem of diversity, attracts empiricists and accounts for the other half of philosophy. The tug of the one and the many has been exercising our minds for more than two and a half millennia. In fact, the so-called "mind" is not quite sure whether it is one or many or both or neither. Consciousness finds diversity inside and outside and immediately sets forth to unify it by some means, perhaps a concept or a "category."

The notion of oneness has exerted a powerful attraction, not only in religion, but also in philosophy and science as Parmenides and his rationalist-realist disciples demonstrate. Nonetheless, it is diversity that we want to understand, and in understanding it we will understand the nature of particular things.

What needs attention, then, in moving forward from the pre-Socratics to Plato and Aristotle and their followers, is the way cosmic diversity is handled. That is, on what basis are admittedly diverse entities unified, categorized, or comprehended as one?

Chapter 3 The Second Major Problem: Plato's Separating Metaphysical "Realities" from actualities, and Socrates' Search for Definitions Requires Plato's Ideal Forms

In the earlier dialogues of Plato, Socrates is in search of definitions. What, he asks, is friendship, justice, beauty, etc.? In fact, he wants to know what common nouns refer to. He prods Euthyphro, in the dialogue of that name, to tell him what is piety or holiness:

> "Well, bear in mind that what I asked of you was not to tell me one or two out of all the numerous actions that are holy; I wanted you to tell me what is the essential form of holiness which makes all holy actions holy. I believe you held that there is one ideal form by which unholy things are all unholy, and by which all holy things are holy. Do you remember?"
> Euthyphro answers, "I do."
> Socrates continues:
> "Well, then, show me what, precisely, this ideal is, so that, with my eye on it, and using it as a standard, I can say that any action done by you or anybody else

is holy if it *resembles* [my emphasis] this ideal, or, if it does not, can deny that it is holy." (Plato, 1964, p. 174)

By the give and take of dialectic, Plato's Socrates implies that we can think our way to intellectually seeing that some action resembles holiness itself, the form, the reality, which makes holy all that can be called "holy." Implied, too, is the notion that each common noun relates a form to its instances. This is the notion of definition. (See Endnote #1) Thus, using the common noun "man" correctly is to relate it to the instances (the particulars) of the form man. Plato is saying that particular men are instances of the form man because that which allegedly makes a man a man "resembles" the form man. To define the word man is to state what its form (or essence) is.

Socrates pursued the definitions of things, mostly virtues, but that pursuit must fail if Plato had not supplied the notion of forms. Definitions tell us what forms particular things and actions are related to (i.e., resemble). Of course, platonic forms are not among the changing particulars of this world. Since they are posits required to have definitions, they are *placed* in a transcendent *m-world* whose objects are not actual, but *m-real*. That *world* is metaphysical.

Readers of Plato often feel they are close to grasping a form, such as truth, beauty, goodness, or justice, but they never actually do. Focusing on definitions of those ideal or abstract forms and hoping they come close by their resemblance to them is all essentialist definers, who are m-realists, can do. Coming close is not to have a definition. To almost intellectually discriminate a form is not to grasp one.

M-realists hold on to their metaphysical posits, nominalists ignore them, while conceptualists feel they can grasp them by means of an intellectual tool they call a *concept*.

We might note that conceptualism is the third way of coming by definitions. If Socrates' eye could have turned to intellectually see the ideal, the form holy itself, then if he had also formed the mental image of that form, he would have a concept of holy. With this concept, he would be able to have that *standard* by which he could measure any action as to whether or not it was holy. Knowing what was holy, he would be in no doubt when applying the concept and the word to particular actions. To have a concept, then, is to have a definition. Of course, if one has trouble seeing the form, the concept of it will be difficult, if not impossible, to form. An incomplete or indistinct concept is no concept at all.

Defining is a veritable industry in philosophy and the sciences. Aristotle tells us that it began with Socrates, and he also incorporated it into his own philosophy. He was an m-realist along with Plato, and differed from Plato in holding that the essences of things are not transcendent forms (i.e., not separated from individuals), but are in each and every individual as its *nature*.

The essence made the individual the kind of thing it became when it was fully developed or realized. Plato's view of forms (separated from the individuals which they *resemble* and of which they are *instances*) is called "Ante Rem" realism. Aristotle's view is called "In Re" realism. Conceptualism, which enters the philosophical scene in the middle ages, is either in-the-head realism (i.e., the concept as a real entity) or logical realism (as with William of Ockham) in which the concept is a sign, of some plurality of things, having no ontological status.

We will critique the various forms of m-realism, but now we will try to dispose of *definition* because its aim of enclosed completeness and validity cannot be achieved.

We understand why Socrates pursued definitions (he wanted to know what the referents are for various common nouns). We understand that Plato wanted to supply what Socrates was looking for: the ideal form, which his definition encompassed, were it complete.

Why are definitions thought to be necessary? Language and its logic require valid categories, and defining is an attempt to classify. We can describe one particular or another, but we can't define one or even more than one of them. We can substitute one word for another, but substitution is not definition.

The particular things, actions, processes, and events in the world differ, but we are in the habit of saying those things, actions, processes, and events, are the *same* or are *identical* or, at least, *resemble* one another. If some of those things, actions, processes, events are the same or are identical or do resemble, then we can use one word for them, a noun "common" to them all. The word refers to what is common to them all, and stating what is common to them all (or stating the respect in which they resemble) is their definition. What's wrong with that? Well, if particulars because of their actual natures won't permit definition, then claiming a definition of them is in error, wrong-headed.

The only way to undermine and dispose of metaphysical realism (and the defining activity which is part of it) is to point to the ontological nature of actualities of things. What is the non-metaphysical nature of actual things?

This cannot be understood until our metaphysical impositions on actual things are removed. What are these impositions? Quite simply, the so-called identities, commonalities, similarities or resemblances. This in turn requires that we see through the illusory nature of each of those metaphysically imposed entities. When we have done the work required, we will understand that each particular or individual thing in the universe is ontologically (i.e., actually) other and different from every other, and that each particular thing is unique, and uniquely changing. If saying this gets to the truth of one thing and another, then definition must fail. If this is the truth of things, then metaphysical posits, those Platonic and Aristotelian forms are unnecessary; more, they falsify the natures of things, for each is unique, not an *instance* of a kind. Definition is the attempt to say what some particular thing is, in terms of something else, namely a class or kind or form or essence. That is surely ridiculous. A particular cow is not something else: it is not a class or a kind or a form or an essence. The particular piety of a particular person is not that of any other. However, traditionally, to define a particular is to classify it: its *form* is its class.

Definitions have been a major problem in philosophy and in the sciences because they are so difficult to come by. We can now understand why. Defining is an attempt to deal with diversity, with otherness and difference, which are insistent traits of the actualities of the cosmos.

Both definition and classification depend on some plurality of diverse particulars having a nature, which is their essence or form. If, however, each particular can be perceived as other and different from every other, then the notions of identity and sameness are called in question as criteria for forming classes and categories as well as in forming definitions. What remains as criteria for forming classes, categories and definitions of diverse particulars are their commonality (which involves identity or partial identity) or their resemblance or similarity. These criteria, and especially resemblance or similarity will be the focus of our attention in this historical review.

Chapter 4 A Third Major Philosophic Problem: The *UNIVERSALS* of Language

Aristotle's Universals and Logic

Aristotle viewed the fully functioning Cosmos as eternal. What he required were explanations of the movements and changes that he observed in terms of causes. He accepts the Empedoclean earth, air, fire, and water, but sees them as formed-matter; the underlying matter of each is unformed simple substance or substrate, which has no opposite and which can receive forms and qualities, even opposing ones such as fire and water. Primary substances are particular men and horses and other things. The genus or species that particular men and horses belong to are secondary substances. It is this secondary sense of substance, the formation of classes or categories of diverse things that requires our attention. These secondaries, the species and genera of particular things, are simply Plato's forms, brought to earth, but not actually, and placed (as posits) in things, and used by Aristotle for his own, especially logical, purposes.

The treatment of species and genera as substances occurs in Aristotle's early work, categories; in a later work, metaphysics, the notion of species and genera as substances is omitted and they are viewed as universals. (See Endnote #2)

What is a universal? Whatever can be attributed to many, says Aristotle. Whatever can be attributed to many is a form, such as a genus or species. On the one hand, then, Socrates belongs to the genus animal and the species man. Socrates can be said to be a man and also an animal, both universals. Whether viewed as secondary substances or universals, saying species and genera (or any classes) are actualities is nonsense; that is, we cannot sense the species, genus, class or category itself. All are m-constructions used for the m-realist's purposes.

Following Socrates, Aristotle focused on definitions and required them. That which made a particular thing to be the kind of thing it became (its form or essence) was its definition. He held that particulars themselves cannot be defined, or even known, but their species or genus are objects to be known and defined. His logic requires particulars to be definable in terms of their kinds (their species or genus) which are secondary substances or universals. Without universals, there simply is no logic, and no science, for Aristotle. This is clear from his remark:

> So demonstration does not necessarily imply the being of Forms nor a One beside a Many, but it does necessarily imply the possibility of truly predicating one of many; since without this possibility we cannot save the universal, and if the universal goes, the middle term goes with it, and so demonstration becomes impossible. We conclude, then, that there

must be a single identical term unequivocally predicable of a number of individuals. (McKeon, 1941, pp. 125-126)

The word "demonstration" here refers to logic, specifically, the syllogism. Note too that the requirement of "a single *identical* [my emphasis] term unequivocally predicable of a number of individuals" implies that some "number of individuals" each have something that is "identical." The notion of identity will be critiqued as we proceed.

Boethius and Porphyry Concerning Genus and Species

That we see particulars but not their species or genus is a fact (unless we can see essences, and we cannot) a truth of human perception. That those forms are intelligible (i.e., mentally apprehended) entities has been claimed by Plato, Aristotle, and Thomas Aquinas, among others. That there is some basis for them in actual particulars is also claimed. If one claims, as Plato and Aristotle and Aquinas do, that knowledge is not the result of the particulars that we see but of universals which particular things belong to or participate in, then we enter that lofty region of philosophy called metaphysics. The Problem of Universals begins with Plato and especially Aristotle, but the debate became heated only in the Middle Ages. Boethius, a 6th century philosopher, quotes a commentary on Aristotle's Categories by Porphyry, a 3rd century philosopher. Porphyry says:

I shall refuse to say concerning genera and species

whether they subsist or whether they are placed in the naked understandings alone or whether subsisting they are corporal or incorporal, and whether they are separated from sensibles or placed in sensibles and in accord with them. Questions of this sort are most exalted business and require very great diligence of inquiry. (McKeon, 1929, p. 91)

Boethius gave Aristotle's opinion of this "most exalted business:"

Since genera and species are thought, there-fore their likeness is gathered from the individuals in which they are, as the likeness of humanity is gathered from individual men unlike each other, which likeness conceived by the mind and perceived truly is made the species; again, when the likeness of these diverse species is considered, which cannot be except in the species themselves or in the individuals of the species, it forms the genus. Consequently, genera and species are in individuals, but they are thought universals; and species must be considered to be nothing other than the thought collected from the substantial likeness of individuals unlike in number, and genus the thought collected from the likeness of species. But this likeness when it is in individual things is made sensible, when it is in universals it is made intelligible; and in the same way when it is sensible, it remains in individuals, when it is understood, it is made universal.

Therefore, they subsist in sensibles, but they

are understood without bodies. ...Once these distinctions are made, therefore, the whole question, I believe, is solved. For genera and species subsist in one manner, but are understood in another; and they are incorporeal, but they subsist in sensible things joined to sensible things. (Ibid, pp. 97-98)

Boethius, I believe, read Aristotle correctly on the issue of species and genus if we also accept perceived identity as well as likeness in the construction of species and genera. Things that are unlike are viewed as having some "substantial likeness" (Aristotle's secondary substance). Thus likeness (similarity or resemblance) bears the burden for justifying our understanding of species and genera as well as for justifying the notion of their subsistence in things.

Boethius also gives his understanding of Plato on the issue of universals:

Plato, however, thinks that genera, and species, and the rest not only understood as universals, but also are and subsist without bodies; whereas Aristotle thinks that they are understood as incorporeal and universal, but subsist in sensibles; we have not considered it proper to determine between their opinions, for that is of more lofty philosophy. (Ibid)

Lofty philosophy, indeed. Of course, if we insist that particulars themselves can be known and species, genera or universals cannot, then we can ignore lofty metaphysics and epistemological life becomes simpler because ontology (the study of what there is) becomes more obvious and parsimonious. A further reward is that the notion of truth is brought down to earth and used with respect to changing actualities and our awareness of them and their changes.

We will argue that life can be simpler, and that the motivation driving the generation of universals is quite understandable: logicians and scientists need them to do their work. I believe major problems in philosophy (problems also inherited in our sciences) stem from the wrong-headedness involved in protecting logic and the classical view of science. The result is that the nature of particulars is ignored, the objects of knowledge are misplaced, and ontology is in a constant state of false pregnancy. To make my case, it will be necessary to look closely at what philosophers say there is (their ontology) and how they deal with it in order to gain knowledge (their epistemology).

Plato and Aristotle: Seeing Particulars and Cognizing "Universals"

We are in a position not too different from the mythmakers, the early Phusikoi, Plato, and Aristotle when it comes to wondering about all the diversity we observe on earth and out there in the unbounded nothingness. As with Plato and Aristotle, we see particular things and call them by individual and specific and generic names: this person, Socrates, is both man and animal; this person, Cratylus, is both man and animal. These particular persons are other and different, but they are said to belong to the same species and genus, and the species and genus are substances (man and animal) and universals. What is more, those substances or universals are not actual, as are the particular persons, Socrates and Cratylus, but are m-real or secondary substances and m-real universals are predicates (for Aristotle) and forms (for Plato). How particulars are related to universal predicates and forms (that is, to species and genera) is for Aristotle and Plato to explain.

Plato's explanation involves the positing of forms, such as species and genera, calling them "kinds," and placing them outside particulars and outside human minds. On the one hand, particulars reflect the eternal forms or kinds that they "are;" on the other hand, the eternal forms or kinds generate the particulars that belong to them. When we look at particular things, we are reminded of the m-real forms to which they belong: we see (perceive) particulars, but cognize (know) their forms.

Aristotle views each particular, formed-matter, such as Socrates or a goat or a tree, as having an essence (form) which makes the individual what it actually is. But Socrates is not entirely unique; that is, he does not have an essence that is only his. His essence (form) is the same as the one belonging to Cratylus and other men: individual essences, in other words, are identical, but there is only one form or essence for all men. Whoa! Only one real form, but a plurality of persons has it. That's a one-many problem. M-realists have some explaining to do. We will hear Aristotle out.

The primary substances of Socrates and Cratylus are other and different, but their secondary substance is the same. According to Aristotle, we see (perceive) particulars (concrete individual objects) but we cognize (know) them only by their secondary substances or what they universally are said to be.

Thus, for Aristotle as for Plato, to see (perceive) is not to know (cognize). Cognition requires the intellectual apprehension of the secondary substantiality or the universal with respect to the particular. A cardinal point in Aristotle's philosophy is that we cannot know particulars as particulars. A cardinal point in Plato's philosophy is that knowing is only related to unchanging, eternal objects, the forms.

How, then, can we cognize the universal or secondary substance when we are looking at particulars? As we indicated, for Plato it is a matter of remembering (for our souls were in contact with the forms before they were embodied; this amounts to innatism, which we will take up down the road). For Aristotle, according to a number of scholars, it is a matter of abstracting. If so, how do we abstract from particulars the secondary substance or universal?

Aristotle's discussion of a thing's nature, which is also its essence or form, clearly requires that it be in the individual, otherwise the individual, say Socrates, will not grow and become an adult (final form). Socrates' nature or essence, while forming his particular matter, is a kind belonging not only to him but to Plato as well; the principle of individuation is matter and that is what makes Socrates other than Plato. The problem here is the claim that a nature or essence is both in Socrates and yet also in others and so shared by all men.

Copleston, a historian of philosophy, has thought much about Aristotle's predicament and has this to say:

Strictly speaking...there is no objective universal for

Aristotle, but there is an objective foundation in things for the subjective universal in the mind. The universal "horse" is a subjective concept, but it has an objective foundation in substantial forms that inform particular horses. (Copleston, 1963, p. 45)

There are no universals out there, but when we look at the (primary) substantial forms of different individual horses, we form a subjective universal in our minds; we form a concept. We will see if this accords with Aristotle's way, but we might note another scholar's interpretation. Zeller remarked that a thing's essence, as a universal, is a concept denoting:

The common nature of particular substances. They can indeed be called unreal and derived substances but they may not be regarded as something subsisting outside the things themselves; they are not a one outside the many, but a one from the many. (Zeller, 1955, p. 192)

Both Copleston and Zeller agree that the common nature or universal does not exist out there (i.e., is not an objective entity); rather, particulars are out there and we form a concept of their individual essences. Aristotle might have accepted these interpretations, for he says, "a secondary substance is not an individual, but a class with a certain qualification; for it is not one and single as a primary substance is; the words 'man', 'animal', are predicable of more than one subject" (McKeon, 1929, p. 12). Zeller (1955) continues, "the essential element has a higher reality than the

33

individual qua individual and is the object of science" (p. 192).

If the essential element, *species*, is a higher reality than the individual organism, then by implication, the genus is even higher on the scale of reality; one can envision hierarchical levels all the way up to the unmoved mover. This is a meta-physics of being in the grand style. (See Ch. 26) However, Zeller responds to this "higher reality" of the essential element:

> It is, of course, a contradiction to attribute a higher reality to form, which is always a universal, in comparison to that which is a compound of form and matter and at the same time to assert that only the universal is the object of knowledge which is in itself the prior and better known. The results of this contradiction are to be observed throughout the whole Aristotelian system. (Zeller, ibid)

Without pursuing the disagreement between Zeller and Copleston (for the latter's response to Zeller, see p. 45ff.), we can make this observation: each of these scholars sees Aristotle as striving to become a nominalistic conceptualist; that is, one who believes only particulars exist and that those particulars can be conceptualized (as species and genera). William of Ockham argued that Aristotle was, indeed, a nominalistic conceptualist (see Tournay's remarks below).

The next, and crucial, point to examine is precisely the manner of obtaining the universal, the concept. How did Aristotle do it?

Sense-perception is innate in all animals, in some the sense-impression comes to persist...animals in which it does come into being have perception and can continue to retain the sense-impression in the soul: and when such persistence is frequently repeated a further distinction at once arises between those which out of the persistence of such sense-impressions develop a power of systematizing them and those which do not. So out of sense-perception comes to be what we call memory, and out of frequently repeated memories of the same thing develops experience; for a number of memories constitute a single experience. From experience again---i.e. from the universal now stabilized in its entirety within the soul, the one beside the many which is a single identity with them all---originate the skill of the craftsman and the knowledge of the man of science, skill in the sphere of coming to be and science in the sphere of being. (McKeon, 1941, p. 185)

As if struggling to make all this clear, he tries again:

When one of a number of logically indiscriminable particulars has made a stand, the earliest universal is present in the soul: for though the act of sense-perception is of the particular, its content is universal---is man, for example, not the man Callias. A fresh stand is made among these rudimentary universals, and the process does not cease until the indivisible concepts, the true universals, are established: e.g. such and such a species of animal is a step towards the genus animal, which by the same process is a step towards a further generalization... (Ibid)

Can the process described by Aristotle in these two quotes be rightly called abstraction? In the latter quote, when one of a number of logically indiscriminable particulars, say individuals among whom are Socrates and Plato and Callias, is present (as an image?) in the soul (mind), that particular (image) is a universal (an early one); viewing more individuals brings in more particulars (images?) to the soul (mind) and the process ceases when an indivisible concept, a true universal, is established. We must note that Aristotle begins not with perception, which can and does discriminate (for we can see that one individual differs from another); he begins with a number of men, whether he knows them or not, for as men, each is logically indiscriminable from another. He might also have started with ducks, goats or trees. From one man, any man, Aristotle notes his form; from other such observations, he notes the forms and finally, somehow, they all merge into one form, and this can be called a concept. Now just how a plurality of forms can unite or merge and become one form is a mystery that remains in Aristotle's account. In fact, it is the problem of one-many all over again, now played out with forms in the mind rather than sensible individuals in nature. As for whether or not the process described is *abstraction*, it is not unless we accept as abstraction that act which is prior to step one in Aristotle's account: ignoring individual differences in order to obtain a number of indiscriminable particulars. This amounts to blinding oneself, perceptually. But, ignoring differences is not a logical process. It is an act of omission, which feeds the needs of logic, namely, inventing a universal, for both logic and science require universals. The lengths to which writers go to manufacture universals and concepts is told in the pages of the history of philosophy dealing with the problem of definition, the problem of universals, the one-many problem, and the problem of species. As indicated, so important to logic and science are universals and concepts that emotions akin to religious fervor are brought forth to save and protect them. The ultimate act, of protection, of course, is to bury them in the deepest recesses of the brain as innate or priori productions. We will have something to say about this, later. (See Part III, Ch. 20)

The first quote adds a factor, identity, which makes the construction of a concept by the mind a little different process. Sense impressions of various individual things are retained in the mind (soul), we repeat sensing individual things, systematize the individuals (e.g., some are of men, others are of goats, still others are of trees), and form memories of these systematized individuals. From repeated memories of these individuals develops experience; that is, the process which develops experience from repeated memories of individuals that are systematized (grouped) also produces the universals as stable entities in the mind. They are the product of *seeing* the identity of some number of remembered sense impressions. A *one*, which is a single identity with them all, has been formed. This one is both concept and universal. We ask, as before, is this process abstraction? It obviously is not. What we have is an alleged seeing of identity in a plurality of differing individuals.

It appears that we must look for abstraction

37

elsewhere, perhaps in Thomas Aquinas or others (e.g., Kant) who came after him. (See Endnote #4)

Clearly, Aristotle, in the first quote, views the construction of a universal or concept as a matter of seeing the identity in some number of particular sense-impressions. This implies some activity on the part of the mind (and so offers a suggestion which may lead to the active intellect of Thomas Aquinas). The second quote suggests that a concept or universal can be formed by the mind, passively; by just allowing the impressions to merge into a oneness, or that any one of logically indiscriminable particulars is an exemplar. Now, just how a one can represent a plurality and so become exemplary of them is also a claim that must and will be examined. (See Part III)

Since we are now in pursuit of concepts as well as universals and the processes alleged to produce them (e.g., abstraction, or perceptual identity and resemblance recognition), we will proceed to Thomas Aquinas. Later, we will pick up the theme and go on to Descartes, Spinoza, Locke, Kant, Hume, Berkeley, and John Stuart Mill before examining post-Darwinian philosophers and scientists with respect to these issues, all foundations for m-realism-rationalism.

Thomas Aquinas: Abstracting Universals from Particulars

Aquinas is clear enough on the matter of knowledge of the universal, and he follows Aristotle for the most part: particulars can be known, but only indirectly, and obtaining a universal involves the process of abstraction. Abstractio (abstraction) is glossed by McKeon as:

The separation of one thing from another; a thing which is taken separately from those things with which it is joined is taken abstractly; particularly the process of deriving the universal from the species of particular things. ... According to Thomas (Sum. Theol. I, q. 40, a 3 concl.), "Abstraction by the understanding is of two sorts: one by which the universal is abstracted from the particular, as animal from man, another by which form is abstracted from matter, as the form of circle is abstracted by the understanding from all sensible matter." (McKeon, 1930, pp. 423-24)

We will follow Copleston's (1963) account of the process by which Aquinas obtains a universal (or species or concept). The steps are in the story, which, roughly, is as follows:

Corporeal objects act upon the organs of sense...The senses are naturally determined to the apprehension of particulars, they cannot apprehend universals...The phantasm or image, which arises in the imagination and which represents the particular material object perceived by the senses, is itself particular, the phantasm of a particular object or objects...the human being in his intellectual operations apprehends the form of the material object in abstraction: he apprehends a universal...Even if we have a composite image of man, not representing any one actual man distinctly but representing many confusedly, it is still particular…The mind, however, can and does conceive the general idea of man as such, which included all men in its extension. An image of man certainly will not apply to all men, but the intellectual idea of man, even though conceived in dependence on the sensitive apprehension of particular men, applies to all men. (pp. 109-111)

The transition from sensitive and particular knowledge to intellectual cognition is effected as follows:

The rational and spiritual soul cannot be affected directly by a material thing or by the phantasm: there is need, therefore, of an activity on the part of the soul, since the concept cannot be formed simply passively. This activity is the activity of the active intellect which 'illumines' the phantasm and abstracts from it the universal or 'intelligible species'. ... the active intellect...renders visible the intelligible aspect of the phantasm, reveals the formal and potentially universal element contained implicitly in the phantasm...To abstract means to isolate intellectually the universal apart from the particularizing notes. Thus the active intellect abstracts the universal essence of man from a particular phantasm by leaving out all particular notes which confine it to a particular man or particular men...As the active intellect is purely active, it cannot impress the universal on itself; it impresses it on the potential element of the human intellect, on the passive intellect, and the reaction to this impression is the concept in the full sense...It is important to realize, however, that the abstract concept is not the object of cognition. If the concept, the modification of the intellect, were itself the object of knowledge, then our knowledge would be a knowledge of ideas, not of things existing extramentally, and the judgments of science would concern not things outside the mind but concepts within the mind. In actual fact, however, the concept is the likeness of the object produced in the mind and is thus the means by which the mind knows the object... As he held that the intellect knows directly the essence, the universal, St. Thomas drew the logical conclusion that the human mind does not know directly singular material things...Thus the sensitive apprehension of Socrates enables the mind to abstract the universal 'man'; but the abstract idea is a means of knowledge, an instrument of knowledge to the intellect only in so far as the latter adverts to the phantasm, and so it is able to form the judgment that Socrates is a man. (Ibid)

Again, we must draw attention to the inventiveness of Aquinas, here, in trying to persuade us that the mind can come up with a universal. Also, we must point out that the reason for all the hard work is simply to save logic and science, as demonstration (i.e., producing logically necessary word truths about the world).

For Aquinas, we know things outside the mind, not just our ideas as the subjective idealists (e.g., Berkeley) would have it, and this is an important claim for sanity. The mire that is subjectivism came after Aquinas, and many are still suffocating themselves in it. But, convinced of Aristotle's claim that knowledge is of the universal, Aquinas proceeds. We know the things out there by means of the universals, the concepts, and the intelligible species that our minds apprehend in the particulars. Those universals, taken directly from particulars, are the primary objects of knowledge. Their abstraction from particulars requires the positing of at least two faculties, a passive and an active intellect, along with a rather Augustinian notion of illumination of the image (phantasm) once it gets into the mind. We must ask: what is it about the particular image (of Socrates) that the active intellect sees and abstracts (isolates from the image)? Is there something else on that image? Is a memory (image) of Socrates more likely to give us that something than Socrates himself, as we look at him? We are to believe that there is a universal on the image of Socrates that can be lifted off (abstracted from him). I have tried it (not with the image of Socrates, of course) but it doesn't work! Neither from my wife, our children, cat or from memory images of them can I get a universal. I have to believe in universals in order to talk about them at all. If I believe in them, then I don't need to play games with my mind or my eyes. If, however, Aquinas is serious about grounding knowledge and the logic of science in universals, and he is, then we must conclude that the process he describes won't work. Aristotle couldn't make it work, the Angelic Doctor can't make it work, the hosts of m-realists who come after them cannot use Aristotelian ways or abstraction and claim they work. Logic and science may require universals, but if we cannot generate them, and there are none to be had, logic and science will just have to make some adjustments. Perhaps pretending to have universals is just as good as having them; that, in fact is the actual situation m-realists are in, and I believe some are even aware of it.

Chapter 5 Looking Back: The Origins of Metaphysical Reality

The rise of universals came with Plato, and especially Aristotle's need for them as he indicated; if the universal goes, so goes the middle term in logic, and if that goes, there is no way for the craftsman and the man of science to get on with their work. What Aristotle had in mind, here, can be seen in that too oft quoted classroom syllogism, invented by him:

> All men are mortal
> Socrates is a man
> Therefore, Socrates is mortal

The second line contains the middle term; *man* is a universal, a class, with Socrates as a member. Without the ability to predicate man of Socrates (m-real definition), there is no syllogism, no way to express the truths of classes and their members.

Universals were logical posits and attempts were made by Aristotle to derive them from particular things, which both he and Plato admitted exist. We have questioned the actuality of the derivations and even suggested that pretending that universals exist is about as good as actually knowing that they do. Even m-realists can be pragmatists; Dewey and James, in putting m-real entities to work, were both. If we want to know the actual world and tell truths about it and our minds that do the truth-telling, we will shun the universals of m-realism as the means to knowledge and truth. Knowledge is about what we can know: particulars.

We must return, now, to the pre-Socratic, Xenophanes, to pick up one of two threads in the story that is metaphysical realism. The thread leading from Xenophanes to Parmenides and on to Hegel and Heidegger and modern continental philosophers is the thread of *being*. The other thread, leading to Anglo-American philosophers has its source primarily in Aristotle who, you will recall, tried to be, as Ockham would have it, a nominalist. In other words, reason and logic and empirical elements in Aristotle are the important ones for Anglo-American philosophers, not being, which played so large a role for idealists and absolutists and existentialists. Xenophanes precedes Parmenides. We will see how being, the grandest m-real entity in philosophy and theology, came into our lives.

Xenophanes

Once upon a time a wise man named Xenophanes criticized the stories of those religious sayers who represented gods in human form. He made fun of the stories of the poets who attributed to the celestials the passions and sins of men. He had a different story to tell. The highest true God is a single God, the original ground of all things, and to this one he gave the attributes the Milesian Phusikoi had

46

assigned to cosmic matter, unoriginated, imperishable, and identical with what there is. God is the cosmic matter or world-all. As Sextus Empiricus put it, "Xenophanes, contrary to the preconceptions of all other men, asserted dogmatically that the All is one, and that God is consubstantial with all things, and is of spherical form and passionless and unchangeable and rational..." (Bury, p. 137).

As Windelband (1956) put it, "World and God to Xenophanes are identical, and all the single things of perception lose themselves in that one, unchanging universal essence" (p. 59).

Whereas the Phusikoi eliminated the religious from their explanations, Xenophanes brings it back and gives the notion of a plural-one a pantheistic aura, which also boosts monotheism. Of course, if Xenophanes' God is the arche, or first principle, of things, then explanation of empirical matters or events becomes impossible, or at least contradictory, because his one is unchanging. We will note, as we have already, that for Xenophanes, "All the single things of perception (i.e., particulars) lose themselves in that one, unchanging universal essence" whereas for Aristotle and Aquinas some of those single things, particulars, gain a species-essence by our ignoring their particularity or abstracting from it.

Appearance versus reality is a theme present in Xenophanes, and Plato will make much of it. The one-many problem was evidently not a problem for Xenophanes or, for that matter, Parmenides, whose story we take up next.

Parmenides: The Creation of Being

Parmenides developed the theme of m-realism and the logic of rationalism in Xenophanes: the "unity" and "singleness" of the Godhead and its "identity" with the world. As Windelband says, "The concept was Being and it was central and drew all into its circle" (Ibid). Of Parmenides, Windelband goes on to say, "The correlation of consciousness and Being hovered before his mind" (Ibid).

That was a small step for Parmenides, a momentous step for the philosophically inclined. With the marriage of thinking (consciousness) and being the hermeneutics of the absolute and subjective idealism, begin in earnest. Being will be used and abused for the next two thousand years. We must take a closer look, first at what Parmenides said, then at a brief overview by Windelband. Parmenides' Way of Truth begins:

> Only one story, one road, now is left: that it is. And on this there are signs in plenty that, being, it is ungenerated and indestructible, whole, of one kind and unwavering, and complete. Nor was it, nor will it be, since now it is, all together, one, continuous. For what generation will you seek for it? How, whence, did it grow? That it came from what is not I shall not allow you to say or think---for it is not sayable or thinkable that it is not. And what need would have impelled it, later or earlier, to grow---if it began from nothing? Thus it must either altogether be or not be. ... Justice has not relaxed her fetters and let it come into being or perish, but she holds it. ... Nor is it divided, since it all alike is---neither more here (which would prevent it from cohering) nor less;

but it is all full of what is. Hence it is all continuous; for what is approaches what is. And unmoving in the limits of great chains it is beginning-less and ceaseless, since generation and destruction have wandered far away, and true trust has thrust them off. The same and remaining in the same state, it lies by itself, and thus remains fixed there. For powerful necessity holds it enchained in a limit which hems it around, because it is right that what is should not be incomplete. For it is not lacking---if it were it would lack everything. *The same thing are thinking and the thought that it is.* [my emphasis] For without what is, in which it has been expressed, you will not find thinking. For nothing either is or will be other than what is, since fate has fettered it to be whole and unmoving. Hence all things are a name which mortals lay down and trust to be true---coming into being and perishing, being and not being, and changing place and altering bright colour. And since there is a last limit, it is completed on all sides, like the bulk of a well- rounded ball, equal in every way from the middle. For it must not be at all greater or smaller here or there... (Barnes, 1987 pp. 134-35)

Those words have been poured over for centuries and pondered by outstanding philosophic minds. Heidegger was so taken with the ancient fragments on being that he tirelessly investigated and subjected them to his uniquely personal hermeneutics. In the fragment just quoted, Heidegger was especially interested in the words I have emphasized, pointing up the correlation, as Windelband puts

49

it, between thinking and being. Here is what Heidegger (1975) says:

> The relation between thinking and being animates all Western reflection. It remains the durable touch-stone for determining to what extent and in what way we have been granted both the privilege and the capacity to approach that which addresses itself to historical man as to-be-thought. (p. 79)

Later we will return, briefly, to Heidegger's comments on Parmenides, but next we will note Windelband's (1956) overview of the fragment:

> It is the greatest of follies to discuss not-Being at all, for we must speak of it as a thought content, that is, as something being, and must contradict ourselves...If all thinking refers to something being, then Being is everywhere the same. For whatever is thought in the particular thing, the quality of Being is in all the same...Being is the last product of an abstraction that has compared the particular thought contents... *being alone remains when all difference has been abstracted from the content determinations of actuality* [my emphasis]...From this follows the fundamental doctrine of the Eleatics, that only the one abstract being is. (pp. 59-60)

Windelband is looking back over the two thousand years of acceptance of being in the philosophic cranium and telling us how we can understand or get a hold on it: abstract all difference from the content determinations of actuality and *being* remains when we have accomplished it. I must emphasize that believing that all difference can be abstracted from the content determinations of actuality is the foremost illusion (erroneous belief) in Western philosophy. It is worth our while to do as Windelband says, although in my many years of philosophic schooling I was never asked to verify the existence of being by getting in touch with it. As with Aristotle's suggestion about how to obtain a universal, I spent some time trying to remove (abstract) all the content determinations of actuality, but being did not remain. I looked at whatever particulars were in view, but they would not go away, leaving an undifferentiated and difference-less actuality I could call being. I closed my eyes and thought of actual things, and tried to remove (abstract) all difference. But, again, I couldn't do it. Of course, what Aristotle and the Angelic Doctor can do with particulars that differ in number, if not as to qualities, in obtaining universals may be just too difficult for my brain. However, if thought is married to being, as Parmenides holds, even I, in thinking about things, should be able to see the *other side* of thought, which is being, for I (and all of us) are so close to it. Presumably, we cannot think about nothing, but we are asked to think just to the point of nothing (thus removing all difference) and there is being. I tried and came up empty minded. I simply can't get in touch with being. Perhaps, as Heidegger suggested, being has had enough of us and won't show itself because for too long we have forgotten it. Perhaps being is angry or speaks only an ancient dialect of Greek.

As with Aristotle's need for universals, I believe that some thinkers need being for their own purposes. We can understand those purposes when we review the philosophies (e.g., Hegel and Heidegger) who use being for their own ends. Again, a pretend being is practically as good as an actual one if you have important work for it to do: theological, historical, political, ethical, social, aesthetic, etc.

I believe the doctrine of being is ontologically empty, epistemologically false, historically illusory, politically and socially dangerous, aesthetically uninformative, and, because of its current and past uses, especially for religious dominance, morally evil.

The confused mess that is Parmenides' thinking about being assuredly needs addressing. Heidegger thought the question of being *the* philosophic question. We ought not ignore it, and it has such deep roots in philosophic history that apparently it cannot be forgotten by philosophers. I believe being needs to be put to rest. I will do my best.

My critique of Parmenides' being rests on this observation: being, as characterized by him, is a mix of notions that are incompatible. Using what Parmenides said of being, I will separate the notions, for they have a legitimacy in their proper spheres: the empirical and the non-empirical. What we have when we are finished is the world or cosmos on the one side, along with the words proper to that empirical sphere; on the other is nothingness and the words proper to it. However, we must pay close attention to key words, especially *one* and *nothingness*. If we do not make sense of being, as I will try to do, the nonsense will continue...through the 21st century.

If we study Parmenides' characterization of his *being*, we find that its *not-being* is unthinkable, that it could not have come from nothing (and therefore it is something), and that it has all these attributes: it is ungenerated, indestructible, whole, one kind, unwavering, complete, continuous, all alike, unmoving, beginningless, ceaseless, the same and remaining in the same state, fixed, thinking and a thought that it is are the same, completed on all sides, like the bulk of a well-rounded ball, equal in every way from the middle.

What Parmenides cannot abide is the notion of nothingness, void, which was introduced, later, by the Atomists. Nothingness is, in my view (and for Leucippus and Democritus), an actuality. It is the ultimate *surround* of whatever contents make up material or wavy or stringy physical universes. In other words, the modern physicists' vacuum with only nothing in it (although a few virtual particles bobbing in and out might be tolerated). Contrary to Parmenides, nothingness can be thought about, can be understood, and we can say something about it. First, it is not, in any sense, a thing. It is also appropriately referred to as: without parts, infinite (without itself being an extended something or with parts), a whole (without parts), eternal (timeless), changeless, fixed, immovable, imperishable, ungenerated, ceaseless, indestructible, unique (no other like it), beginningless, the same and remaining in the same state, complete, shapeless. In other words, most of what Parmenides said of his being applies to nothingness and only to nothingness. To apply the above terms to any thing (with one exception I will mention) is simply a mistake leading to most of the problems we are confronting in this essay. The mistake Parmenides makes is dismissing the notion of a comprehensive actual nothingness and treating his being as a comprehensive actual thing. Clearly, if we separate those of his attributes for being, as I have, which only apply to nothingness (i.e., to no thing), then the mess that is Parmenidean being is cleared up. Whatever is not infinite, not eternal, not changeless, not fixed, is a thing, part of the contents of the cosmos. Thoughts, as energy products of brain functioning, are parts of what there is, parts of the cosmos, however fleeting. Thoughts are things, and so are finite and destructible. They cannot be bound to a changeless, eternal, nothingness. We do consciousness or thought no favor by thinking it a part of something eternal and unchanging. We need not think nonsense.

The result of our examination of being is that it is actually nothing. Put another way, being is the grand metaphysical nothingness. Nothingness is the only meta-physical (i.e., non-physical) actuality. May being, excuse me, nothingness, rest in peace, free from reification. (See Endnote #5)

Chapter 6 The Ontological Status of Mathematical Entities and Systems

Mathematical physicists aim to understand the cosmos, its contents, and the laws which have generated (exemplify) the processes we observe in nature. A stated aim of this work is to understand what there is and the character or *nature* of each thing, large or small. The major tools of mathematical physicists are, of course, mathematics. Although there are no observable mathematical entities such as numbers, figures, and systems as constituents of the cosmos, some philosophers, mathematicians, and physicists are Platonists (e.g., Godel, Hawking, and Penrose) when it comes to what there is and admit into their ontology mathematical ideas and relations (e.g., numbers, figures, and systems), believing that while such entities may not exist in our world, they exist in some other objectively m-real world.

We are out to critique the incorporation of metaphysical entities in our view of what there (actually) is. The one-many problem is generated, at bottom, by *seeing* or intellectually *abstracting* a one from a many. This *one* is a *m-one* (a plural one) and can also be treated mathematically as one even if it is a plurality. The solution to the one-many problem does not require explication of the notion of one in a mathematical context. In answer to the question of how many, one is a mathematical notion appropriately used to refer to any thing that is not two or more, however simple or complex. Exceptions abound (e.g., Siamese twins, etc.). Mathematicians do not determine the ontology of the universe or of any particular thing. Nothingness as ontological actuality is unknowable as a totality, as a one. It is knowable only relative to physical things and by their absence in some finite location. But it is up to the ontologist to argue the character of nothingness (void). That is, it is self-evident that it can be characterized as having no parts. Hence, the use of the mathematical expression, one, in that instance must respect the non-divisible nature of nothingness (void) and not treat it as a thing which can be divided. Physical space, which can bend, carries the burden of geometrization and is viewed by physicists as something, not nothing. Nothingness is unique (nothing else is even like it), non-physical ontologically, and incomparably other and different from whatever is a thing.

It is my belief that mathematical entities are not part of what there is in our cosmos, and talk of their existence or being in their own metaphysical universe is in itself harmless but unnecessary. To believe mathematical entities are part of our universe is a mistake which leads to confusion and paradox. To make my point, I will only discuss Zeno's Paradoxes and go no farther into the status of mathematics and its entities than is necessary to undermine metaphysical realism as it relates to our categorical attitude and the nature of things. We will, however, look into the notion of whole-part (in Part V) where the whole, an alleged one, involves unity and identity with its parts but is also distinguishable (and perhaps separable) from them. First we will go on to Zeno and note how certain m-entities of mathematics, inserted into the actual world, generate paradoxes.

Zeno's Paradoxes: The Misapplication of Pure Math

Zeno's paradoxes are a staple in the field of paradoxes, but there is great uncertainty as to what he was actually intending when he formulated them. Some believe he was defending his elder friend, Parmenides who, surely, needed a little help with the contradictory notions he used to characterize being. If being is as fixed as he claimed, how is motion possible? One way out is simply to say that the empirical world, where motion occurs, is not a part of being and therefore we can go on out-running tortoises and shooting arrows through the air. Sticking with the paradoxical, we can deny that running gets us anywhere and that arrows don't actually move, if time and motion and space and matter are assumed to have certain mathematical characteristics. Zeno seems to have been exploring the consequences of certain assumptions. Since we all know that walking and running do get walkers and runners from one place to another and that arrows leave the bow, arc into the air, and fall somewhere to earth, we can't take too seriously the claim that movement doesn't occur.

We will take a look at four of Zeno's paradoxes, indicate their solutions, and then wonder what Zeno had in mind by formulating them. As with the problems of universals and being, we might suspect that the paradoxes harbor still more metaphysical nonsense; this time nonsense emanating from thinking that is m-mathematical.

Since time as well as motion, space (or place), and divisibility (finite and infinite), are factors in Zeno's paradoxes we will begin with some clarifications.

Just as actual particulars have suffered from their alleged tie to being which we now correctly understand is a term empty of content and without reference, they also suffer alleged ties to time. At this point in our essay, it may be clearer that what there is, actually, comprehends only the multitudinous, dynamically interacting, unique, and uniquely changing particulars and void (i.e., nothingness). Whatever we would understand is in terms of those particulars and their relatively empty indivisible surround. What then is time? First of all, it is no thing. It is nothing. It is an illusion. Thinking time a reality makes of it a metaphysical being. In actuality, there are particulars which move and change. Our notion of time comes from changes, from motion and movements of things. But things don't move and change in something called time. They just move and change. We add the metaphysical entity time and believe that things have their existence in it, but metaphysical temporal entities don't exist. There is no actual entity whose continuity comprehends a universal past, present, and future. Our clocks do not tick off time, they just tick, tick, tick. The Big Bang did not begin time, it began movements and changes of things. It did not create the uncreatable void in which it banged.

Space, if something which can curve, or is a field of force, is not nothingness, void. Scientists don't have much use for nothingness, but not mentioning it is only a problem if, when pressed, they deny its actuality or identify it with physical space; that is the space of physics. Scientists, of course, have long given up the notion of time as an absolute; married to space and particular matter, the temporal is dependent and relative.

Temporal sequences, then, are our selections of changes arranged in terms of before and after. Measuring the temporality of anything from before to after is difficult, for it is dependent both on the stick or clock used and the temporal extent to be measured. Where the before begins and where the after ends.

Time, then, is no actual thing, and no infinitely divisible line can be divided into instants or nows or seconds or parts thereof.

If there are only dynamically unique particulars, their interactions and processes, and nothingness, there is also no such thing as place. Since nothingness has no parts, it cannot be divided into places. The surfaces of things can be places in the sense of a material place, but place is not something added to that surface and distinct from the matter. Place is an imaginary or real entity, the offspring of the old absolute space and its subdivisions. No particular is in a real entity called place. Is a particular in nothingness, then, no place? No, it is wherever it is, relative to other particulars, wherever they are.

Particulars (matter-energy entities) are finite; they are quantitative (i.e., things or their processes) and have least bits which cannot be further divided. That is, least quantitative bits, or minima, cannot be reduced to energy but not to nothingness, for this would either create a bit of nothingness out of it or make something disappear without consequence. In the first, it makes nothingness a plurality which, in part, is created, in the second, a mystery is created.

The simplest belief is the one we already have; matter-energy is transformable but indestructible.

That least bits can be infinitely divided goes against the notion of particulars as finite quantities. The only infinite, if such there is, is the non-material, non-thing nothingness. Our cosmos offers a discontinuity of diverse, finite entities. Could there be an infinite number of differing cosmoses? Infinity is a mathematical notion which is both real and metaphysical.

We are ready for Zeno. Aristotle dealt with three of the four paradoxes which interest us and felt that he had disposed of them, but many doubt it. (McKeon, 1941, pp. 239-40) Some mathematicians feel that they persist as paradoxes, but that Kantor has, perhaps, the proper approach to their solution, but I doubt it. The first is the arrow. Aristotle gives this account: if a flying arrow is always at the place in which it is, then it is always at rest. Zeno is saying that the arrow cannot move in the place in which it is not, nor can it move in the place in which it is, a place equal to itself. But, Zeno asks, is not every thing always at rest when it is at a place equal to itself?

To understand what Zeno is driving at, we will assume an arrow to move uniformly through an extended space and during an extended time. If the course through space is a mathematical line composed of points (the beginning and end of which define a place) and the time is a mathematical line composed of nows (defining a time), then the arrow must be in some place, in some time, otherwise it is no place, no time. But, if the arrow is in a place and in a time, it is at rest there. If it is not there, now, it is no place, no time. If space is composed of places, defined by points, and if time is the correlative extension of space, but composed of nows, then the arrow while there, in the place-now of space-time, is at rest. The moving arrow is motionless.

The solution to the arrow paradox is as follows, first and foremost, arrows, do not, in actuality, move along m-mathematical lines, curved or straight. Secondly, space, if nothingness, is an actuality having no parts. In other words, space cannot be treated as a mathematical line divisible into points or places, and time cannot be treated as a mathematical line, divisible into nows. The paradox is not linguistic, it is the result of mathematical assumptions which do not apply to actual objects and their contexts.

The second paradox is that of dichotomy and involves a race course: starting from some point, a runner runs toward the finish line but cannot reach it unless she traverses successive halves of the total distance to be run. To reach the half-point of the total distance, half that distance must be run; but, to reach that point, half that, etc. etc., must be run...or an infinite number of halves must be traversed, in some finite time...which is impossible. The result: a runner cannot reach the finish line.

We know of course that runners do reach finish lines, but not by running along m-mathematical lines. They get to the finish line because they run a finite distance, composed of finite parts. Actual race courses are not infinitely divisible, nor are the runner's efforts produced in infinitely divisible units corresponding to the infinitely divisible course. Quite simply, runners don't run m-mathematical lines which are infinitely divisible. Again, the paradox stems from the inapplicability of mathematical notions to an actual event in the actual world.

The third paradox is the Achilles; as the fastest runner of the Greeks moves from the starting point, the tortoise, already ahead, traverses some distance. The distance between Achilles and the tortoise is shortened, but whatever the remaining distance between them, it is infinitely divisible. So in trying to get to where the tortoise begins, Achilles must traverse that distance first, then the distance the tortoise has travelled in the meantime, etc. over an infinitely decreasing distance, but one in which Achilles cannot catch up with the tortoise.

The problem here is that of the second paradox, but instead of traversing an infinite distance by halves, the distance is reduced by unequal amounts, but still is infinite in extent. The error is as above, runners, whether Greek athletes or tortoises, do not run m-mathematical lines, which, by definition are infinitely divisible.

The forth and last paradox is the stadium. Two columns of men are ready to march in opposite directions from a point or marker in the stadium. The two lead men stand side-by-side, facing in opposite directions, at the marker and when the signal is given, move in opposite directions, an equal number past an equal number at equal speed. If the one column starts from one end of the stadium, the other from the middle, Zeno asks, does not half the time equal its double?

Simplified, we have a fixed line for distance, right and left of the marker, over which the men in the two columns will walk. We also have a fixed line for time correlated with the distance. If, at the mid-line marker for both distance and time, we have Man-A and Man-B ready to proceed, uniformly, in opposite directions, then in one unit of time, A and B will be one distance unit right, one distance unit distance left but two distance units apart in one-unit time, or one-unit distance apart in one-half unit time. Zeno asks how is it possible that half a unit of time is equal to double the unit of time?

The solution is, actual men move actual distances which can be clocked. Man-A moves an actual distance, say one unit, when clocked in a unit of time (tick-tocks). Man-B moves an actual distance, as with Man-A. Each covers a unit distance in a unit time, judged by the fixed distance line. However, when A moves right one-unit distance and B moves left one-unit distance, an apartness distance is created of two distance units in one unit time. The error is that the apartness, emerging in clock-time, is not the actual distances A and B traverse. The apartness distance of one unit, judged by another clock keyed to the newly emerging distance line is, indeed, created in one-half the time. If the actual distances traversed by A and by B and the apartness distance emerging from their opposite movements are viewed on the same distance line, using the same clock, the mathematical contradiction, or paradox, will emerge. If A and B are runners, each can understand that the distance covered in a unit-time, when they run at the same speed in opposite directions, will be equal while also understanding that the emerging distance of one unit between them will be created in one-half the time. Neither will believe that half the time is equal to double the time, for it is not. Again, the problem is applying m-mathematical notions to a situation (actuality) in which it does not apply.

There are, then, answers to the paradoxes Zeno put forth. But, why did he formulate them? I don't know. I would like to believe, however, that the answer is: he wanted to demonstrate that mathematical notions require realities which do not apply to the actual world. Paradox arises when two different systems seem to be compatible but generate both truth and falsity: the arrow moves, the arrow is at rest; the runner runs, the runner cannot reach the finish line. Or, to use another example, if what you say is true, then it is false (all Cretans are liars). If, in the case of Zeno, we eliminate the assumption that the mathematical treatment of real entities by mathematicians can also apply to movements over actual distances and clock-tics, we are mistaken. As one mathematician put it:

> ...the value of the Arguments lies precisely in the fact that they forcefully bring out the position which mathematics occupies in the general scheme of human knowledge. The Arguments show that space and time and motion as perceived by our senses (or for that matter by their modern extensions, the scientific instruments) are not co-extensive with the mathematical concepts which bear the same name. The difficulties raised by Zeno are not the type to alarm the pure mathematician---they do not disclose any logical contradictions, but only sheer ambiguities of language; the mathematician may dispose of these ambiguities by admitting that the symbolic world in which he creates is not identical with the world of his senses. (Dantzig, 1959, p. 123)

Mathematicians in Zeno's day, as well as in ours, apply their mathematics of real or imagined entities to things in the actual world. Modern science was created, largely by Galileo, who believed that nature was a book to be read in terms of mathematics. Mathematicians are not ontologists, and ontologists are, or should be, concerned with the characteristics of particular things for they and their processes are the components of the cosmos. Mathematicians also know that any mathematical system, whether of arithmetic or geometry, generates notions (operations) whose relevance is a matter internal to itself. Its truths are matters of self-consistency having nothing to do with an actual world. Different mathematical systems can be, and are, developed and applied to the cosmos, but not one of them can be said to apply because it fits the ontological character of the particulars of the cosmos. Why? Because mathematical entities (numbers, figures, etc.) are real or pretend entities and actual entities are things involved in causal events and processes and those things, events, and processes are unique and non-recurrent. Thus, no real or pretend entity, such as one (or a number series) or triangle, circle, point, line, recurrence, and no real or pretend claim of identity or equality apply, in fact, to ontological actualities. It simply is not true that $1 + 1 = 2$ when it comes to actual things. The two ones of this addition are, for mathematicians, identical. But no two actual things are identical, or equal to one another, for each is other and different, actually. The definitions of numbers are legislated by mathematical logic and they must behave (in the system), in specified ways; two numbers that are the same or substitutable are legislated to be identical or equal. Each operation of addition, subtraction, etc., is, in terms of the system, identical regardless of who does it, when or where it is done.

I certainly am not saying we should give up the theoretical application of mathematics to the world. That is unnecessarily hobbling. Rather, the basis for its truth, in application (which is not a matter of consistency), is not present in the actual world. It is one thing to use mathematics as a logical system, and it is another to say that there are real mathematical entities and that they provide ontological knowledge and truths of the things of the world.

All this is not too strange, perhaps, to those who incline to Platonism. Platonists always believed that the reality of the forms was elsewhere than this world, and that their relation to the things of this world, the particulars, could not be given a satisfactory explanation. The forms and the actual world just don't connect. If the forms are more attractive than a very messy world of differing particulars, then the world of actuality fades away, to appearance, and becomes unimportant, for knowledge and truth are elsewhere. That's a pity. But mathematicians are not at fault for having a lock on certainty. It belongs to them as a result of the systems they have created. Most are aware that the truths and certainties of mathematics rest on the logic inherent to the systems, along with the notions of identity and definition. Applied to the actual world, mathematical systems run into problems. But, that's because of the way things are.

We know why metaphysical realities were posited; they were needed either to explain how particular things got here or to do the logical work needed to establish logical truths. Those m-realities, being and the forms, are still with us as the subject matter of metaphysics. The forms, especially, have been criticized, but have not been driven from philosophy and science. Aquinas, as we saw was an upholder of Aristotle's forms and universals and the manner of obtaining them from particulars and understanding them. Abelard came before Aquinas and Ockham came after him. We will look at their views, for nominalism is in the air, coming from Roscelin, and Abelard was his student. Ockham will deliver a devastating, if incomplete, critique of the m-real entities, the forms, of Plato and Aristotle.

First, A Word More About Time

From the Big Bang came what there is. Being was not involved and nothingness was not a constraint. What about time? We would like to understand the temporal aspects of the Big Bang. Was there time before the Bang, a futural flow in which the Bang was immersed and out of which came temporal distributions of what there is right to the present moment (i.e., my now, your now)? Scientists, viewing the cosmos produced by the Bang, say time did not exist before the Bang simply because the Bang created time and space, which Einstein combined into an inseparable pair, space-time, coupled with matter and energy.

The question of the existence or non-existence of something called time has been dampened in science because scientists don't, for the most part, do philosophy. The current scientific thinking is that the question of time is a settled matter securely attached to Einstein's four-dimensional space-time geometry; three spatial dimensions tied to one temporal dimension, also treated as a spatial dimension.

In a recent book on the legacy of Godel and Einstein, Palle Yourgrau, a philosopher, reminds us that the question of the existence (the reality) of what we call time is alive but largely ignored by both scientists and philosophers. He points to Kurt Godel who wrote an essay for a volume on his friend Einstein for his 70th birthday. His essay concluded that if Einstein's relativity theories (special and general) are correct (and he believed they are), then intuitive time, the time we are aware of as flowing from our nows and receding into our pasts as we face the future, is an illusion. The felt-temporal-nows of multitudes of people cannot be combined into a single directional time having objective validity. There is no universal now, no present state of the universe, only an *unreal time* cosmologists call "the mean cosmic time."

Godel's argument is complex (and nicely reproduced in Yourgrau's book) and I have no need to go into it, here. However, just as I have indicated that *being* is a metaphysical non-entity, time is also a metaphysical non-entity, an illusion, as Godel concluded using Einstein's work and his own view of possible worlds, but my argument differs from his. Godel is deep into metaphysics, in two ways. First, as a mathematical Platonist who believes in the reality of numbers. Secondly, as a philosophical idealist who believes in being. My aim in dealing with the question of the reality of time is simply to alert us to the fact that we should be aware that it is in consciousness that we imagine and so invent the metaphysicals such as being and time. We believe them to be realities which are somehow actual.

As a subjective feeling attached especially to clocks, but also to cycles of night and day, the seasons, and movements of things that we sequence as changes that are *befores* and *afters*, what we sense as stretching from a before to an after is a bit of metaphysics we call time. The habit of temporal awareness becomes fixed, providing inarguable truths about nature and ourselves. Eternity was pondered and clarified before anyone thought to question the actuality of something called time. Time became a stretch of eternity which involved the creation of the world by a biblical God. Time would end when and if God eliminated that stretch of it which he allowed to exist for his own purposes. With the elimination of time, everything in the worldly world would be thrown back into eternity, a timelessness which cannot be clocked off. However strange it may sound, that is where we are now, now, now. . .

Einstein's four-dimensional space-time in which time (little-t) is treated as a spatial dimension has to do with clocks, not with anything actual which can be called time. Clocks simply tick, tick, tick (or digitally change, change, change). They do not tick-off something called time. Further, even if there were something called time, we cannot say what it is in terms of something else, such as a distance. That is analogy, perhaps metaphor. We know what a spatial distance is; it is a length or width or depth. Space-distance is not temporal distance because time is not space. As Godel indicated, time vanishes in the special and general theories of relativity. Behind the illusion of time in these theories is the old metaphysical entity, time, along with the belief that clocks tick it off. Although Godel believes that the illusory nature of time gives us a world without time, as Yourgrau put it, Godel was a Platonist who believed in the reality of numbers (and other mathematical objects) and the ideality of time. So, time disappears from our world only to find a fixed heaven, an eternity if you will, where it can be called upon to explain that insistent temporal habit we humans have formed of it.

Chapter 7 Looking Forward: Undermining Metaphysical Reality

Abelard's Way with Particulars

Abelard is the first of the Latin writers, after Boethius, to make much of the notion of *concept* and also of the notion of *abstraction*. Both notions arise in his treatment of universals and his attempt to solve that problem. We have already seen how Aristotle, presumably, and Aquinas, used abstraction in obtaining concepts or universals. Of Abelard, McKeon (1930) says, "The solution of Abailard is an Aristotelian moderate realism" (p. 104); he explains:

> There are, strictly, no universal things, for only individual things exist. Human language however is composed of conventional words which are general in form. Such words (voices) cover general and abstract notions...the universal word does not indicate a universal thing, rather it forms a certain conception which is common to the individuals it names. Its universality consists in the multitude of individuals named by it in that common likeness. (Ibid)

Thus, we find Abelard asking:

> What the conception of the understanding of the
> common likeness of this is, and whether the word is
> called common because of a common cause in which
> the things agree or because of a common conception
> or because of both at once. (Ibid, pp.104-5)

Abelard argues that while Socrates and Plato agree in that they are men:

> We understand nothing other than that they are men,
> and in this they do not differ in the least, in this, I
> say, that they are men, although we appeal to no
> essence. We call it the status itself of man to be man,
> which is not a thing and which we also called the
> common cause of imposition of the word on
> individuals, according as they themselves agree with
> each other. (Ibid, p. 237)

Since he insists that we appeal to no essence in applying the word man to both Socrates and Plato, the explanation for the imposition of the common noun must lie elsewhere. Abelard locates the basis of that explanation in the human understanding. He says:

> The understanding...does not need a corporeal
> instrument, so it is not necessary that it have a subject
> body to which it may be referred, but it is satisfied
> with *the likeness of things* which the mind constructs

for itself [my emphasis], into which it directs the action of its intelligence. (Ibid, p. 238)

However, Abelard goes on to say this formed-likeness, or simply form of things and toward which it is directed is:

A certain imaginary and fictive thing, which the mind constructs for itself when it wishes and as it wishes...like...that form of the projected building which the artist conceives as the figure and exemplar of the thing to be formed, which we can call neither substance nor accident. (Ibid, pp. 238-9)

We will note, here, that Ockham will also use the notion of the concept as being *fictive* and an *exemplar*. What Abelard has done, in following, loosely, Aristotle's way of obtaining a universal, is to tighten the process into an active constructing by the mind, which is the formation of a concept. But, Abelard is careful not to make this likeness constructed by the understanding into a real, or metaphysical thing or essence. He says, "just as the quality is fictive, a fictive substance is subject to it...the image in a mirror too, which seems to be the subject of sight, can be said truly to be nothing..." (Ibid, p. 239).

He follows with these remarks on the understandings of universals and particulars:

That which is of the universal noun, conceives a common and confused image of many things, whereas that which the particular word generates...restricts itself to only one person. Whence when I hear man a certain figure arises in my mind which is so related to individual men that it is common to all and proper to none. (Ibid, p. 240)

We may wonder what figure arose in Abelard's mind upon hearing the word man; a figure which is common to all and proper to none. We may note, here, that Berkeley ridiculed Locke for suggesting that we can have an idea of triangle which is no particular triangle at all. The problem with Abelard's concept constructed by the mind out of perceived individuals or which is the confused image of many things, is simply this: how did he form it? That is, how did his mind make a diverse plurality into a one? His answer involves the notion of abstraction. His claim is that "the conceptions of universals are formed by abstraction, and we must indicate how we may speak of them alone, naked and pure but not empty" (Ibid).

We are left wondering, as we were when we tried to understand Aristotle and Aquinas. How is abstraction actually achieved, and how is universality conferred and conveyed by this so-called abstraction? Indeed, why didn't Abelard stop with the clarification he achieved, namely that only particulars exist and that universals are merely fictions formed in the brain? The answer, of course, is that like Aristotle and Aquinas he needed something, a concept, in order to make the inferences of logic. Simply put, reasoning depended on them.

Ockham: Logical Universals and Concepts

William of Ockham is often given credit for two achievements: a view of particulars which undermines the two major forms of m-realism and a forceful nominalism. In truth, he became a Conceptualist (the doctrine that abstracting from particulars results in a mental entity which is their common form or universal) while holding, too, to his nominalism (i.e., the doctrine that only particulars exist). The view of particulars which undermined the metaphysical realism of Plato (Ante Rem Realism: the doctrine that universals or forms are realities outside nature and the human mind) and the metaphysical realism of Aristotle (In Re Realism: the doctrine that universals or forms are realities in particulars), was extraordinarily simple: we intuit (perceive) particulars directly and we can know particulars, contrary to the wisdom of Aristotle and Aquinas.

If we can know particulars, then we can stop trying to apprehend Platonic and Aristotelian universals. Unfortunately, Ockham needed universals for the same purposes that Aristotle and Aquinas needed them: to reason. So, while making ontology (what there is) more parsimonious, he did not go far enough. His universals have the ontological status of concepts, mental constructs. If a universal has even a psychological existence (or reality) we must be concerned and inquire into how we come by it, if, indeed, we can. If it is only an erroneous bit of psychological debris, we need not worry.

Ockham used a number of alternative expressions in stressing ontological parsimony. In exploring his natural philosophy, Tournay (1938) says, "The famous razor (frustra fit per plura quod potest fieri per pauciora) is always in readiness to cut out imaginary, supersensuous, or occult elements from physical problems" (p.31).

The heart of Ockham's nominalistic approach to the solution of the problem of universals is his notion of concept. Tournay's assessment of the importance of this notion is worth quoting:

> The story of philosophical development in the West centers, undoubtedly, in the problem of the nature of conceptual thought. The universal or class concept, discovered by Socrates as the rock of knowledge, extended by Plato to metaphysical dimensions, and developed by Aristotle as the indwelling principle of all actuality, was eagerly accepted by both Augustinian and Thomistic lines of thought as the surety to guarantee the solidity of science and life. Logic was projected into ontology as a pertinacious pursuit of self-assertion to impose a human perspective upon the world. (Ibid, p. 1)

What a wonderful distillation of philosophical thinking! The universal or class concept, in the Aristotelian sense quoted by Tournay, is of course, the heart of m-realism. Roscelin and Abelard, in the 12th century, made the first telling attacks on it, Ockham followed and dispatched Platonic and alleged Aristotelian metaphysical forms and essences and thereby undermined the foundations of m-realism. Left in the wake of his nominalistic approach, however, is the notion of a concept, which does the logical work of universality, predicating one of many, just as Aristotle required. We must ask, is Ockham's concept itself an m-real entity? The answer, given by Tournay, is in the negative. "Every universal is one singular thing and is universal only by signification of many things. In so far, however, as it is a single form subsisting really in the intellect, it is called singular" (Ibid).

The universal, which is a concept, is, as Ockham put it, a second intention of the soul or mind, hence a particular. We must now ask, how does the universal get into the mind, and whence comes its universality? Tournay answers, "The universals and second intentions simply appear in the mind as mental products caused spontaneously by the particular objects as heat is caused by fire, to use the very words of Ockham" (Ibid, pp. 10-11). Tournay continues, "Repeated causal actions of the external object...create in us in Ockham's expression 'a certain habit,' with an inclination to revisualize the previously sensed object" (Ibid, p.11).

This comports well with Aristotle's way of obtaining universals through what he calls experience. But is it "abstraction?" Tournay continues:

> The process of abstraction in these words is described entirely in terms of similar experiences caused by objects, through intuitions or habits resulting in a new or second intention: the universal. The distinctive mark of every universal is to be a sign for all the individuals involved in the abstraction. (Ibid, p.12)

Is having similar experiences caused by objects, through intuitions or habits resulting in a new or second intention, the universal called *abstraction*? It would seem that from Ockham's description (conveyed by Tournay) of intuiting particulars, which are directly known, no process of abstraction has occurred. Aristotle, we will recall, noted the single identity of a plurality of particulars---which is why he considered them logically indiscriminable---but no abstracting has taken place (unless we infer it as the step leading to the view of particulars as indiscriminable, as we have before indicated). Ockham follows Aristotle precisely in the way of obtaining a universal. Although the universal is embedded, here, in the psychological act of intuiting, it is a logical entity, not a psychological reality. Ockham says:

> The universal is not some real thing having a psychological being (esse subjectivum) in the soul or outside of the soul. It has only a logical being (esse objectivum) in the soul and is a kind of fiction...Figments have no psychological being [otherwise] chimera and centaur and other such things would all be real things. There are, then, certain entities which have only logical being. In the same way, propositions, syllogisms, and such other things as logic treats, have no psychological being, but only a logical being: and so *their being is their being understood* (my emphasis). (Ibid, p.13)

Frege, who threw psychology out of logic, must have read that. In any case, the universal has been transplanted from the realm of ontology to that of logic. Still, we must ask, has a concept (a one over many) been validly formed in the mind? We must answer, no. Ockham does not say he sees, as Aristotle does, the identity of a plurality of particulars. What he does say is that the universal is an exemplar or likeness.

Tournay says, "The two apparently realistic expressions which occur here: EXEMPLAR and SIMILITUDO, may be taken for the fact that Ockham was willing to adopt the very words of his adversaries rather than to give up the objective validity of his universals" (Ibid, p.15).

Tournay asks of Ockham, "What is, then, that similitude in the logical realm, on the basis of which the universal can stand for external things and can be predicated of them." And answers:

> After what we know about his views on the superiority of inner experiences, we will find it quite consistent when he says that it lies *in the similarity of experience*. Repeated impressions of stones, for instance, produce in us a reiteration of the original experience when we touched stone for the first time. Because of the similarity of these impressions and on the basis of such repeated and resembling experiences the intellect molds them into an *exemplar*, a logical *fictum* (my emphases), into a meaning... (Ibid, p. 16)

We have been heading toward meanings ever since Abelard and the nominalistic approach to universals, especially by Ockham. Meanings, as logical and fictive creations in the mind will be raised by realists into metaphysical (i.e., real) existence by contemporary philosophers. However, back to Tournay's remarks, above.

Again Tournay has, as in using abstraction, above, taken a step not mentioned by Ockham when he says the intellect molds the repeated and resembling experiences. Whereas Aristotle sees identity in a plurality of impressions, Ockham sees resemblance and accords it the status of a logical fictum. For neither is identity or resemblance an actual entity, an ontological universal; for both, there is only logical being. What is *logical being*? Simply the use of a word predicating one of many (i.e., universality). The word is not a universal, its use is to universalize. Ontology has not been enlarged. We must ask, however, what is the status of a logical entity such as a meaning or a concept? For Ockham, as for Aristotle, only particulars exist. Meanings and concepts, if they exist, are particulars. Whence comes their universality? They can be predicated of many. Why can a particular meaning or concept be predicated of many? Ockham answers, because they are exemplars. If meanings or concepts are universals because they are exemplars, then we are involved in circularity. To break the circle, we need to know how an exemplar becomes an exemplar, how a universal or concept becomes a universal or a concept.

For Ockham, the focus must be on his notion of similarity, for it is from the similarities of experience that the exemplar emerges by the action of the intellect. Now, Copleston agrees that similarity is the crucial notion for Ockham:

> The universal concept arises simply because there are varying degrees of similarity between individual things. Socrates and Plato are more similar to one another than either is to an ass; and this fact of experience is reflected in the formation of the specific [species] concept of man....there is no nature common

to Socrates and Plato, *in* which they come together or
share or agree; but the nature which is Socrates and
the nature which is Plato are *alike* [my emphasis].
(Ibid, p.17)

This solves the problem we noted in our discussion of
Aristotle: how, if form or essence is one, it can be in many,
Socrates and Callias or, if one, how it is the case that Socrates'
form or essence is not completely his. Continuing
Coppleston's discussion, he compares the approach of
Ockham with Aquinas and says:

But it must be remembered that St. Thomas gave a
metaphysical explanation of the similarity of natures;
for he held that God creates things belonging to the
same species, things, that is, with similar natures,
according to an idea of human nature in the divine
mind. Ockham, however, discarded this theory of
divine ideas. The consequence was that for him the
similarities which give rise to universal concepts are
simply similarities, so to speak, of fact: there is no
metaphysical reason for these similarities except the
divine choice, which is not dependent on any divine
ideas. (Copleston, 1963, p. 69)

Indeed, Ockham discards divine ideas and refuses to
generate real entities in or out of the human mind. Similarity
is not a real or metaphysical entity, for him, only a physical
or particular fact.

Now, we must emphasize at this point a matter of the
greatest importance; if a resemblance is not a metaphysically

real entity (as Ockham believes, along with Aristotle and others who are nominalistically minded), then it must, as Ockham says, be something, if only a physical fact. Resembling particulars may just resemble, or their resemblance may give rise to an m-real entity. These two poles of thought are the points of oscillation between nominalism (which does not explain resemblance, but only claims that resemblance is resemblance, a matter of (perceptual) fact, and m-realism (which insists that an m-real entity is seen in resembling particulars). Between these two views is conceptualism, which can lean toward nominalism (by claiming that the resemblances of particulars are just resemblances) or toward m-realism (by claiming that the concept derived from resembling particulars is, or harbors, an m-real entity).

Ockham does not further explicate similarity. It is left to oscillate one way or another, or simply continue as an unexplained, and perhaps unexplainable fact for the next 600 years. Moving on from Ockham, we may be left with, as Copleston says, the notion that similarities are simply similarities with no satisfactory metaphysical or physical explanations given. Leaving the notion of similarity unexplained won't do. It is too important to intellectual thought to leave it in obscurity.

I will claim that the basis for deriving or constructing m-real entities, whether they are called universals, concepts, forms, ideas, generals, numbers, figures, or relations, is either the incoherent notion of identity or the so far unexplained notion of similarity or resemblance, or commonality. Further, I will claim that the unexplained notion, usually similarity or resemblance, generates metaphysical realism throughout the history of philosophy. Wittgenstein's *family resemblance* notion is not only important in philosophy but it became foundational for cognitive psychologists and at least one Nobel Neuroscientist who tell us about the formation of concepts and categories. I will tell that story as we proceed. We will follow, then, the history of similarity or resemblance, for it is the thread along which the one-many problem and the problem of universals, categories, concepts, kinds (e.g., species, race) proceeds. The problems are handled in terms of m-realism, nominalism, conceptualism. Many along the way, from Ockham to Wittgenstein, will try to honor Ockham's nominalistic (and conceptual) approach; these include: Hobbes, Locke, Berkeley, Hume, Mill, and Goodman. Others will honor the creation of m-real entities, such as universals. These include: Descartes, Spinoza, Leibniz, Kant. It is the nominalists and nominalistic conceptualists against the m-realists, the empirically-minded against the rationalists (whose abstract and abstracting reason is grounded in, and the ground of, metaphysical realism). We will take up the thread of resemblance with Locke.

Locke's Conceptualism and Nominalism

We must remember that Locke's nominalism (only particulars exist) goes back to Aristotle. This claim was made in the Middle Ages by Roscelin, who is sometimes given credit for being the first nominalist if, indeed, he shunned all m-real entities of any stripe. The Church so disliked his saying that universals were mere flatus vocis, yakety-yak, as Quine, an outstanding contemporary philosopher put it, that he was excommunicated and his writings destroyed. Why?

Perhaps the doctrine of the Trinity was put in peril. Abelard, as we saw, was his pupil and the nominalism he espoused was the likely result of that association.

With the coming of Ockham, nominalism was a doctrine m-realists had to deal with. His conceptualism was also attractive, but for different reasons, both to m-realists and to the nominalistically minded.

Locke shows where he is coming from and then asks the crucial question, "Since all things that exist are only particulars, how come we by general terms; or where find we those general natures they are supposed to stand for"(Locke, 1974, p.264)?

His answer is that words are general by being signs of general ideas. The next question is how we form those ideas. As with others, he believes we form them by abstraction, which is separating an idea from "the circumstances of time and place, and any other ideas that may determine (it) to this or that particular existence" (Ibid).

Thus, a common noun can represent a number of individuals by standing for an abstract idea. This, of course, is conceptualism, for the universal or general element is said to reside inside the head, in those ideas which are the result of collecting, by abstraction, the common feature in a plurality of individuals. Those ideas are concepts. An entity called an abstract idea is now added to the other real entities we have noted.

Locke is not emphasizing the logical nature of his abstract idea. He emphasizes the abstract idea as an entity, an m- real one. His abstract idea is also a concept, and has the same function as Ockham's concept, namely to name, define, predicate, and generalize over, particulars; these are

84

the four functions---we might say, the four horses---that m-realists ride. So, Locke retained Ockham's notion of concept, and for those reasons given first by Aristotle; knowledge, science, and communication were at stake:

> ...a distinct name for every particular thing would not be of any great use for the improvement of knowledge, which though founded in particular things, enlarges itself by general views; to which things reduced into sorts, under general names, are properly subservient. These, with the names belonging to them, come within some compass, and do not multiply every moment beyond what either the mind can contain, or use requires. (Ibid, p. 264)

Mentally reducing things (particulars) into sorts or kinds is, of course, the creation of concepts.

Communication is an important function in our lives, and Locke (1974) maintains that, "For every particular thing to have a name is impossible" (p.263). It would also, according to him, be useless, because, as he put it, "...it would not serve to the chief end of language. Men would in vain heap up names of particular things that would not serve them to communicate their thoughts" (Ibid).

He continues:

> This cannot be done by names applied to particular things; whereof I alone have the ideas in my mind, the names of them could not be significant or intelligible to another, who was not acquainted with

all those very particular things which had fallen under my notice. (Ibid, pp. 263-64)

Locke very clearly demonstrates in these passages that while only particulars actually exist, we are forced by our circumstances and that of nature to rise above the level of particulars for our knowledge of them and for intelligible communication. Indeed, each particular might have a name, but who could do the naming? The implication, of course, is that we don't have to do it because we can reduce the impossible numbers of particulars, and therefore the names to be given, by a mental process, abstraction, which gives us the needed intellectual instrument, a concept. General words become the signs of these general or abstract ideas. Abstract ideas in fact are the essences comprising genera and species. Locke admits that the essences are, as he puts it, "the workmanship of the understanding, but have their foundation in the similitude of things" (Ibid, p.268).

With that remark, he shows his kinship with Aristotle, Aquinas, and Ockham. Similitude is not explained, but its importance is foremost; it is the founding principle of m-realism.

Returning to Lock, we may focus, momentarily, on his notion of essences. If, as Locke maintains, the essences of things are abstract ideas, then such entities cannot be outside the head. But Locke insists that things do have m-real essences, "the real internal, but generally (in substances) unknown constitution of things, whereon their discoverable qualities depend" (Ibid, p. 270).

Since these real essences cannot be the same ones as the

abstract ideas, Locke evidently believes in two sorts of essences, real and nominal, and he does. Whether real or nominal, the fact is Locke is unable, or unwilling, to give up realism. His nominalism seems only skin deep, but his conceptualism is firmly rooted in the mental. I might add that this is true of most of the empiricists, right down to the present. They hanker after nominalism, speak the language of a nominalistic conceptualism, and when pressed, fall back on m-realism. This is exhibited in Locke's remarks about essences being ingenerable and incorruptible, the view poor Darwin had to oppose:

> That such abstract ideas, with names to them, as we have been speaking of are essences may further appear by what we are told concerning essences, viz. that they are all ungenerable and incorruptible. For, whatever becomes of Alexander and Bucephalus, the ideas to which 'man' and 'horse' are annexed are supposed nevertheless to remain in the same; and so the essences of those species are preserved whole and undestroyed, whatever changes happen to any or all of the individuals of those species. By this means the essence of a species rests safe and entire, without the existence of so much as one individual of that kind. (Ibid, p. 272)

How marvelous! We have, in these words, an example of the belief that a whole, such as a kind, can exist or have some ontological being without any of its parts, the individuals which make it up! We have, thus, still another notion to subject to analytic scrutiny: Whole-part, the subject of Part V. Why? Obviously some believe (some contemporary biological systematists, among others) that such wholes as described by Locke are real, are entities that can and do exist, with and without their members.

Locke goes on to repeat, were it possible, what will be enunciated ad nauseum right to the edge of the 2lst century, the m-realists' belief about geometrical figures and numbers:

> For, were there now no circle existing anywhere in the world, (as perhaps that figure exists not anywhere exactly marked out), yet the idea annexed to that name would not cease to be what it is, nor cease to be as a pattern to determine which of the particular figures we meet with have or have not a right to the name 'circle', and so to show which of them, by having that essence, was of that species...it is evident that the doctrine of the immutability of essences proves them to be only abstract ideas, and is founded on the relation established between them and certain sounds as signs of them, and will always be true, as long as the same name can have the same signification. (Ibid)

There seems little difference, here, between Locke's abstract ideas and the eternal ideas or forms of Plato. Yet there is a difference. In Locke's controversy with Stillingfleet, he said that the same name (for example, 'man') can have different significations. And that each of these significations, being an abstract idea, is both real and constitutes a distinct kind. In his words, "The truth is, every distinct, abstract idea, with a name to it, makes a real, distinct kind, whatever the real essence (which we know not of any of them) be" (Ibid, p. 453). That remark is noteworthy; not only has Locke transgressed against Ockham's principle of parsimony, the classification of natural things in the world is now up for grabs! How so? Anyone who declares having a distinct, abstract idea of some number of individuals, plant or animal, can declare them a real, distinct kind. Who is to say someone's abstract idea is not distinct? Paleontologists dig up remains which give them ideas about kinds all the time. Is Lucy one of a kind? Or is she still another individual related, more or less, closer or more distantly, to other individuals? Someone apparently saw her bones and got the idea that indeed she is, but also gave those bones the proper name, Lucy. There is a problem, here, because the notion of kinds or species is an unsolved problem. If there are no kinds or species, only differing individuals each other and different from every other, then there is no problem. Scientists need only ask what other bones differ little from (not similar to) those of Lucy's. Bones in comparable anatomical positions may be homologous and therefore suggest genetic relationship. We want to know actual relationships among organisms, but that does not require classes or natural kinds. Taxonomies can be viewed as holding pens for diagnostic information concerning organisms and their interrelations, and not be viewed as realities, whether they are called species or other kinds. (We will pursue taxonomic diagnosis and the species problem in other sections, below.)

It was the arbitrariness of Locke's way with nominal essences that made Stillingfleet nervous. He complained that if the differences of kinds were real then that which makes them all one kind must be a real essence, not a nominal essence.

As indicated, above, in Locke's remark about real essences, we can never know those essences. They underlie the qualities of individuals, make them what they come to be (after the fashion of an eternal idea). Left to figure out the demarcations of natural kinds by forming some (nominal) idea of the individuals which would make them up, we head for an unknown destination without knowing which of many roads to take. We sense the arbitrariness of Locke's way with nominal essences while knowing that real essences, if undiscoverable, are of no value to scientists, but helpful to m-realists and innatists. We sense that Locke's ideas, abstracted from particulars and which serve to represent them generally is still part of the m-realist's paraphernalia to control thinking, especially logical and rational thought. The tie to particulars by means of the paraphernalia is becoming more and more questionable. It is our job to make this apparent and to break the tie. On the way to cutting m-realism's tie to the world's particulars, we will briefly demonstrate how firmly it was attached by several rationalists who, of course, might well be expected to avail themselves of the universals, concepts, forms, and ideas, of m-realism, for reason itself (the apparent creator of real entities) requires them.

Chapter 8 Looking Forward: Strengthening Metaphysical Reality

Descartes: The Eternal Immutable Triangle

Before we go on to Descartes, we will stop, momentarily, to note a remark of his contemporary, Thomas Hobbes. Hobbes (1964) was a nominalist when he said, "...there being nothing in the world universal but names; for the things named are every one of them individual and singular" (p. 16). But he accepted the universals of mathematics, which also makes him a rationalist. Locke, as we saw, also oscillated between an empiricism of particulars and a rationalism of universals, especially in mathematics.

For the rationalists, particulars are either mental ideas or, as objects of sense, are hidden under the primary qualities---those rational, which is to say, realist ideas of---number, figure, motion, and extension all of which are universals.

In the Fifth of his Meditations, Descartes (1927) says:

But before examining whether any such objects as I conceive exist outside of me, I must consider the ideas of them in so far as they are in my thought...I discover an infinitude of particulars respecting numbers, figures, movements, and other such things. (p. 137)

Meditating was especially rewarding for Descartes, and we will note that he begins in a subjective state, not with things out there, and discovers an infinitude of particulars (mental entities) respecting numbers, figures, and movements---all universals or concepts in the mind. He does not tell us how, in this short spate of meditating, he came up with those universals or concepts, so we will assume he imposes them on the particulars. Of the universals he describes, none are more real than the mathematical:

> For example, when I imagine a triangle, although there may nowhere in the world be such a figure outside my thought, or ever have been, there is nevertheless in this figure a certain determinate nature, form, or essence, which is immutable and eternal, which I have not invented, and which in no wise depends on my mind, as appears from the fact that diverse properties of that triangle can be demonstrated, viz. that its three angles are equal to two right angles, that the greatest side is subtended by the greatest angle, and the like, which now, whether I wish it or do not wish it, I recognize very clearly as pertaining to it, although I never thought of the matter at all when I imagined a triangle for the first time, and which therefore cannot be said to have been invented by me. (Ibid, p. 138)

Divine triangles have been hanging around since

Plato. The triangle is a real (i.e., metaphysical) form Descartes sees reflected in any triangle he draws or imagines. Of course, he could imagine a triangle (or any other figure) and that triangle, imagined or drawn would be other and different from any other imagined or actual triangular figure. His actually imagined or drawn triangles have no need of a metaphysical or ideal or real form in order to exist and have the properties triangles have. Clearly, we don't need divine or real entities. Descartes need not invest his imagined triangle with a certain determinate nature, form, or essence, which is immutable and eternal. His imagined triangle doesn't have a nature, form, or essence...which is immutable and eternal. What for Descartes (and other m-mathematical realists) seems immutable and eternal about any imagined triangle is simply his alleged ability to repeat certain operations: e.g., that the three angles of his triangle are equal to two right angles. Indeed, although we never have the one and only real triangle to work with, more mundane triangles, imagined and actual, lend themselves to such near-perfect demonstrations. So what? It certainly does not prove that each triangle has a nature, form, or essence which is immutable and eternal. We simply cannot imagine that performing the operation showing that the three angles of a triangle are equal to two right angles would not give us that result if carried on one more time. We won't, of course, be able to prove that, but we need not. What may be clear, now, is that repetition (of the operation) and imagined repetition are the only bases for assuming mathematical universals (such as triangles). But, please note, each repetition (actual or imagined) is a different one, and to assume that all such different ones can be generalized over to give us the

93

universal (triangle or properties) depends on the validity of generalization (analyzed below), which must be proven, in order for m-realism to make its claims about the eternal and immutable natures of triangles, imagined and actual. We have already indicated that mathematicians don't need real triangles in order to fiddle around with triangles. If they cannot see that the universals of figures and operations are grounded in actual or imagined repetitions---which cannot generate real entities (forms, natures, essences) ---more is the pity. realities, or pretend objects, can be dangerous fictions, but I don't include numbers and triangles as fictions we need worry about.

Spinoza: Knowledge of Reality by Degrees

Spinoza seems to have been suspicious of abstractions, and he sounds like a nominalist when he insists that, for example, it is Peter and Paul who exist, not the universal man. Nonetheless, he is a rationalist and he does recognize universals.

He comes to them in a rather different manner than do other rationalists. Writing of our notion of a universal such as man, he says:

.

> So many images of men, for instance, are formed in the human body at once, that they exceed the power of the imagination, not entirely, but to such a degree that the mind has no power to imagine the determinate number of men and the small differences of each, such as color and size, etc. It will therefore distinctly imagine that only in which all of them

agree in so far as the body is affected by them, for by that the body was chiefly affected, that is to say, by each individual, and this it will express by the name MAN, covering thereby an infinite number of individuals; to imagine a determinate number of individuals being out of its power. (Ratner, 1927, pp. 179-80)

Our minds will distinctly imagine *that only* in which all [men] agree. We know, admittedly, that each man differs from every other (in color, size, etc.), but if we imagine (not abstract) *that something* in which they agree (that which is identical in them all?), then we can express that something by the name man (i.e., the common noun). These images coming from so many men that we see are said to be confused; they are low-level universals gained by imagination. These universals will differ in people, for each person forms them on the basis of particulars in his or her experiences. They are quite close to particulars.

The universals determined by our understanding, ratio, are more clear and distinct. These are the abstract universals of mathematics; figures and numbers, which we met with in Descartes.

Knowledge obtained at the third and highest level of thinking, *Scientia Intuitiva*, is knowledge of the essences of things themselves. For our purposes, and as Spinoza allowed it as adequate, we will rest with the claims of the first and second levels, and not climb higher into metaphysics, where the necessary and certain have their lodgings. Intuiting the essences themselves is not for the likes of most of us, for it is pure definition; or pure ontological nonsense.

Leibniz: Resemblance is a Reality

Leibniz is so full of interesting notions that one hardly knows where to begin. On the issues we are interested in: universals, concepts, kinds, species and how we come by them, Leibniz should be viewed as looking over his shoulder at Locke's Essay. Leibniz's *New Essays* (1982) are the source of the following remarks. We will follow, especially, the thread that is resemblance, "generality consists in the resemblances of singular things to one another, and this resemblance is a reality" (p.292). Increasingly, it will be seen that rationalists will use the notion of resemblance in order to tie particulars together into a reality as Leibniz does in his remark. Further characterizing singular things, Leibniz says:

> If by 'particular things' you mean individual ones, then if we only had words which applied to them--- only *proper names* and no *appellatives*---we would not be able to say anything. This is because new ones are being encountered at every moment---new individuals and accidents and (what we talk about most) actions. But if by 'particular things' you mean the lowest species, then, apart from the fact that it is often difficult to determine them, it is obvious that they are themselves universals, founded on *similarity* [my emphasis]. (Ibid, p. 275)

In the first half of that remark, Leibniz is agreeing with Locke: not every particular can have its own name, and we agree. Particulars are too numerous, too changing, for the human mind to keep track of them. The fastest computers are but hopeless dummies when it comes to recognizing ontological entities in their actuality.

Leibniz settles on the traditional way of handling all the diversity presented by particulars; note their similarity and divide them into groups (species) accordingly. That process will give us a manageable unit, even if, as Leibniz admits, it is often difficult to determine a species. Difficult or not, a species is, for him, a universal for he follows Aristotle's doctrine of predicating one of many. Further, we form the species or universal by noting its foundation in the similarity of particulars. Similarity is a reality as we noted in the first quote.

Particulars and their individuality is an important issue, for ontology and epistemology, and Leibniz is especially aware of them:

> You see, paradoxical as it may seem, it is impossible for us to know individuals or to find any way of precisely determining the individuality of any thing except by keeping hold of the thing itself (except by keeping it unchanged)...individuality involves infinity, and only someone who is capable of grasping the infinite could know the principle of individuation of a given thing. This arises from the influence---properly understood---that all the things in the universe have on one another. The case would be otherwise, it is true, if the atoms of Democritus existed, but then there would be no difference between two different individuals with the same

shape and size. (Ibid, p. 290)

To know the career (entirely) and individuality (totally) of any individual is indeed doomed. We can know an individual as the individual it is (however recognized) for the duration (i.e. over the changes) that we perceive it, but its full career, however long or fleeting, and its complete characters, cannot be determined. We will just have to forgo determining or knowing the full individuality of any particular. We can know something about it, not all that might be known about it.

Leibniz is aware (perhaps as a result of Newton's work on gravity?) that the individuation of a given individual "arises from the influence...that all the things in the universe have on one another." This is an important point. But why does he say: "The case would be otherwise...if the atoms of Democritus existed?" His answer: "then there would be no difference between two different individuals with the same shape and size." That answer would, presumably, be true if the atoms were, as Leibniz assumed, identical. That is, the individuals would, for Leibniz, differ only in number (i.e., in being two, not one). That is the famous problem, stated by Leibniz himself, of the principle of the identity of indiscernibles; two objects are identical if we can discern no differences between them (i.e., if they have all properties in common). The notions of identity and commonality will be explored below.

The Notion of Identity: Analysis and Critique

This will be a good place to analyze the crucial notion

of identity. I will argue that, in actuality, no two particulars (whether least matter-energy bits or complexes of them) are identical. Each particular is other than any other, and however little it differs (or is viewed as not differing to our eyes and instruments), it differs ontologically in that it is the particular it is, and not another. Number, is thus relevant to otherness, which is ontological difference. Thus, no two or more particulars (or any of their particular characters or properties) are the same or identical or held in common.

Now, the question may be asked: is identity a coherent expression? I answer that it is not. Does it denote an actuality of some sort? The answer is no. An identity alleged of two or more things is something legislated by m-realists in order to manage diversity and guide our thoughts along m-rational lines such as generalization.

M-realists make two claims: that a thing can be identical with itself and that two things can be identical, as with Leibniz, above. We have dismissed the second claim as ontologically false. The first claim can be shown to involve incoherence; a particular cannot be identical with itself simply because it has no self to be identical with. Particulars don't come in doubles, the particular and its self. The claim is ontologically false. Nor does a particular remain identical with itself during any change it may undergo; if it changes, it is not the same as it was before.

The notion of identity, then, is still another tool in the kit of m-realists: a thing's identity with itself and the identity of two, or more, things make identities m-real entities. Such pretend entities are of use to the logic of m-realism (which is embraced as rationalism).

I can now make an important announcement; if there

are no identities in the natural world, the natural world of things is utterly diverse. But, wait, you may say, what about samenesses and resemblances? Each of these would reduce some of the diversity and generate clumps of non-diversity. No. Sameness must go the way of identity if it excludes all difference; if it includes some difference, then the sameness that is also included is still, as with identity, inadmissible, for it simply plays on identity without claiming to be so. Partial sameness of two particulars would be partial identity; the play is transparent. It won't work. What about resemblance? Will that not undermine my claim of utter diversity? The otherness and difference of particulars? No, not unless resemblances can be seen and the very word implies that they can. We will delay our analysis of resemblance (or its alternative expression, similarity) until the rest of its history has been reviewed.

Returning to Leibniz. Leibniz actually holds that the particulars he calls *monads*, the metaphysical entities making up the universe, are unique; each offers a perspective on the universe which, in their totality, is reality (the Mind of God). Those real entities, the monads, are obviously not the particulars we run in to.

Had Leibniz not believed so firmly in reality, he might well have made the announcement, above, concerning diversity. Believing in real entities, he takes the traditional way out with actual particulars; he recognizes them, as he said, as belonging to species, which are universals, founded on similarity. Particulars are stepping-stones to m-real entities for Leibniz as for Aristotle, Aquinas, Descartes, Locke. Since particulars belong to species, they can, as with all realists, be defined nominally, if not *really*. Leibniz says, "nominal definitions...pertain to logical specific [species] differences as well as to physical ones" (Ibid, p. 327).

And:

> In the logical, or rather the mathematical sense, (of species), the least dissimilarity is enough, so that each different idea yields a new species, whether it has a name or not. However, in the physical sense, we do not give weight to every variation; and we speak either unreservedly, when it is a question merely of appearances, or conjecturally, when it is a question of the inner truth of things, with the presumption that they have some essential and unchangeable nature, as man has reason. (Ibid)

Leibniz is agreeing with Locke that, nominally, we can have any number of classifications, but underneath it all, so to speak, are real essences. Here are his remarks on species:

> One can understand species mathematically or else physically. In mathematical strictness, the tiniest difference which stops two things from being alike in all respects makes them of different species. It is in this sense that in geometry all circles are of a single species, because they are all perfectly alike... Two physical individuals will never be perfectly of the same species in this manner, because they will never be perfectly alike; and, furthermore, a single individual will move from species to species, for it is never entirely similar to itself for more than a

moment. But when men settle on physical species, they do not abide by such rigorous standards; ...in the case of organic bodies---i.e. the species of plants and animals---we define species by generation, so that two similar individuals belong to the same species if they did or could have come from the same origin or seed. (Ibid, 308-9)

The application of mathematics to ontological particulars in order to derive species is inadmissible, as we discussed regarding Zeno, above. Pure mathematics cannot discover ontological differences with respect to any particular. The mathematical approach to individuals in deriving species is also the approach leading to real definitions. But, real definitions are equally unavailable due to the actual natures of particulars; each is other and different. We are left with nominal definitions, but they are necessarily imprecise. It should be clear, however, that because of the diverse natures of particulars, no definitions are possible respecting them.

To define some number of particulars in terms of a real entity which allegedly covers them, say, the common noun 'cow,' is to say what something is in terms of something else (an m-real entity). Think about that. How can a particular cow be something else, something not that cow? Definition is, of course, still another tool in the m-realist's kit. Clearly, the work of biological systematists can proceed without definition and without identifying classes. Actual genetic or phylogenetic relationships (what came from what and when) are not a matter of definition and not a matter of classification.

102

A further point with respect to the above quote from Leibniz. We might pause to reflect on this, "in the case of organic bodies---i.e. the species of plants animals---we define species by generation, so that two similar individuals belong to the same species if they did or could have come from the same origin or seed" (Ibid, p. 309).

Did Leibniz come up with that definition of species (by generation) all by himself? He might have read John Ray. Ernst Mayr used it to make history in the 1940s; it is the core of the modern species definition. We will examine it down the road. Of great interest is Leibniz's understanding of species mathematically. He says, "...the tiniest difference which stops two things from being alike in all respects makes them of different species." If all things differ in all respects (i.e., having no identities, similarities, or commonalities) there can be no species! And, of course, no categories. Mathematics cannot resolve the species problem, but empirical methods, based on the perception of ontological otherness and difference, can.

Liebniz is a great mix of insights. To be sure, he is correctly labeled a rationalist, but he thought of particulars more clearly than any of the empirical philosophers, before or after him. The following quotes will help to support this claim, "every body is changeable and indeed is actually changing all the time, so that it differs in itself from every other". (Ibid, p. 231)

This Heraclitean view of the material world wreaks havoc with category formation. Again, it is evident in this remark, "So we must acknowledge that organic bodies as well as others remain 'the same' only in appearance, and not strictly speaking. It is rather like a river whose water is continually changing" (Ibid).

Of course, what is unchanging for Leibniz, and which makes him an m-realist-rationalist, is equally evident in this remark, "one can rightly say that they [substantial beings] remain perfectly 'the same individual' in virtue of this soul or spirit which makes the I in substances which think" (Ibid, p. 232).

As we shall see, David Hume will look inside, at his I-Substance, and come to a different conclusion about the self.

Chapter 9 Conceptualism Digs in

Kant and the Formation of Concepts

After Leibniz, the increasing interest in the natural world, especially of plants and animals, gave empiricism a boost. Hume reflects some of this. His published skepticism concerning rational knowledge may have awakened Kant from his dogmatic slumber. In trying to do justice to the rights of reason (m-realism-rationalism) and the rights of empiricism (perceived particulars), Kant centers his thought on *concepts*. We intuit (or perceive) particulars, but our minds order sensations in terms of concepts. A concept is what the mind adds to particulars to make them *one, whole, knowable*. That notion was already present, in germ, in Aristotle; concept was also made explicit in Ockham as a logical factor having no ontological status. The concept seems to rise to some ontological status in Locke, and definitely has ontological status in Leibniz' notion of *resemblance as a reality*.

We need to investigate the status of the concept in Kant, and especially his manner of obtaining one, for with him, generating concepts becomes a permanent feature of the human mind over the next couple of centuries. Since they are reason's work, they will occupy a generating/apprehending chamber in the brain called the apriori. Whatever is innate (such as Chomsky's grammatical rules and Quine's quality spacings for similarities and kinds and Fodor's concepts) will find a home among the fibers of that chamber.

Some of what we are looking for is in Kant's logic, the work which sets the stage for his critique. Kant almost never speaks of particulars. The alpha of his philosophy is the concept of the understanding, the omega is the idea of reason, the even more abstract concept. Kant is a rationalist, even if a critical one. He never shows the slightest unease with the formation of concepts and ideas. Kant (1974) justifies reason's ways to man. In the logic he has this to say:

> All cognitions, that is, all presentations consciously referred to an object, are either intuitions or concepts. Intuition is a singular presentation, the concept is a general or reflected presentation.... Concept is opposed to intuition, for it is a general presentation or a presentation of what is common to several objects, a presentation, therefore, so far as it may be contained in different objects. (p. 96)

To understand presentations, we need only remember that Kant lives in a subjective bubble inside his head; that is where sense-data coming from the perception of things arise, that is where the mind generates concepts to deal with the sense-data, ordering them for our understanding. Of the utmost importance is how the mind forms a concept. He says:

> In order to make our presentations into concepts, one must be able to compare, reflect, and abstract, for

106

these three logical operations of the understanding are the essential and general conditions of generating any concept whatever. For example, I see a fir, a willow, and a linden. In firstly comparing these objects, I notice that they are different from one another in respect of trunk, branches, leaves, and the like; further, however, I reflect only on what they have in common, the trunk, the branches, the leaves themselves, and abstract from their size, shape, and so forth; thus I gain a concept of a tree. (Ibid, p. 100)

Kant must have been a great teacher. What could be clearer than those words? A student is assured of generating a concept. Students, but especially professors, have been forming concepts ever since Kant issued his recipe. With such clarity as to their formation, students and professors in Germany have been constructing concepts and ideas in great abundance, some beginning with humble particulars outside the head, others beginning with particulars or other concepts already inside the head. Hegel loved them.

Having shown that abstraction was in trouble when we tried to follow Aquinas, we might expect some trouble here. But we must try to form a concept in the way Kant has stated it can be done. We see three trees; we notice differences; we reflect on what they have in common; we abstract from their differences; and we gain a concept. We won't worry whether three different trees are enough or whether we should include borderline cases of trees; perhaps we can get a complete concept with no more than three trees. But, we will get on with our task of forming a concept. There is no problem in looking at three different trees, especially if you are in a tree nursery or in Central Park where I often go to look at them. I like trees. We might, then, substitute a eucalyptus, a white oak, and a gingko. 1. I look at each one. 2. I notice differences (and they are many with respect to the trees I am using: bark, color and shape of leaves, configuration, height, etc.). 3. I am asked to reflect on what they have in common. Now I have a problem. They don't have anything in common. We can say each has a trunk, branches, leaves...but each has its own trunk, branches, and leaves. So, saying that they have something in common does not generate a something... which they have in common. 4. I am asked to abstract from their differences. I noted, above, several differences, and could have gotten multitudes had I investigated closely the gross and microscopic structures of leaves, branches, trunk, and roots. I admitted difficulty with abstraction earlier and, again, I find that however long my list of comparative differences, I cannot abstract from them, for those differences are, in each case, inherent to the actual tree. Each of those trees can only present (for comparison) its differences for me to cognize! I know the particular gingko, eucalyptus, and white oak I am looking at, closely and in some detail. I could compare two gingkoes, but each is different, but to a lesser degree than they are to other trees. I cannot abstract from the actual differences of my three trees. I could pretend to do it and say that I have some mental image or something that is of no particular tree but is treeness itself since all tree-differences have vanished. But I would be involved in an untruth. I fail, again, to come up with a concept. I was an agreeable student in philosophy and accepted what professors told me, in their lectures and in their writings. Since Kant (and certainly Aquinas) was a wise man, I assumed that if he formed concepts in the way he described, there was little need for me to try, although I never felt that I had more than the word, concept. (I remember worrying over not actually having the concept of democracy in political philosophy, and in the philosophy of science I despaired when it came to the concept of species). Others, too, may not have much more than words about notions. It is my guess that most evolutionary theorists have never ever worried over forming an actual concept of a species.

My coming out of the philosophic closet with respect to forming concepts may help others to be honest about what they can and cannot do in their heads while perceiving particular things. Abstraction, if it can be done, is an important process. Higher intelligence depends on it. Countless thinkers take for granted that it can be done. Isn't it about time someone put that to a test? In *Logic* (1974):

> A concept is either empirical or pure, and the pure concept, so far as it has its origin in the understanding only (not in the pure image of sensibility) is called notion (notio). A concept formed of notions and transcending all possible experience is an idea, or a concept of reason. (Kant, p. 97)

Those words are mindful of Spinoza and his view of levels of knowledge (imagination, ratio, scientia intuitiva). Kant has levels of abstraction too, and we may recall Windelband's remark that Parmenides' being is what we finally arrive at when all difference has been abstracted from the things of this world. Such is our power of abstraction! To contemplate being is surely a godly thing, if we can do it. Kant was not in doubt that we could climb the ladder from concepts to notions to ideas. Heidegger denied that we could have a concept of being, but Kant implies that we can have an idea of God. "By continued logical abstraction originate ever higher concepts, just as on the other hand ever lower concepts originate by continued logical determination" (Ibid, p. 105)

Kant imagines a hierarchy of nested concepts, a notion given considerable attention by taxonomists and biological systematists. If concepts are real entities and can be nested, a metaphysical taxonomic hierarchy might be claimed to exist in nature. Such a claim has been made by some modern evolutionary theorists (e.g., Ghiselin, Hull, Eldredge, Gould), making them, of course, metaphysical realists. Kant (1974) describes such serial nesting as follows:

> There must be in the end a highest concept (concept summum) from which as such no further abstraction can be made without making the entire concept disappear. But there is no lowest concept (concept infimus) or lowest species in the series of species and genera under which not yet another would be contained, because it is impossible to determine such a concept. For even if we have a concept that we apply immediately to individuals, there may still be present in respect of it specific differences which we either do not notice or disregard. Only relative to use are there lowest concepts which have received this meaning, as it were, by convention, to the extent that one has agreed to go no further down. (pp. 103-4)

Kant is following Aristotle's method of division in those remarks. What is of interest here is the admission that, respecting actual individuals we have conceptualized, we are never sure that over-looked differences among some may exclude them from the concept. Low-down concepts are in peril of not being concepts at all. If you think about it (as I did with those trees in the park), the actual differences of individuals forbid our conceptualizing them! Recall Leibniz' approach to species that differ even slightly, mathematically or physically. To conceptualize is to ignore differences, which is to say, it is to pretend sameness of some plurality of individuals. Finding actual relationships of things is not impaired by denying the formation of concepts.

The admission, above, about the indeterminacy of species-level concepts is correlated with Kant's (1881) view of definition.

> To define, as the very name implies, means only to represent the complete concept of a thing within its limits and in its primary character. From this point of view, an empirical concept cannot be defined, but can be explained only. For, as we have in an empirical concept some predicates only belonging to a certain class of sensuous objects, we are never certain whether by the word which denotes one and the same object, we do not think at one time a greater, at another a smaller number of predicates. Thus one man may by the concept of gold think, in addition to weight, colour, malleability, the quality of its not rusting, while another may know nothing of the last.

We use certain predicates so long only as they are required for distinction. New observations add and remove certain predicates, so that the concept never stands within safe limits. (pp.623-24)

Empirical concepts, then, are as indeterminate as their definitions. Much time and effort wasted on defining in the biological arena could have been avoided if the definers had known that empirical definitions must be as arbitrary as the concepts (or classes) on which they are based. A clear definition is an oxymoron. (Recall, the substitution of one word or a phrase for another as in dictionaries is substitution, not definition.)

Chapter 10 Where have we been? Where are we going?

At this point in our review and critique of m-realism and rationalism, we will pause, briefly, and determine where we have been and where we are going.

In a sense, the story in philosophical texts is the one-many story, the story of how the diverse many, the particulars, we see as the contents of the cosmos or nature are viewed as plural ones or kinds. The story also includes the development of the rational way of viewing actual things so as to make nature intelligible. Needed for this rational view were clearly defined categories of things (i.e., the overcoming of their actual differences by notions of identity, sameness, resemblance or likeness and commonality). This step-in rationality introduced m-realism, the doctrine of metaphysical or real entities as part of what there is (given that ontology includes both real and actual things). Belief in metaphysical entities gives rise to a two-tiered epistemology of how and what we know. Metaphysical entities are apprehended differently from rocks and snowflakes for they have virtues of permanence, fixity, timelessness because of their alleged linguistic repeatability. Knowledge of metaphysical objects is the highest type of knowledge or, for some, true knowledge. Since m-real entities are not part of the furniture of the actual world they must be constructed by those who claim to know them. Non-metaphysical objects, the actual particulars of nature, are known directly, and our knowledge of them is not metaphysically constructed but reported. M-realists believe that their metaphysical objects are easily obtained by the process of abstraction. This is more easily said than done. Whether by abstraction or other alleged ways of creating m-real entities, it is apparent that the reason for all the hard work in obtaining and defending their existence is a simple one; the traditional logic generating our rational view of the world requires them. This view is related to the macro-world of things, not the micro-world encountered in quantum mechanics. In the everyday world, particular things are used as stepping stones to generate m-real entities.

So-called pure thought or reason is the legislator of logic. We may wonder if this reason is an attitude each of us has, more or less, toward particular things and particular processes. Is reason a reality demonstrated in the process that is logic? Is it capable of generating the real entities, such as universals, concepts and categories? Is reason simply still another real entity generated by the habit of categorical and inferential ways of behaving? Are we in need of a broader and deeper notion of rationality, a revised notion, or should we discard it in favor of some other process? Would a broader and deeper understanding of what can be experienced be of value in deciding about rationality?

To help answer these questions, we will jump from Kant to C.I. Lewis, an insightful logician and Kantian. We want to pursue the attitude that is reason and note how it creates a rational view of the universe using metaphysical elements.

PART II   Logic, Philosophy, and the Structure of Science

Chapter 11 Experience, Knowing, and The Categorical Attitude

C. I. Lewis and Logic

Lewis (1923) is especially clear about logic, how it is generated, its laws, and what it comprehends:

> That is a priori which is true, no matter what. What it anticipates is not the given, but our attitude toward it: it concerns the uncompelled initiative of the mind or, as Josiah Royce would say, our categorical ways of acting....The traditional example of the a priori par excellence is the laws of logic. These cannot be derived from experience since they must first be taken for granted in order to prove them. They make explicit our general modes of classification....The laws of logic are purely formal; they forbid nothing but what concerns the use of terms and the corresponding modes of classification and analysis....Laws of logic...are principles of procedure the parliamentary rules of intelligent thought and speech. Such laws are independent of experience because they impose no limitations whatever upon it.

They are legislative because they are addressed to ourselves---because definition, classification, and inference represent no operations of the objective world, but only our own categorical attitudes of mind. (p.16)

I devised the title of this essay from, especially, the last lines of the above quotes. It is our categorical attitude, exhibited in definition, classification, and inference which dominates rational thinking. The given (the particulars we experience) are forced into manageable sets by disregarding their individuality. Quite simply, as Lewis points out, we behave categorically.

If we did not behave categorically, we would not generate the logic we do; and we would not think and behave rationally. Many of our actual behaviors have nothing to do with categories, their construction, and the logical inferences using them. It is in using language, in speaking and writing, that the categorical attitude is manifested.

Lewis, we will recall, insists that logic (and its fundamental operations: defining, classifying, and inferring) is a matter of mind, and its operations *represent no operations of the objective world*. Further, he says that definition is classification, a view held by other philosophers and which we have mentioned before. But Lewis adds, "the manner in which the precise classifications which definition embodies shall be affected is something not dictated by experience" (Ibid, p.17). To define is to classify. But the manner of obtaining precise classifications embodied in definitions is not dictated by experience? Who or what dictates those classifications, then? The answer is, the mind dictates the classifications when the particulars, or their impressions, are in its presence, i.e., presented to it. Why? Because the mind has a categorical attitude toward the things we experience. Kant said it. The mind not only dictates the classifications, it also constructs the definitions and makes the inferences.

I will now ask a question that is of the utmost importance in our pursuit of understanding the world and ourselves; why has experience failed to dictate in this most important matter of classifications and definitions and therefore allowed realists to dictate independent of experience, i.e., by an a priori faculty of mind?

To answer that question, I will remind the reader that we first met the philosophical notion of experience in Aristotle's forming a universal. Kant's notion of experience was taken from Aristotle, and Lewis's is taken from either or both. Quite simply, experience has been viewed (and conceptually defined) as an internal affair, an affair of mind, its impressions and memories, touched off by the perception of stimuli from objects in the natural world. Is experience correctly viewed by these philosophers? I think not. Their view of experience is too shallow. 1. They do not persist in the perceptual phase, hence they do not go deeply enough to discover more details of the actual character of each particular and the comparative otherness and difference of each. 2. Their view of perception is faulty; it is viewed as a subjective process from beginning to end, whereas in actuality it begins with an external object and ends with that object, thus making it an objective process of knowing particulars, as they are and can become. 3. Lastly, perceiving is the process of knowing; knowing actualities as they are and become, for it is the process of discriminating actual differences. To know is to perceive a thing as it is, over the period of our perceptual scrutiny of it. Comparative scrutiny, in the context of extended experience reveals its otherness and differences out there, in the world of objects. Hence, short-circuiting the process of perception from its termination in the external experience is stopping short, in the subjective arena of mind where labels are put on things: a similarity, a commonality, an identity.

Traditionally, perception has been viewed as the first phase, or psychological base, on which knowing, the second phase of empirical knowing, develops. It is during the second phase that the mind allegedly operates on the psychological materials (sensations, stimuli, sense-data, or whatever) and, noting similarities or identities or commonalities and classifies them. Knowing thus becomes that internal affair of mind: the imposition of a metaphysical reality (i.e., a class, kind, etc.) on particulars. If experience involves perceptual discrimination of the otherness and difference of actual particulars, knowing them as they are, then no imposition of real entities is required. If perception is viewed as a psychological event separated from the particulars and terminating in the mind, rather than terminating in, while persisting in examining, the object(s), then we will proceed with the traditional recipe; perceive, then operate on the perceptual materials, then know...which is the result of those operations. If perception begins with objects and terminates with our knowing them, then experience is a richer process than philosophers have imagined. Returning to Lewis:

If experience were other than it is, the definition and its corresponding classification might be inconvenient, fantastic, or useless, but it could not be false. Mind makes classifications and determines meanings; in so doing it creates the a priori truth of analytic judgments. (Ibid, p. 17)

We have decided that experience can be other than the traditional way of viewing it. If so, then the definitions and the corresponding classifications are not true of the particulars defined and classified. This means there is a disconnect between the mind, as Lewis (and every m-realist) views it, and the particulars of the world (outside and inside the head).

Lewis might well ignore our new way of experiencing which terminates in objects outside the head and refuse to change his categorical habits of defining and classifying in which experience is short-circuited and thus favor subjective reason. If experience and its determination of the actual natures of particulars can be perceived, then the philosophic stance in the metaphysical is an error. If it is the case that we can know the natures of particulars if we try, then the metaphysical ground on which scientists construct their theories and rest their laws is called in question. *Definitions* and *classifications* yield pretend objects, objects not true of the actual world. Furthermore, the logic using those pretend objects can be shown to be without foundation, incapable of validation. The result is that generalizations, as well as inferences, deductive and inductive, fall apart.

Here is Lewis on the relation of concepts, definition, naming, and classification to science:

All science is based on definitive concepts. The formulation of these concepts is, indeed, a matter determined by the commerce between our intellectual or our pragmatic interests and the nature of experience. Definition is classification. The scientific search is for such classification as will make it possible to correlate appearance and behavior, to discover law, to penetrate to the "essential nature" of things in order that behavior may become predictable....if definition is unsuccessful, as early scientific definitions mostly have been, it is because the classification thus set up corresponds with no natural cleavage and does not correlate with any important uniformity of behavior....A name itself must represent some uniformity in experience or it names nothing. What does not repeat itself or recur in intelligible fashion is not a thing.... In scientific classification the search is, thus, for things worth naming. But the naming, classifying, defining activity is essentially prior to investigation. We cannot interrogate experience in general. Until our meaning is definite and our classification correspondingly exact, experience cannot conceivably answer our questions. (Ibid, p. 19)

For Lewis, as for his student Quine, science has the burden of discovering natural laws, of finding those natural cleavage(s) which enable us to create precise scientific definitions and classifications, of penetrating to the essential nature of things and behaviors that are uniform, that can be named, that can be predicted.

Certainly, Lewis is saying, a name must represent some *uniformity* in experience, something which is repeated, which recurs in intelligible fashion. *Cow, electron, thunder* do not represent some uniformity in subjective experience, they represent uniquely changing things out there whose behaviors or changes are not so extensive as to have us withhold the same names for them. It would be better to say the name points to, or points up (not represents) a discontinuous bit of matter-energy, not a uniformity. The word thunder does not represent a uniformity (which is a generalization) in nature, it represents events which are other and different each time they occur; and thunder and Bessie the cow do not recur. Nor does the same electron recur; we are not, now, sure that the same electron can occur again or what it may be like when we are not seeing it (which we haven't yet been able to do). If quantum theory is to be believed, electrons are rather perverse little entities anyway, and especially when confronted with a slit or two.

As for the relation of scientific laws to concepts and categories, Lewis says, "the fundamental laws of any science...are a priori because they formulate just such definitive concepts or categorical tests by which alone investigation becomes possible." (Ibid, p. 19)

He continues:

At the bottom of all science and all knowledge are categories and definitive concepts which represent fundamental habits of thought and deep-lying attitudes which the human mind has taken in the light of its total experience...and no experience can conceivably prove them invalid. (Ibid, p. 23)

The last quote sends a strong message: all science and all knowledge are based on categories and definitive concepts. This is the Kantian way with philosophy and science. The categories and concepts are produced by the mind in its response to its total experience, a notion of experience which, I contend, is incomplete. As for the categories and concepts we produce:

> Our categories and definitions are peculiarly social products... Conceptions, such as those of logic, which are least likely to be affected by the opening of new ranges of experience, represent the most stable of our categories; but none of them is beyond the possibility of alteration. (Ibid, p. 24)

The categorical attitude is a permanent (A Priori) feature of mind, but particular categories and concepts and definitions may be altered or even discarded. Logic itself is subject to change, but Lewis cannot imagine that the categorical attitude will ever be given up.

My Question: Under what circumstances would we be willing to suspend our categorical attitude toward nature? The best answer I can come up with is, if nature is falsified in our experience of it by holding to the categorical attitude, then we must first suspend---think through the consequences---and then give it up.

Lewis and most philosophers hold to a view of nature and experience quite other and different from mine. "Mind contributes to experience the element of order, of classification, categories, and definition. Without such, experience would be unintelligible" (Ibid).

That is a not only a Kantian view of mind and experience, it is an Aristotelian and Thomistic view. Those views are wrong because they do not penetrate to the natures of actual particulars although a more open mind and experience could reveal those natures.

Nature, the cosmos, does not need the mind to order it. Whatever order or chaos it has is what it developmentally and changingly has. That order or disorder is understandable without the screen of concepts and categories our minds can erect to view nature through. Intelligibility is a word in the tool kit of m-realism. Its original utility is over now that we no longer need to abstract the images and phantasms from faceless particulars.

I am calling the status of the A Priori function of mind into question. If the natures of multitudinous particulars of the cosmos, inside and outside heads, are as I am indicating, there is no need for the A Priori as it would relate to actualities. The cosmos is not logical (quantum mechanics is making this more than abundantly clear), the cosmos offers no basis for concepts and categories and for inferences between and among them and particulars. If Reason is the primary occupant of the A Priori, then, with respect to the cosmos, Reason can relax; it needn't formulate scientific laws, for the cosmos doesn't have any. At least it has none that fit our rational description of what laws must be. No laws can be derived or apply simply because the cosmos never in any of its particulars recurs or presents a uniformity. Oddly enough, and this is one of the extraordinary things about the cosmos, it differs so little at times that we think expectantly in terms of similarities, identities, uniformities and recurrences. Indeed, there are good reasons why our categorical attitude is a habit. But it is a bad habit. Fortunately, habits can be changed.

Chapter 12 Quine: The Structure of Science and its Relation to Experience

Traditional Notions of Experience and Perception Criticized

We might begin with this remark by Quine (1953):

The totality of our so-called knowledge or beliefs from the most casual matters of geography and history to the profoundest laws of atomic physics or even of pure mathematics and logic, is a man-made fabric which impinges on experience only along the edges. (p. 62)

For Lewis experience cannot undermine the authority of the a priori. Quine allows that experience could undermine it, although it is not likely that it will do so. The *could* is important, for it makes this great logician something of an empiricist! In fact, Quine says he is:

No statement is immune to revision. Revision even of the logical law of excluded middle has been proposed as a means of simplifying quantum mechanics...As an empiricist I continue to think of the conceptual scheme of science as a tool, ultimately, for predicting future experience in the light of past experience. (Ibid, p. 63)

This does not mean, of course, that Quine cannot also be a rationalist, which he is, and an m-realist to boot.

Quine's view of experience is the traditional view, of Aristotle, Kant, and Lewis that we have addressed. It does not go deeply enough into the experienceable , it does not come up with the actual natures of particulars. At the same time, shallow experience has a minor role to play in an empiricism whose logical statements are in a close-knit holistic structure open to experience only at the edges. As Quine says:

Total science, mathematical and natural and human, is...extremely underdetermined by experience. The edge of the system must be kept squared with experience; the rest, with all its elaborate myths or fictions, has as its objective the simplicity of laws. (Ibid, p. 64)

What myths or fictions is he talking about in his view of total science? Perhaps this will help:

Physical objects are conceptually imported into the situation as convenient intermediaries---not by definition in terms of experience, but simply as irreducible posits comparable, epistemologically, to the gods of Homer. For my part I do, QUA lay

130

physicist, believe in physical objects and not in Homer's gods; and I consider it a scientific error to believe otherwise. But in point of epistemological footing the physical objects and the gods differ only in degree and not in kind. Both sorts of entities enter our conception only as cultural posits. The myth of physical objects is epistemologically superior to most in that it has proved more efficacious than other myths as a device for working a manageable structure into the flux of experience. (Ibid, p. 64)

So, the myth of physical objects and the myths of the Greek gods are comparable, epistemologically. Sounds strange. We must remember, however, that Quine's fabric of sentences (total science) will include anything as the value of a variable. We can speak knowingly (i.e., epistemologically) about the Rocky Mountains, electrons, quarks, and Zeus. Those who want to claim Zeus lives can make the claim in a logically valid sentence. Whether Zeus actually lives or not is another matter, but Quine will not disallow the ontological implication of the valid sentence. For him, Zeus and Numbers have ontological rights. I would prefer to say Zeus has mythological rights and that Numbers have pretend rights, but that's because I'm inclined to be ontologically parsimonious. But ontology is not just a matter of taste! What we claim exists, or say is *real*, (i.e., actual) makes a difference. Metaphysical realities have proven to be a troublesome lot. Ask Darwin about species. Ask those who have been victims of religious or racial or political realities. All that, however, is another story. We will get on with this one. Quine says:

131

Positing does not stop with macroscopic physical objects. Objects at the atomic level are posited to make the laws of macroscopic objects, and ultimately the laws of experience, simpler and more manageable; and we need not expect or demand full definition of atomic and subatomic entities in terms of macroscopic ones, any more than definition of macroscopic things in terms of sense data. Science is a continuation of common sense, and it continues the common-sense expedient of swelling ontology to simplify theory. (Ibid, p. 64-5)

Plato posited forms, Aristotle posited forms and essences, mathematicians posit m-real numbers and figures, Quine posits whatever he needs to obtain simple laws, to simplify theory, to work a manageable structure into the flux of experience. We are not to worry. We benefit if science helps us to expedite our dealings with experience. After all, science is a continuation of common sense (as Scott Atran has shown) and it continues the common-sense expedient of swelling ontology to simplify theory. Perhaps, then, we should take a closer look at common-sense.

Common-sense is hardly something to be proud of, judged by the accounts of the tribes and clans, and even larger social groups, who possess it. I have already indicated that, other than the Phusikoi---who gave up common-sense to ask the question concerning what is the nature of Nature--- most peoples' common-sense is awash in the pseudo-ontologies of religion, mythology, the occult, the astrological. It is common-sense, in modern folk, that tells them that there are commonalities, identities, resemblances which allow them to define and classify plants and animals (and other things); in other words, that species and races exist. Epistemologically, Quine is aware that physical things and the gods of Homer are posits, but he is also aware that the gods don't exist, they are not part of his ontological world. But, as we shall see down the road, Ghiselin, Hull, Eldredge, and Gould declare species to be individuals and also real; that is, they exist in their ontological world along with this and that particular plant and animal. I can understand Quine's way with ontology; the mythical is tolerated along with the non-mythical. But he knows the difference between Zeus and the Empire State Building. Ghiselin, Hull, Eldredge and Gould don't seem to understand the difference. They claim that scientific theory is better if their particular mythical entities are used. Are we to tolerate any and everything for the sake of theory, for the sake of laws? What Ghiselin, Hull, Eldredge, and Gould sense in common (their individuals) is, admittedly, common-sense; but so are UFOs and ghosts and souls headed for reincarnation. Nothing prevents ghosts and souls from being ontological objects used in theories; are those theories scientific? Given the epistemological equivalence of mythical entities and physical objects, who's to say? Are souls useful in simplifying theory? Perhaps they are, for those who use them. Are the boundaries between the scientific and the non-scientific so vague? Perhaps they are, perhaps they don't exist. If souls help us to expedite our dealings with experiences, why not use them? Sticking pins in dolls helps some to expedite their dealings with experience. Killing people helps others. I should think that it makes an important difference whether some alleged objects do, in actuality, exist, and I should think that it makes an important difference as to whether we believe in non-existent objects. Ontology aims to encompass every thing, and not also every non-thing we may care to believe in. We must be tolerant of people, but not of any and all of their beliefs, for some beliefs are fatally important to those who may want nothing to do with them.

Quine's view of experience is not only shallow, it is a peripheral matter with respect to the so-called fabric that is science. Common-sense plus the hard work of scientists over the last five hundred years, especially, have woven sentences into logical concepts, theories, and laws. All that is, as Quine said, rather stable. New experiences, he says, may turn up items which may simply further corroborate what we already have or cause us to change some of the lower-level concepts or theories. Most laws he believes will probably remain or, at most, be encompassed by more general ones. Quine doesn't expect experience to change, and he certainly doesn't expect experience to undermine science as a totality.

That brings us to ask a crucial question; what makes the fit between experience and science? That is, where does the linguistic (a sentence) attach to the experiential? If total science is a fabric touching experience only at the edges, I want to see where a sentence (a scientific claim) attaches to sensory materials. If experience is to undermine the metaphysics in Quine's notion of total science, then I suspect that the alleged point of attachment of a word to its sensory object is the place to focus on. Let us see.

Chapter 13 Kuhn's Second Thoughts on Paradigms

The Point of Attachment of Words to Things

Quine is quite clear; it is observation sentences (e.g., 'the swan is white') that are made, and they are made on the basis of stimuli. Kuhn is clear as to how this is done, for it involves his notion of a scientific community and the steps a little boy takes in becoming a prospective member of the larger community in which the activities called science are embedded. He says, "A paradigm is what members of a scientific community, and they alone, share" (Kuhn, 1997, p. 460). And, "A scientific community consists...of practitioners of a scientific specialty...typically...perhaps 100 members" (Ibid, 461-62).

Having second thoughts after having received some criticisms about his use of "paradigm," Kuhn says, "less confusion will result if I...replace [paradigm] with the phrase 'disciplinary matrix'" (Ibid, p. 463). And what are the constituents of such a matrix? "Symbolic generalizations, models, and exemplars" (Ibid).

Generalizations are extremely important in doing science. They are either symbolic (f ' ma) or non-symbolic (action equals reaction, all cells come from cells). Kuhn says, "without a shared commitment to a set of symbolic generalizations, logic and mathematics could not routinely be applied in the community's work" (Ibid, p. 464).

What we are interested in is how scientists attach symbolic expressions or words to nature. Kuhn's answer involves turning away from the customary notion, that of correspondence rules. Such rules are, "operational definitions of scientific terms or else a set of necessary and sufficient conditions for the term's applicability" (Ibid, p. 467).

However, for Kuhn, the correspondence rules do not connect symbolic expressions directly to nature, they connect words to other words, "theoretical terms acquire meaning via the correspondence rules that attach them to a previously meaningful vocabulary. Only the latter attach directly to nature" (Ibid, p. 467).

Thus, the meaningful vocabulary attaches directly to nature, and this all-important attachment is not only of interest to us, it is of importance to Kuhn. "...I am...concerned to inquire how direct attachment may work, whether of a theoretical or basic vocabulary" (Ibid). Kuhn is critical of the accepted view that implicitly assumes "that anyone who knows how to use a basic term correctly has access, consciously or unconsciously, to a set of criteria which define that term or provide necessary and sufficient conditions governing its application" (Ibid).

That remark goes to the heart of definition. We all certainly assume that we know how to use basic terms such as 'duck,' 'goose,' and 'swan,' for example, but we also assume that our use follows upon our knowledge of criteria for defining the terms and, perhaps, our ability to provide necessary and sufficient conditions governing their application. Kuhn is saying that the use of a set of criteria to define a term or provide necessary and sufficient conditions for its application, "make the deployment of language seem more a matter of convention than it is" (Ibid). The deployment of language is less conventional than definition, etc., because for Kuhn, "a man who acquires either an everyday or a scientific language simultaneously learns things about nature which are not themselves embodied in verbal generalizations" (Ibid).

The key to the attachment of basic terms to nature, then, involves our learning certain things about nature. What can they be? Kuhn is emphasizing a firmer linkage, a linkage firmer than convention, that will nail down the term, so to speak. Philosophers of science have not, according to Kuhn, given sufficient attention to the language-nature link. He believes the transition from a sense-datum language to a basic vocabulary has resulted in a loss, epistemologically. As he puts it, "'green patch there' scarcely needed further operational specification; Benzene boils at 80 degrees centigrade is, however, a very different sort of statement" (Ibid, p. 468).

Kuhn's clarification of the language-nature link, the attachment of basic terms to nature, resides in this, "an acquired ability to see resemblances...an acquired perception of analogy" (Ibid, pp. 471-72). Philosophers of science agree that the old sense-datum language was too private. As Kuhn put it, "it is stimuli, not sensations, that impinge on us as organisms" (Ibid, p. 473).

The switch to a basic vocabulary that we all use, and in which the (basic) terms are linked not to subjective factors but to objective resemblances and acquired perception of analogy, makes the language-nature link a public and community affair. Presumably, all of us can see resemblances and even acquire the needed perception of analogy. Clearly, if we can see a resemblance, we can see where a basic term attaches to nature. Let us see.

The alleged language-nature link must involve particular things and the singular or proper terms we use for them or the common nouns used in reference to them. But since to see resemblances involves some number of particulars, it is common nouns and their use that is the focus for Kuhn. This is the traditional problem of universals. This is the problem that we have seen Plato, Aristotle, Aquinas, Ockham, Locke, Leibniz, Spinoza, and Kant grappling with, more often in terms of the process of abstraction. Quine grapples with this, too, and we shall see how he fares after we understand Kuhn's way with the language-nature link (i.e., his settling on m-realism as the solution to the problem of universals).

We will take a walk with Kuhn, Johnny, and Johnny's father. We will receive a lesson in the educational program of m-realism. Johnny goes to the Zoological Garden with his father, says Kuhn, and learns how to use, that is attach, the word-labels swans, geese, and ducks, to the feathered particulars in the garden. Kuhn says, "Anyone who has taught a child...knows that the primary tool is ostension" (Ibid, p. 473). By pointing and correcting Johnny's responses, Johnny learns to use/attach the words to his father's satisfaction.

Johnny did not discover for himself that there were

138

swans, geese, and ducks. Rather, he was taught....Since Johnny's father has, in effect, told him that ducks, geese, and swans are members of discrete natural families, Johnny has every right to expect that all future ducks, geese, and swans will fall naturally into...one of these families....By being programmed to recognize what his prospective community already knows, Johnny has acquired consequential information. He has learned that geese, ducks, and swans form discrete natural families and that nature offers no swan-geese or goose-ducks. (Ibid, pp. 474-75)

We might be curious enough, at this juncture, to ask whether Johnny knows the meanings of the terms goose, duck, or swan? It would seem that Johnny doesn't need, or use, meanings when, under the guidance of his father, he is correlating a word and a feathered particular. Shaving meanings, as possible m-real entities, is our obligation to ontological parsimony. Kuhn, however answers our question:

In any useful sense, yes, for he can apply these labels unequivocally and without effort, drawing from their application, either directly or via general statements. ...he has learned all this without acquiring, or at least without needing to acquire, even one criterion for identifying swans, geese, or ducks. Johnny, in short, has learned to apply symbolic labels to nature without anything like definitions or correspondence rules. In their absence he employs a learned but nonetheless primitive perception of similarity and difference. While acquiring the perception, he has learned something about nature. This knowledge can thereafter be embedded, not in generalizations or rules, but in the similarity relationship itself. (Ibid, pp. 475-77)

There we have it. Anyone who can unequivocally apply the label 'duck' to a duck knows the meaning of duck and such application does not require criteria, definitions, or correspondence rules. But, how does someone manage to apply such labels? He employs a learned but nonetheless primitive perception of similarity and difference; he perceives the similarity of ducks and their difference from geese and swans. These perceptions of similarity and difference are the way we learn about, and gain knowledge of, nature. Knowledge of nature, then, resides not in each particular, but the similarity relationship itself, which is a matter of two or more particulars.

We must turn to that similarity relationship and examine it. But the truth is, we can't find it. Nor have we any hope of finding it. We understand why Kuhn makes the claim of its existence: it is necessary if we are to have science. The problem is a simple one. There is no resemblance entity or relationship to be seen. To see a resemblance between or among two or more things is, presumably, to also see the resemblance relationship itself. That factor or entity or relationship must be something (else how could we see it), and the particulars who share that something must resemble in that respect, else there is no resemblance relationship at all. Now, Kuhn insists that the respect in which some

140

number of things (say ducks) resemble cannot, or must not, be specified, for to do so is to immediately make possible the invocation of correspondence rules. That is, if we can state the respect, we can thereby state criteria and so make possible definitions and necessary and sufficient conditions for the application of a common noun. Kuhn, having learned about family resemblances from Wittgenstein, leaves open what is perceived or seen when we know the resemblance of particular things. We must wonder whether having actually failed to see the respect which unites two or more things in their similarity, he decided to shun stating the criteria and its path to definitions and the necessary and sufficient conditions for the application of common nouns. We will get around to Wittgenstein, but there may be a better way with resemblance, or similarity, than making it an open mystery. What Kuhn focuses on is the nub of the problem, but he fails to solve it: Similarity claims regarding two or more particulars must establish that there is a similarity relation between those particulars. It is not sufficient to say of this particular's x, y, and z characteristics that they are alike x, y, and z of that particular where x, y, and z refer to, say, size, shape, and color. To validate the claim of the existence of the similarity relationship, we must see not the size, shape, and color of each particular but what makes the size, shape, and color of each (individually or in toto) similar. This requires that we see that in respect of which two or more things are said to be similar. But, we never see anything other than the individual traits of each, never the similarity relationship which establishes their similarity. Assuming that we can see a similarity of two or more things is an assumption that has been with us for more than two thousand years.

Chapter 14 Quine's Reflections on "Natural Kinds" and "Similarity"

Before Kuhn pointed to the language-nature link and pronounced it to be in the perceived resemblance of things, Quine wrote an important essay in which he discussed the notions of similarity (or resemblance) and kind. The outcome of that analysis indicates that, for Quine, similarity is not merely a psychological aspect of perception; it is rooted in our biology:

> ...the innate sense of perceptual similarity has, for all its subjectivity, a degree of objective validity... Our innate standards of perceptual similarity show a gratifying tendency to run with the grain of nature...Natural selection will have favored green and blue, as avenues of inductive generalization, and never grue. (Quine, 1973, p. 118)

And,

> If an individual learns at all, differences in degree of similarity must be implicit in his learning pattern. Otherwise any response, if reinforced, would be

conditioned equally and indiscriminately to any and every future episode, all these being equally similar. Some implicit standard, however provisional for ordering our episodes as more or less similar must therefore antedate all learning, and be innate. (Ibid, p. 119)

Quine's remarks on the innate sense of perceptual similarity has been accorded dictum status, and it reinforces the views of linguistic innatists as with Chomsky and Fodor. Plato, in explaining his forms, looked toward the Divine; Quine looks toward Darwin and genetic installation in the human brain. Darwin has an answer for him.

We need to understand Quine's analysis and conclusions regarding similarity and natural kinds.

...there is nothing more basic to thought and language than our sense of similarity; our sorting of things into kinds. [And,] The usual general term, whether a common noun or a verb or an adjective, owes its generality to some resemblance among the things referred to. (Ibid, p. 116)

Clearly, Quine is in accord with Professor C.I. Lewis on the matter of the categorical attitude. However, unlike Lewis, Quine aims to understand the notion of a kind and of similarity. "The notion of a kind and the notion of similarity or resemblance seem to be variants or adaptations of a single notion. Similarity is immediately definable in terms of kind; for, things are similar when they are two of a kind" (Ibid, p. 117).

Some progress will have been made if similarity can be defined in terms of kind; that is, things are similar when they are two of a kind. We see that two things are similar, so we can say that they are two of a kind. If we know their kind we will know why they are similar. Can we know their kind? It seems that even for Quine, we cannot; "...we are baffled when we try to relate the general notion of similarity significantly to logical terms" (Ibid). That is, "One's first hasty suggestion might be to say that things are similar when they have all or most or many properties in common" (Ibid). However, "...any such course only reduces our problem to the unpromising task of settling what to count as a property" (Ibid).

Quine tries to deal with the nature of the problem of what to count as a property, explicating it in terms of set theory. "Things are viewed as going together into sets in any and every combination, describable and indescribable. Any two things are joint members of any number of sets" (Ibid, pp. 117-18).

He admits that set theory fails in solving the problem of what counts as a property in defining similarity. So he goes on, "If properties are to support this line of definition where sets do not, it must be because properties do not, like sets, take things in every random combination. It must be that properties are shared only by things that are significantly similar" (Ibid, p. 118). However, he finds 'similarity' is inexplicable without its connotation of shared properties. "Properties in such a sense are no clearer than kinds. To start with such a notion of property, and define similarity on that basis, is no better than accepting similarity as undefined" (Ibid).

145

Up to this point in Quine's discussion, similarity has been treated as a dyadic relation and simply means belonging to some one same kind. Moving up to the more serious and useful triadic relation of comparative similarity forces a correlative change to take place in the notion of kind. At this point, the trivial definition of similarity as sameness of kind breaks down, and defining triadic similarity works only for finite systems of kinds. Quine sums up:

> The notion of kind and the notion of similarity seemed to be substantially one notion.... They resist reduction to less dubious notions, as of logic or set theory....That they at any rate be definable each in terms of the other seems little enough to ask. (Ibid, p. 119)

However:

> Definition of similarity in terms of kind is halting...definition of kind in terms of similarity is unknown....Still the two notions are in an important sense correlative. They vary together.... I have stressed how fundamental the notion of similarity or kind is to our thinking, and how alien to logic and set theory. (Ibid, p. 121)

It seems that *similarity* and *kind* remain opaque to our understanding. Still, for Quine and all scientists, they are of fundamental importance. We know that logic itself is at stake and therefore our view of science. Quine goes on in his discussion to point up how the notion of similarity is used in the ostensive learning of language; we learn by ostension what presentations to call yellow; more samples and hearing 'yellow' applied to them reinforce the learning; then, all one has to go on is the similarity of further cases to the samples; similarity is a matter of degree; the process is mostly unconscious, but what one uses here is a fully functioning sense of similarity; needed as they are for all learning, the distinctive *spacing of qualities* cannot all be learned; some must be innate; in fact, a standard of similarity is in some sense innate.

Quine also goes on to relate the notions of similarity and kind to the process of induction. He says, "Induction itself is essentially only more of the same: animal expectation or habit formation. And the ostensive learning of words is an implicit case of induction" (Ibid, p. 125). And:

> The brute irrationality of our sense of similarity, its irrelevance to anything in logic and math, offers little reason to expect that this sense is somehow in tune with the world---a world which, unlike language, we never made. Why induction should be trusted, apart from special cases such as the ostensive learning of words, is the perennial philosophic problem of induction. (Ibid, pp. 125-26)

The problem of induction, then, as with the problem of one-many, universals, and species, is related, ultimately, to the natures of particulars. The problem of induction was an albatross around the collective neck of the logical positivists; it is a problem created by belief in the doctrine of m-realism and remains because of the opaqueness of the notions of similarity and kind. We will consider it briefly after we leave Quine and return to Kuhn and his computer modeling of similarity.

Quine is sure that one part of induction, the question why there should be regularities in nature at all---can be dismissed: "That there is an established fact of science." That assumption, unexamined by Quine, is related to the problem of similarity, kinds, universals, and, of course, induction itself. Quine says, "...the other part: why does our innate subjective spacing of qualities accord so well with the functionally relevant groupings in nature as to make our inductions tend to come out right" (Ibid, p. 126)

His answer is that we and the world somehow match and that our expectations along certain inductive lines will be satisfied. Faith in induction is a deeply rooted feeling and, for Quine, justified by our tendency to get things right. Whence comes such a fit between man and nature? The answer, for Quine, is rooted in the neuro-physiology of human evolution. Had we gone along with grue, early on, rather than with blue, we probably would not be around to praise ourselves for our inductive intuition.

Not only our inductive procedures are based on kinds, cause also turns on the notion of kinds. "A singular causal statement says no more than that one event was followed by the other.... To say that one event caused another is to say that the two events are of KINDS between which there is invariable succession" (Ibid, p. 132).

Thus, the notion of kinds brings out the "needed link between singular and general causal statements" (Ibid). In addition to cause, other notions rest on kind or similarity, "the notion of kind, or similarity, is crucially relevant to the notion of disposition, to the subjunctive conditional, and to singular causal statements" (Ibid, pp. 132-33).

How important, then, are kind and similarity? "Some such notion, some similarity sense, was seen to be crucial to all learning, and central in particular to the processes of inductive generalization and prediction which are the very life of science" (Ibid, p. 132). Those notions are at the core of science. Still, Quine admits that he has failed to make them intelligible, so, "science is rotten to the core...yet, science reveals hidden mysteries, predicts successfully, and works technological wonders" (Ibid).

Quine wants us to believe that our similarity sense is responsible for our success in scientific prediction. If we have no such sense---because the natures of particulars in the world are never similar, only different in various ways and degrees---then our success in predicting must be tied to the tendency to ignore certain differences. Scientific inductions are, therefore, based upon untruths. Telling untruths has never much bothered humans and especially if doing so makes for some measure of success. But if we know better, we might want to tell truths.

To broaden our survey, we will look into some of Goodman's views on the notion of similarity and its relation to induction.

Chapter 15 Goodman on Similarity and Induction

Nelson Goodman is a nominalist who managed to keep afloat in the sea of m-realism which surrounds us all. His rejection of classes still stands, and he rejects much else besides: intensions, modalities, analyticity, synonymy, and properties. His view of similarity is consistent with his nominalism: the rejection of Platonism and the construing of classes as individuals. Parenthetically, this construal is taken up by Michael Ghiselin in his *solution* to the problem of biological species. Goodman's construal is invalid and so is Ghiselin's solution.

Quine says that Goodman's nominalism has managed to subjugate only a small part of what is required in doing math and science. Quine himself has disavowed nominalism and opted for the richer domain that abstract entities affords. In other words, Quine is an m-realist.

Since Goodman allows commonalities between and among particulars, he does not dig far enough into ontology to come up with a correct view of the actual natures of particulars. His nominalism aims at parsimony, but it does not close the door on m-realism.

As for his view of similarity, Goodman says, "As it

occurs in philosophy, similarity tends under analysis either to vanish entirely or to require for its explanation just what it purports to explain....statements of similarity...cannot be trusted in the philosopher's study" (Goodman, 1972, p. 446).

Goodman rejects the notion of similarity, whereas Quine makes it an innate sense on which Science is based. The disagreement with Quine may be noted in his statement, "Similarity does not account for our predictive, or more generally, our inductive practices" (Ibid, p. 441). It is not often that a philosopher's remarks can be the source of enjoyment; however, the following remarks on the relation of similarity to induction, may be an exception.

> That the future will be like the past is often regarded as highly dubious---an assumption necessary for science and for life but probably false, and capable of justification only with the greatest difficulty if at all. I am glad to be able to offer you something positive here. All these doubts and worries are needless. I can assure you confidently that the future will be like the past. I do not know whether you find this comforting or depressing. But before you decide on celebration or suicide, I must add that while I am sure the future will be like the past, I am not sure in just what way it will be like the past. No matter what happens, the future will be in some way like the past. (Ibid)

> Thus our predictions cannot be based upon the bald principle that the future will be like the past. The question is how what is predicted is like what has already been found. Along which, among countless

lines of similarity, do our predictions run? I suspect that rather than similarity providing any guidelines for inductive practice, inductive practice may provide the basis for some cannons of similarity. (Ibid)

That is the similarity or likeness view of the world and our inductive practice. I will append my diversity view of the world and relate it to inductive practice:

I can assure you confidently that the future will differ from the past. I do not know whether you find this comforting or depressing. I must add that while I am sure the future will differ from the past, I am not sure in just what ways it will differ. No matter what happens, the future will differ from the past.

Our predictions cannot be based upon the bald principle that the future will be like the past, for that is illusory. The question is, then, how, or to what degree, what is predicted differs from what has already been found. Along which, among countless lines of difference can our predictions run? I suspect that since difference cannot provide for the entrenchment of predicates or the construction of "kinds," it also cannot provide secure guidelines for inductive practice. Inductive practice, however useful, is without rational foundation. (The author)

Goodman's resolution of the new riddle of induction distinguished between projectable lawlike hypotheses and those that merely resemble them. The solution depends upon the relative entrenchment of predicates. As another philosopher, Margolis, put it, entrenchment "constitutes...a pragmatic confirmation of the fruitfulness of certain favored predicates" (1978). Green, in the matter of emeralds, for example, rather than grue. My question is, is entrenchment merely instrumental or is it, at bottom, simply m-realism? Let us turn to Goodman's account:

> What, then, is required for inductive validity? Certain formal relationships among the sentences in question plus what I shall call right categorization. Now a category or system of categories---a way of sorting--- is not sentential, is not true or false; but use of wrong categories will make an induction invalid no matter how true the conclusion. (Goodman, 1984, p. 37)

He then gives his *grue emeralds* example and says:

> "Grue" picks out a category wrong in this context, a nonrelevant kind. Valid induction runs within---is constrained by---right categories; and only through distinguishing right categories from among classes in general can we distinguish valid from invalid induction. But what makes a category right? Very briefly, and over simply, its adoption in inductive practice, its entrenchment, resulting from inertia modified by invention. Why some categories rather than others have become entrenched---a subject of avid philosophical debate---does not matter here; the entrenchment, however achieved, provides the required distinction. Rightness of categorization, in my view, derives from rather than underlies

entrenchment. (Ibid)

How, then, is our question, above, answered? Is entrenchment merely instrumental or is it m-realism? Margolis believes, and we may agree, that Goodman's solution to the riddle of induction stops short of "specifying the actual basis of an epistemically operative [m-] realism" (1978). We may also agree with Margolis's observation that "entrenchment and projectability presuppose a solution to the problem of similarity rather than supply it" (Ibid).

Quine's analysis of similarity and kind did not remove their obscurity, it left us not understanding either of those crucial notions. Goodman points to entrenchment as the basis for rightness of categorization and for our practice of induction. But, do we understand entrenchment? It remains quite as obscure as similarity and kind in Quine's analysis. We are left to believe that inductive validity rests on right categories and that right categories rest on their entrenchment. Unless I am mistaken, this leaves us to conclude that we do not know why correct categories are *correct* other than the fact that they are the ones we usually use, and the ones we usually use are those that are entrenched. And, again, unless I am mistaken, entrenchment remains unexplained. Margolis put Goodman's ultimate stance in entrenchment this way, "The epistemic viability of nominalism directly depends on [m-]realism, without which it must be either vacuous or arbitrary" (Margolis, 1978, p. 390).

Margolis, I believe, has correctly described Goodman's nominalism and, for that matter, traditional nominalism from the standpoint of one who is an m-realist.

Traditional nominalism is not incorrect; it and Goodman's are simply incomplete. We are left hanging between the vacuous and the arbitrary. Margolis is saying that when we fall, we will land on an m-real entity. Goodman refuses to be an m-realist. His nominalism doesn't simply shun m-real entities, such as species and classes, he incorporates them into his system as individuals; they are particulars among the other particulars that the nominalist already acknowledges. That solution, however will not do; there are no m-real entities, call them individuals or what you will.

We might pursue, briefly, Margolis's unhappiness with Goodman's view of similarity and stance in nominalism. Margolis insists that there is a, "disposition toward [M-]Realism that is inherent in the very use of language, facilitating our movements within an actual world encountered" (Ibid, p. 397). He continues:

> It is quite impossible to treat the use of language either instrumentally or conventionalistically. This is precisely what undercuts Quine's skepticism and Feyerabend's anarchism. It must also, as matters stand, expose the profound gap of Goodman's system. Linguistic behavior cannot but be [m-]realistic. But if it is, then conventionalism, instrumentalism, anarchism, skepticism must be at least minimally constrained. If so, then it is entirely fair to demand an account of the epistemically operative notion of similarity. (Ibid)

"Linguistic behavior cannot but be [m-]realistic." That is a very entrenched attitude and it explains his earlier remark, "The epistemic viability of nominalism directly depends on [m-]realism, without which it must be either vacuous or arbitrary" (Ibid, p. 390). Recalling that the problem of universals touches on both epistemology and ontology, we might note Margolis's remark to the effect that the problem is entirely a matter of ontology. "...we may say that the problem of universals concerns the [m-]ontological conditions of cognition, that it does not concern at all the epistemic, semantic, or methodological conditions of cognition" (Margolis, 1982, p. 218).

We agree. Unfortunately, Margolis believes that the ontological conditions involve the reality of resemblances. In truth, it is a matter of the natures of actual particulars and whether or not they are cognized as the particulars they are: i.e., without the imposition of m-realism's real entities.

Although we can accept Margolis's criticism of Goodman, it is equally clear that Margolis's m-realism depends on non-existent entities. Thus, the ontological conditions m-realism proclaims for cognition are illusory.

PART III   Metaphysical Realism and the Formation of Categories and Concepts

Chapter 16 Cognitive Psychology: Its High Ways are Paved with Similarity

Pursuing, as we are, the career of similarity, we must keep in mind how important the notion is: Logic and Science require it. Otherwise there are no categories, no concepts, no valid generalizations, no valid inductions, no valid construction of theories, no laws.

We have focused on the notion of similarity in visiting a number of philosophers. We will make a slight detour and pursue the work done by similarity for cognitive psychologists and neuroscientists. It may be that without similarity, cognitive psychology has little or nothing to cognize, and therefore no valid way to categorize or form concepts or kinds. Let us see.

Kuhn's Computer Modeling of Similarity

When we left Kuhn and Johnny in the Zoological Park, we understood Johnny's learning process; it was based on Johnny's ability to see particulars and place them in a category (natural family, or kind), using his sense of their similarity. seeing their similarity is necessary in order to link language and nature. Kuhn went on to model Johnny's learning process on a computer. I will briefly describe Kuhn's computer modeling of similarity, for it will be used by Edelman, a Nobel neuroscientist. Says Kuhn:

> Every datum obtained is a string of n numbers, a position in what I call an n-dimensional quality space....In this space the distance between two data...represents their similarity....If the machine is given stimuli which can be grouped in clusters and it is informed which stimuli must be placed in the same and which in different clusters, it can design an appropriate set of transformation functions for itself. ... The machine, like the child, must be told at first which ones belong together and which apart. (Kuhn, 1997, p. 474)

What are we to make of all this? Do we see a similarity...on the computer screen? No. We see clusters of dots or images representing water birds. We see the clusters and are to understand that, for example, some represent ducks, others represent geese and swans. What Kuhn wants to represent is similarity, and that is a matter of the space between two data points. To see space is not to see a similarity. Nor can one see a species or a genus or a kind. We would have to read those real entities into the clusters. Since the computer, as with Johnny, must be told how to categorize ducks and geese and swans, we would not be surprised at a program which allowed the machine to find a new quality space for cormorants. That m-realism can be reproduced by a machine in the representations of similarity is not surprising. What would be surprising is a machine that produces and lets us see, a similarity.

Ethnobiology and the Formation of Concepts and Categories

Berlin is an ethnobiologist whose contributions to cognitive psychology are recognized. He has studied two preliterate societies and drawn some conclusions about the nature of man's folk classification of plants and animals. Respecting his studies, he lists two conclusions:

> The first and most obvious...is that the basic principles of classification of biological diversity appear to arise directly out of the recognition by man of groupings of plants and animals formed on the basis of such visible similarities and differences as can be inferred from gross features of morphology and behavior. This is simply to say that organisms are grouped into named classes primarily on the basis of overall perceptual similarities. (Berlin, 1978, p. 10)

Indeed, perceptual similarities appear to be at work even among the folk. One might say, even at this point, that some kind of common sense is at work which continues right on into science. Atran has argued this in a most impressive essay. Berlin continues:

> The second fundamental pattern that has emerged from the work on ethnobiological classification...is that recognized classes of plants and animals

(hereafter referred to as TAXA) are organized into a taxonomic hierarchy whereby taxa of greater and lesser inclusiveness are related by the logical relation of class inclusion. (Ibid, p. 11)

Surely, the Tzeltal Maya of Southern Mexico and the Aguaruna Jivaro of North Central Peru do not talk about classes and the logic of class inclusion. Berlin supplies the linguistic paraphernalia of categorization. What we would like to know is whether or not he is also supplying, in his interpretations, his own obvious belief in the doctrine of m-realism. He continues:

> The taxon of the most inclusive rank is not named with a separate word. ... The domain of plants is usually referred to in Hanunoo as "those elements that germinate and grow in place." In Tzeltal, it is possible to elicit the descriptive phrase "those things that don't move, don't walk, possess roots, and are planted in the earth." (Ibid, p. 12)

He says:

> In spite of the lack of a single linguistic designation for the kingdom as a whole, considerable behavioral evidence can be amassed in these situations to show that the domain of plants is nonetheless *conceptually* [my emphasis] recognized. (Ibid)

Not having a general name for plants, and describing individual things (comprehended by Berlin as plants) as

164

"those things that don't move, don't walk, possess roots, and are planted in the earth" sounds rather vague to me, a description quite lacking in demarcation, not intended as a classification at all. And, it is clear he wants to view these preliterate minds as functioning quite like his own mind; he has concepts, they must also have concepts (even if they don't recognize them as such). He goes on, "In Tzeltal, for example, all names that later proved to refer to plants occur with the neutral classifier TEHK, whereas all animal names occur with the contrasting classifier KOHT" (Ibid, pp. 12-13). From that, Berlin infers that those folk conceptualize plants as a domain.

Berlin is so entrenched in m-realism that he cannot allow himself to believe that a mind can function any other way. If not explicitly, then implicitly, minds function in terms of m-realism. Western minds do function that way. Minds in folk elsewhere may not, and I am not convinced that from TEHK and KOHT we can infer a perceptual sense involving classification. We can surely infer that for them some things that walk are different from some things that don't move and possess roots; that is, they recognize that a goat is not a tree. Berlin tends to see these folk as incipient m-realists; I tend to see them as disinterested nominalists; they use some words in ways that leave denotations vague, open, without boundaries. To convince non-m-realists, Berlin must show that his folk are not using non-inclusive ways of looking at the things in their environment, for non-inclusive ways give rise to no concepts, classes, domains, categories. Most folk are viewed as prescientific simply because they do not form hierarchies of such alleged inclusive entities. We know that western science requires them for dealing logically with the things of our world. Preliterate folk don't seem to need them nor can they, any more than literate folk, have them.

Rosch: The Principles of Categorization

We have come a long way since Rosch published her "Principles of Categorization." But she laid down the broad principles still followed by researchers. Rosch states that the psychology of categorizing can be studied scientifically. She says there are concepts and categories and tells us how we come by them. Since cognitive psychology claims to be a science largely on the basis of the principles she enunciates, it will be worth our while to understand them. I list 11 items (with some comments), 1) "By category is meant a number of objects that are considered equivalent. Categories are generally designated by names (e.g., dog, animal)" (Rosch, 1978, p. 30).

Comment: The notion of objects that are considered equivalent is the basis of the formation of a category. The category dog is composed of dogs which, in her considered opinion are equivalent. If dogs were like mathematical numbers, they might very well be so considered. Since no two dogs are identical or the same or have anything ontological in common, they cannot in any legitimate sense be considered equivalent. Equivalence is a mathematical and logical term and must be used with care in other contexts. In logic, the notion of identity of two or more terms or expressions hinges on their equivalence, so one can be substituted for the other. See our discussion of Zeno.

(2) A taxonomy is a system by which categories are related to one another by means of class inclusion. The greater the inclusiveness of a category within a taxonomy, the higher the level of abstraction. Each category within a taxonomy is entirely included within one other category (unless it is the highest-level category) but it is not exhaustive of that more inclusive category. (Ibid)

Comment: If actual objects to be categorized are not equivalent, and they are not, then a category cannot be formed. A taxonomy made of categories cannot represent the actualities it presumes to categorize. Further, we are told, here, that abstraction is used to form the taxonomic system. Again, no one can actually abstract from anything actual and obtain a cognitive entity which represents some number of particulars. She is correct that a taxonomy is indeed established in the manner she has indicated. Such a system of included categories would, if it were true of the way things are, establish hierarchies in nature. But since nature does not contain the where-with-all for categories, it also does not contain hierarchies of them. 3) "the most basic level of categorization will be the most inclusive (abstract) level at which the categories can mirror the structure of attributes perceived in the world" (Ibid).

Comment: One wonders what it is about a basic category of living things that Rosch perceives and has in mind and which also mirrors the structure of attributes perceived in the world. What structure is she seeing? Anyway she looks at the structures of living things, those structures are unique, ontologically, to each of the individuals she would categorize. Paraphrasing Darwin, we do vaguely know what our common nouns (e.g., those related to what we call species) refer to. 4) "categories tend to become defined in terms of prototypes or prototypical instances that contain the attributes most representative of items inside and least representative of terms outside the category" (Ibid).

Comment: Traditionally, classes are defined in terms of their members. Rosch is using that approach to categories. If one member is as good as another as a bearer of attributes, it and its attributes become prototypical. This allows Rosch to move away from the metaphysical something that is being defined and focus on something else; namely, the prototypes or Proto-typical instances. It is easy to see an instance, but not the something the *instance* is an instance of (i.e., the category).

> (5) A working assumption of the research on basic objects is that (1) in the perceived world, information-rich bundles of perceptual and functional attributes occur that form natural discontinuities, and that (2) basic cuts in categorization are made at these discontinuities. (Ibid, p. 31)

Comment: There is no mention, here, of things (e.g., dogs, trees) having those bundles of perceptual and functional attributes, no mention of legs and mammary glands or leaves and lenticels. An attribute is what we say of some thing; presumably, as a psychologist, Rosch wants to leave the legs and lenticels out there for biologists to worry about and talk of perceptual bundles. The problem is that bundles of perceptual attributes are rather mysterious things and their ontological status is quite unclear; certainly they are not the same thing as a leg or a tenticle. Rosch believes that nature provides us with things that have natural discontinuities. True enough. Organisms are naturally discontinuous. Why not make the cuts between one organism and another? Should we make the cuts between two organisms that are non-sexual? Between two organisms that are male and female, child and adult? Between some number of closely related organisms (e.g., the Jones family and their relatives, only Albanians, all humans, living and dead)? All this is silly, isn't it? Don't we know what Rosch is talking about? Indeed we do. We have been educated in m-realism. But that is false doctrine. If there were natural kinds whose members are the same and whose sameness formed a discontinuity because that collective sameness made them distinctly different from other kinds, then we would be in business in category formation. Nature, Plato suggested, has joints. The problem is that they don't occur around what we call kinds. Ultimately, it may be that the joints are around each of the least bits of what there is. That makes a mess of category construction and concept formation. 6) "Most, if not all, categories do not have clear-cut boundaries. To argue that basic object categories follow clusters of perceived attributes is not to say that such clusters are necessarily discontinuous" (Ibid, p. 35).

Comment: We, of course, make the cuts. Boundaries that are not clear-cut are indeed a problem in category formation. The boundary problem is alluded to below.

(7) Categories tend to be viewed as being as separate

from each other and as clear-cut as possible. One way to achieve this is by means of formal, necessary and sufficient criteria for category membership. The attempt to impose such criteria on categories marks virtually all definitions in the tradition of Western reason. The psychological treatment of categories in the standard concept-identification paradigm lies within this tradition. Another way to achieve separateness and clarity of actually continuous categories is by conceiving of each category in terms of its clear cases rather than its boundaries. As Wittgenstein (philosophical investigations) has pointed out, categorical judgments become a problem only if one is concerned with boundaries---in the normal course of life, two neighbors know on whose property they are standing without exact demarcation of the boundary line. Categories can be viewed in terms of their clear cases if the perceiver places emphasis on the correlational structure of perceived attributes such that the categories are represented by their most structured portions. (Ibid, pp. 35-36)

Comment: Again, there is trouble finding clear boundaries or joints in subject matter that is now less discontinuous than was originally hypothesized. In fact, obtaining clarity and distinctness and separation for categories takes two routes: the criterial route (stating necessary and sufficient conditions for inclusion) and the Wittgensteinian route of family resemblances. The criterial route achieved success in mathematics; we tell perfect triangles and circles what they are because we create them, using imagination and especially notions of identity and definition within the m-mathematical system we have constructed. The ontological status of perfect triangles and circles is that of the Tooth Fairy. We will examine Wittgenstein's family resemblance notion later.

> (8) By prototypes of categories we have generally meant the clearest cases of category membership defined operationally by people's judgments of goodness of membership of the category. ...the Wittgensteinian insight [is] that we can judge how clear a case something is and deal with categories on the basis of clear cases in the total absence of information about boundaries. (Ibid, p. 36)

Comment: If prototypes are defined as the clearest cases, what, we may ask, makes a case clear? That is, what is it that we see that makes the case clearly a prototype? What is it that we see that makes us know that a prototype is a prototype?" What is it about a prototype that makes us see that it links others to each other and they, in turn to something called a category? If we are to rely on people's judgments of goodness of membership, then let the people who judge be non-m-realists, otherwise the outcome is not only predictable, it is self-fulfilling prophecy. Is that science? M-realists who perform experiments on m-realists are likely to get the results they want. Rosch is building categories without asking the crucial question, is it possible that the world of things is such that categories cannot be validly constructed?

(9) "Tversky formalizes prototypicality as the member or members of the category with the highest summed similarity to all members of the category" (Ibid, p. 37).

Comment: Here, the notion of prototypicality rests on similarity and our ability to see it. We will examine this alleged ability.

> (10) To speak of a prototype at all is simply a convenient grammatical fiction, what is really referred to are judgments of degree of prototypicality... For natural-language categories, to speak of a single entity that is the prototype is either a gross misunderstanding of the empirical data or a covert theory of mental representation. (Ibid, p. 40)

Comment: However, formed, Rosch speaks a lot about something called a prototype and judgments of prototypicality. To be able to see that something is a prototype or to be able to see degrees of prototypicality in a plurality of things is no escape from the problem of one-many and the problem of universals. That Rosch's subjects can say they can see that something is a prototype or that they can see that some number of entities carry/have prototypical traits is not to the point. We are not interested in continuing demonstrations of metaphysical realism in category formation.

> (11) one purpose of categorization is to reduce the infinite differences among stimuli to behaviorally and cognitively usable proportions. It is to the organism's advantage not to differentiate one

stimulus from others when that differentiation is irrelevant to the purpose at hand. (Ibid, p. 29)

Comment: We are aware that the categorical attitude in Western philosophy and science is to reduce the infinite differences respecting the things of our universe. We may also understand that it is not always to our advantage to differentiate two bananas when we are hungry. But the purpose of constructing categories and defending them psychologically and philosophically and scientifically is also a matter of truth. Can we do it, actually, validly, truly? Reducing the infinite differences of things may be a pragmatic necessity from some point of view, but from an ontological point of view it is disastrous and, in fact, leads to falsifying the things of nature, things we really care about. For those engaged in telling us about ourselves and the world, differences must not be ignored. It is ignoring differences that makes cognitive psychology as a science of knowing a non-science, an un-paid servant of the doctrine of philosophical m-realism.

What is apparent in Rosch's approach to categorization is that while she has a lot to say about categories, we never actually get a handle on one; they are always approached (as with definitions) in terms of something else. She is aware, more than others, that categories are beclouded objects: most, if not all, do not have clear-cut boundaries. Prototypes or judgments of degree of prototypicality are called upon to point to categories. Similarity measurements and attributes in common are the means to prototypicality and thus to categories. In other words, Rosch has called on Wittgenstein to furnish a way for our grasping categories, not by defining their necessary and sufficient conditions for membership---a route to categories beset with difficulties---but by grasping the clear cases, the prototypes of categories. Thus the boundary problem is circumvented. A prototype is, of course, Berkeley's representative-one. Just what makes the representative-one, or prototype, represent is the issue. Is it similarity? If so, then do we see a similarity? If so, then we must see it (the similarity) emerge when viewing two (or more) particulars and which clearly unites them, in that respect. Rosch, as we indicated, is aware that representation presents problems, for she says, "Prototypes do not constitute a theory of representation of categories" (Ibid, p. 40). This leaves her with the Wittgensteinian way with similarity or family resemblance. Just how similarity (with or without Wittgenstein) generates categories is left by Rosch for others to explain.

Tversky and Gati on Similarity

In a work authored by Rosch and Lloyd, they state that the approach to categories in cognitive psychology assumes, "a category processor who is able to perform at least three primitive functions: He can judge between stimuli, he can perceive and process the attributes of a stimulus, and he can learn" (Ibid, p. 73). The authors continue, saying both Rosch and Berlin believe, "the basic level of abstraction in taxonomies can be derived from considerations of the perceived similarity between objects. Neither, however, offers a theory of the nature of similarity judgments" (Ibid). It is just such a theory that Tversky and Gati offer, "a new set theoretical approach to similarity in which objects are represented as collections of features, and similarity is described as a feature-matching process" (Ibid).

The old approach was one in which similarity is treated in psychological theory as distance between stimuli in Euclidean space. This is the approach we discussed in Kuhn's grouping of waterfowl. Rather than that geometrical model, Tversky offers a feature-metric model which treats similarity as asymmetrical rather than a symmetrical distance relation. This, according to Tversky and his colleague, Gati, gives predictions not possible by the geometric model. The two researchers believe that there is a dimension of particular things called similarity. Oddly, they do not search and find this dimension in the domain of psychology, although they admit its importance to psychology. How important is the notion of similarity? According to Tversky and Gati (1978), it is, "fundamental to theories of perception, learning, and judgment" (p. 79).

If this fundamental notion is not grounded in psychology, we might wonder where Tversky and Gati got it. It appears that it came from Quine whom they quote, "There is nothing more basic to thought and language than our sense of similarity; our sorting of things into kinds" (Ibid). Philosophy, then, is the source of the notion of similarity. As I have pointed out throughout this section of the essay, Tversky and Gati are also aware of the importance of the notion of similarity in explaining, "inductive practices such as concept formation, classification, and generalization" (Ibid, p. 98).

Quine, again is also a major source of this information. We must try to understand, then, the set-theoretical approach to similarity. The formulation is this, "each object-a is characterized by a set of features, denoted A, and the observed similarity of a to b, denoted s(a, b), is expressed as a function of their common and distinctive features" (Ibid, p. 79). This gives three arguments: A and B, the features shared by a and b; A - B, the features of a that are not shared by b; B - A, the features of b that are not shared by a. As the authors put it, "thus the similarity between objects expressed as a feature-matching function (i.e., a function that measures the degree to which two sets of features match each other) rather than as the metric distance between points in a coordinate space"(Ibid, pp. 79-80).

The studies of Tversky and Gati in feature-matching to establish similarity by measuring the degree to which two sets of features match each other is still another study in futility. The problem is not in the model used, whether geometric, set-theoretical, or whatever. The problem is the standing one of whether or not anyone can see a similarity or, in this study, see degrees of similarity. Certainly if we are able to see a similarity we should be able to see degrees of it. If, for example, we note that ducks have feathers, geese have feathers, that is a similarity, is it not? No, it is not. We see the feathers of the duck, we see the feathers of the goose, we do not see the similarity which bridges the two. We say the feathers are similar. If asked about the degree of similarity of the feathers of the duck and the feathers of the goose, we may say, the structures of the feathers are similar, their colors are somewhat similar. Is that seeing degrees of similarity? No. If we want to point out that the structures of the feathers are similar we see that they may not differ very much. That is, we can see difference, but we cannot see similarity...or even degrees of it. Why? Put simply, there is no similarity object to be seen. If we ignore all or most differences (as Rosch set forth in her principles, above), as to structure, we can say, the feathers are similar. Thus, Tversky and Gati, in obtaining data (the observations of subjects matching features of objects) on similarity are actually obtaining data on how m-realist experimenters and their m-realist subjects talk about things they are matching. But there is nothing new in that. These studies in cognitive psychology tell us what experimenters and their subjects have been taught about things and the application of their language to those things. They demonstrate that this is the way we use our language. Unaware that they cannot see a similarity, they are unaware that they are misusing their language and also demonstrating false notions about the nature of objects, our perception of them, the nature of learning, and the status of categories.

Smith and Medin: Cognizing Concepts and Categories

The authors begin with a statement on the importance of concepts:

> Without concepts, mental life would be chaotic. If we perceived each entity as unique, we should be overwhelmed by the sheer diversity of what we experience and unable to remember more than a minute fraction of what we encounter. And if each individual entity needed a distinct name, our language would be staggeringly complex and communication virtually impossible. Fortunately,

though, we do not perceive, remember, and talk about each object and event as unique, but rather as an instance of a class or concept that we already know something about. (Smith and Medin, 1981, p. 1)

They have been reading Locke. As with Rosch, we are counseled to ignore some measure of difference. But is it the case that we do not perceive each object as unique, but rather as an instance of a class or concept that we already know something about? Given our education in m-realism, that is the case. We don't perceive the uniqueness of each object, although we might make progress in understanding that such is the case for they are unique (i.e., other and different), each and every one. But, since we are not only m-realists but also lazy, we find it easier to follow tradition and allow others to tell us how to think about things. In Rosch's (1978) words, "the task of category systems is to provide maximum information with the least cognitive effort" (p. 28). Least cognitive effort. That's what we want and the tradition, as Rosch also points out, saves us a lot of trouble by serving up categories. "One purpose of categorization is to reduce infinite differences among stimuli to behaviorally and cognitively usable proportions" (Ibid, p. 29).

Those messy differences need to be reduced or abstracted from in order to avoid the chaos the mind would otherwise experience! Would our mental lives, as Smith and Medin declare, be chaotic without concepts? It is my opinion that we don't have concepts, can't form them in our minds, and that we pretend we have them in order to accomplish certain ends (e.g., logic and a rational approach to science). I cannot agree that the objects in the environment, living and non-living, would be viewed as chaotic if concepts were absent. Those objects, with whatever differences they present to us or however different each would be were we to examine them, are not affected by what we think about them. I cannot agree that if each individual entity received a distinct name our language would be staggeringly complex and communication virtually impossible. Smith has his own name, Medin too; why not each and every individual thing? We don't have to try to remember all of them. Taxonomists haven't ruined communication by the multitudes of names they have given to plants and animals. Every person has a name. Every frog is not important enough to be given a name, nor every insect, but why not? Language would bear up. But I am not arguing that point. Rather, agreeing with the observation that grouping individuals and naming groups is an efficient way to deal with non-human particulars, my point is that there is no valid basis for forming groups (categories) and we need not, and should not, ignore the fact that particular things are unique, different, each and every one. If that complicates language, which I deny, so be it. Smith and Medin (1981) maintain that:

> Concepts give our world stability. They capture the notion that many objects or events are alike in some important respects, and hence can be thought about and responded to in ways we have already mastered. …In short, concepts are critical for perceiving, remembering, talking, and thinking about objects and events in the world. (pp. 1-2)

Again, concepts are not involved in giving our world

stability. It is just as stable or unstable as we find it, without the help or interference of concepts. If we want to believe that many objects or events are alike in some important respects, then we can tie the belief to something we call a concept. It is just as easy to remember that we have beliefs as to remember things we don't have, but say we do, namely concepts. When we say that some objects or events are alike in some important respects, and believe it, we have learned to transmute the belief into a concept because we have learned that concepts are more stable than beliefs. We can change our beliefs about things (and scientists are constantly making us do it), but when we have a concept, it seems to remain as part of our mental hardware. Smith and Medin maintain that concepts are critical for perceiving objects and events in the world. Not true. If we use concepts as the screen through which we see things, we will falsify their natures, while, perhaps, confirming our conceptual system. Nature is what we must try to understand, not confirming what we already believe.

To understand more about concepts and categories, we must give Smith and Medin an opportunity to tell us about them. "Until recently the dominant position---which we will call the classical view---held that all instances of a concept shared common properties, and that these common properties were necessary and sufficient to define the concept" (Ibid, p. 2). They continue:

> In the past decade the criticisms have become more frequent and intense, and three views have emerged. Perhaps the most prominent of these assumes that instances of a concept vary in the degree which they

share certain properties, and consequently vary in the degree to which they represent the concept. (Ibid)

Tying particulars together into the oneness that is a concept and therefore enabling a definition of those particulars was the classical way, but as we learned from Rosch, unclear boundaries and absence of some properties by members made the classical view a more limited way with particulars. The most promising alternative, mentioned above, is what Rosch and Tversky called prototypes. Smith and Medin call that view *probabilistic*. The third way with concepts they call the exemplar view; it is described as follows, "there is no single representation of an entire class or concept, but only specific representations of the class's exemplars" (Ibid).

The question they attempt to answer is, what is the correct view of concepts? We will give their conclusion and then review their observations:

> It [is] clear that there will likely be no crucial experiments or analyses that will establish one view of concepts as correct and rule out all others irrevocably. Although the evidence we have sifted through in this book has generally been more favorable to the probabilistic and exemplar views than to the classical one, we think there are aspects of the classical view that will doubtless find their way into any comprehensive theory of concepts. In effect, then, what we have done in this book is to examine in detail some components of a comprehensive theory. The theory itself will take a little longer. (Ibid, p. 7)

Since, as I have tried to indicate, the actual natures of particulars resists categorization and concept-formation, a theory about how to come by correct categories and concepts must fail. Whatever use of categories and concepts we insist upon in the future must proceed as an entirely arbitrary imposition on things. I am arguing that the claim that there is a valid (non-arbitrary) basis for concept and category formation is false. I am arguing against the claims that we have concepts as mental entities validly formed on any basis. However, let us listen to Smith and Medin and especially to their claims about concept-formation. "Most would agree that people use concepts to provide a taxonomy of things in the world and to express relations between classes in that taxonomy" (Ibid).

They continue:

This function [categorization] involves determining that a specific instance is a member of a concept (for example, this particular creature is a guppy) or one particular concept is a subset of another (for example, guppies are fish). …This function [conceptual combination] is responsible for enlarging the taxonomy by combining existent concepts into novel ones (for example, the concepts pet and fish can be combined into the conjunction pet-fish). (Ibid, pp.7-8)

Again, we agree with their description of how we use concepts. How do we come by a concept? They answer, "To have a concept of X is to know something about the properties of entities that belong to the class of X, and such properties can be used to categorize...objects" (Ibid, p. 11). As for properties:

> A component property is, roughly, one that helps to describe an object but does not usually constitute a complete description of the object. ... For one's concept of car, the component properties might include...having wheels, having a motor, the average shape of a car, and the fact that its major function is transportation. (Ibid)

And, "a holistic property offers a complete description of the object. For example, your concept of a car might be represented by some sort of template of an ideal car" (Ibid). As to representation of concepts, "If we decide to represent object concepts in terms of components, we have a choice of how to characterize these components---either by quantitative components, called dimensions, or qualitative components, called features" (Ibid, p. 23). As to features, the claim is that they can be both perceptual and abstract.

The three views of concepts are described and critical comments are made by the authors. The first or classical (or unitary) view goes back to Aristotle. "The classical view is a proposal about representations, not about processes" (Ibid). The representational assumptions are described and then critical comments follow:

> The first assumption is as follows: The representation of a concept is a summary description of an entire class, rather than a set of descriptions of various subsets or exemplars of that class. To illustrate, in

representing the concept bird we would not list separate descriptions for different species (like robin and chicken) and for specific instances (like our pet canary Fluffy), but rather would give a summary representation for all birds. (Ibid)

And:

The heart of the classical view is contained in its second assumption: The features that represent a concept are (1) singly necessary and (2) jointly sufficient to define that concept. For a feature to be singly necessary, every instance of the concept must have it; for a set of features to be jointly sufficient, every entity having that set must be an instance of the concept. (Ibid, p. 24)

Finally, "We shall sometimes refer to such necessary and sufficient features as defining ones" (Ibid, p. 62).
Their criticisms of the classical view of concepts:

(1) the existence of disjunctive concepts (which is prohibited by the view's assumption that features are defining; (2) the existence of unclear cases (which is difficult to reconcile with the view's assumption that a concept's defining features are nested within those of its subordinates); (3) the general failure to specify defining features for most concepts. (Ibid)

The second or probabilistic view has two important assumptions regarding its featural approach:

The first assumption of the featural approach is again that of a summary description for the concept. That is, the representation of a concept is assumed to be the result of an abstraction process; not necessarily realizable as an instance; and used whenever a decision must be made about membership in that concept. (Ibid, p. 62)

The second assumption...is the critical one: The features that represent a concept are salient ones that have a substantial probability of occurring in instances of the concept. ... An example is "flies," which is listed for birds. Though some birds do not fly (chicken and penguin), flying is a very salient property that is true of most things called birds. (Ibid, p. 65)

A third assumption, regarding categorization, is added to obtain the general featural model. "An entity X is categorized as an instance or subset of concept Y if and only if X possesses some critical sum of the weighted features of Y" (Ibid, p. 83).

The general featural model, according to the authors, can handle all the problems that embarrassed the classical view. Unfortunately, perhaps, the model has short-comings, "thus far [it] has failed to provide constraints on what features may be posited" (Ibid, p. 164).

This criticism points to a concept which is open. An open concept is not a concept, just as a bucket with no bottom is not a container. To close the concept the authors resort to reintroducing some of the constraints of the classical view; some features should be necessary, but not sufficient. It seems that the probabilistic approach to concepts approaches the closed approach of the classical view on one end and total openness on the other.

The third, and last way with concepts, is the exemplar view. It holds that, "a concept is represented not by a summary representation but rather by separate descriptions of some of its exemplars" (Ibid, p. 143). The authors add, "the term exemplar is often used ambiguously; it can refer either to a specific instance of a concept or to a subset of that concept" (Ibid, p. 144). And, "There is probably only one assumption that all proponents of the exemplar view would accept: the representation of a concept consists of separate descriptions of some of its exemplars (either instances or subsets)" (Ibid, pp. 159-60).

Presumably adding up the separate descriptions, conjunctively, is no problem in obtaining one and the same concept. Just how this unification is achieved is left for our imaginations. What if the concept is represented by a disjunction of exemplars? The authors admit two problems: one concerning the relation between the disjuncts, the other the learning of summary information. They continue:

> The only relation between exemplars in a given representation is that they all point to the same concept. But "exemplars that point to the same concept" can be a trait of totally unnatural concepts. For example, let furds be the concept represented by the exemplars of chair, table, robin, and eagle; again each exemplar points to the same concept but this collection of exemplars will not meet anyone's

pretheoretical notion of a concept. The point is that the exemplar view has failed to specify principled constraints on the relation between exemplars that can be joined in a representation. (Ibid, p. 160)

It is a fortunate fellow who has formed a furd. In truth, perhaps, if you have formed one furd you have formed all that could ever be a concept. Still, there is unhappiness in the Exemplar Camp. Representation in the exemplar view of concepts, can be too open, hence requires constraints. As to that, the authors say:

Since any added constraint must deal with the relation between concept exemplars, the constraint must be something that applies to all exemplars. ... Positing such a constraint therefore amounts to positing something that summarizes all exemplars. In short, any added constraint forces a retreat from a pure exemplar representation toward the direction of a summary representation. (Ibid, p. 166)

The authors conclude:

Too few constraints on the properties used in probabilistic representations, too few constraints on the relations between the exemplars of a concept in the exemplar view. These problems deprive models based on the probabilistic and exemplar views of any true explanatory power; with no constraints on possible features, for example, probabilistic models can explain virtually any result. (Ibid)

And:

A lack of constraints means that the probabilistic and exemplar views are telling us little about what constitutes a concept or a categorization process. (In contrast, the classical view told us a lot---namely, that a concept must have necessary and sufficient properties.) (Ibid, p. 175)

Finally, "The major conclusion to emerge from this book is that the facts about object categorization fit the probabilistic and exemplar views better than they do the classical view" (Ibid).

Smith and Medin fairly conclude that there are problems with all views of concepts and categories, respecting their formation. Those damn differences of things in the world are, of course, the problem. Each of the approaches to a concept or category requires a representation of them. The representation, coming from some number of differing particulars, is supposed to point to the concept. Surely we are in trouble when, not having any notion of the concept, a psychological whatever, we are trying to represent, we try to gather a representation from the particulars which will point to the concept. All we actually have are the differing particulars, and they don't seem to cooperate in our efforts at unification and closure, the end-result required to obtain a representation. If the exemplars of the particulars used in trying to form the representation are too diverse, unification is a problem and the concept remains open. Closing an open concept tilts the process in the direction of the classical way of forming concepts, the most satisfactory way, but the way which cannot be used on the world's particulars. Why? The classical way requires necessary and sufficient properties. The best candidates for classical conceptualization are in the realm of mathematics; numbers and figures, such as the triangle. A mathematician can state precisely what is necessary and sufficient to construct a triangle; a closed figure with three sides whose interior angles equal 180 degrees. I did not say that the mathematician, in stating precisely what is necessary and sufficient to form or construct a triangle, also has a concept of triangle. He can no more have that than anyone else, for they are not to be had. Each triangle he constructs is other and different from every other, actually. Each triangle he imagines is other and different from every other, actually. All the triangles he may construct or imagine will never add up to one unified triangle or represent the concept triangle or the divine or universal triangle. Representation is something an actual triangle, or other so-called exemplar, cannot do. we may want a triangle or picture of a car, etc., to represent a concept, but it cannot oblige. If the classical view of concepts fails to generate a concept, there is even less hope that a probabilistic view can succeed; for it is a view which accepts different sets of features or average, or mean, dimension values of a class, and so must make sense of disjuncts. If disjuncts are to constitute a concept, what is the basis for their unity. If there is no ontological commonality for the disjuncts, what makes such a loose arrangement a concept? Placing constraints on such concepts is to reintroduce some tautness enjoyed by the classical view, but probabilistic concepts are necessarily open concepts, and open concepts are not concepts at all. The exemplar view, being also disjunctive, suffers this fate too.

What value have all these studies in a psychology that aims to be cognitive? If knowledge of the actual bases for concepts and categories and an understanding of how they are formed is the aim, then these studies fail. What the studies tell us, if that is of value, is the following: 1. how the experimenter's subjects think about objects (i.e. how they conceive or categorize them); 2. what the experimenters take concepts and categories to be; 3. that both subjects and experimenters have been educated to accept m-realism in these matters as their dominant mode of thinking about objects; 4. that problems encountered with the formation of concepts and categories are always seen as problems of disunity, where objects tend not to fit, are not clear cases, break down boundaries or extend them indefinitely, and where objects are so disjunctive that no boundaries are possible, thus the rallying around a prototype or exemplar; 5. that the firmest hold on concepts and categories is within the classical view which cannot accommodate all that needs conceptual attention; 6. and most importantly, they tell us that the search for unity in difference is their obsession and, we might add, the obsession of philosophers who believe the doctrine of m-realism.

Chapter 17 Edelman and Neural Darwinism: The Bases of Perceptual Categorization and Generalization

Continuing our pursuit of the careers of concepts and categories, we now leave the outer perceptual areas of cognitive psychology and enter the brain itself. Edelman (1987) asks, "What are the bases in neural structure of perceptual categorization and generalization" (p. xix)

If Edelman can pull it off, demonstrating the bases for perceptual categorization and generalization in neural structure will resolve the innateness issue raised by Quine and make Kantians of us all. For, relating neural structure and perceptual categorization and generalization will establish a synthetic a priori state between brain and objects. We will proceed slowly and give this neuroscientist an opportunity to prove his case. Edelman says:

> The theory of neuronal group selection...was formulated to explain how perceptual categorization could occur without assuming that the world is prearranged in an informational fashion or that the brain contains a homunculus. ...To account for categorization without assuming information

191

processing or computing, the theory proposes that the key principle governing brain organization is a populational one and that in its operation the brain is a selective system. (Ibid, p. 4)

In moving toward his accounting for perceptual categorization, Edelman remarks on perceived differences in human brains:

The diversification is such that no two individuals are likely to have identical connectivity in corresponding brain regions. …Although structures in a particular area of the brain are modally similar among con-specific animals, at the level of fine axonal and dendritic ramifications and connections, there occurs a very large degree of individual variation in shape, extent, and connectivity. (Ibid, pp. 5-6)

In the development of the brain, two phases are described. In prenatal development, a primary repertoire of cells is selectively laid down: the original ensemble of anatomically variant groups. Then, during postnatal behavior:

a second selective process occurs...through epigenetic modifications in the strength of synaptic connections within and between neuronal groups. As a result, combinations of those particular groups whose activities are correlated with various signals arising from adaptive behavior are selected. This selection occurs within the original ensemble...and it results in the formation of a secondary repertoire consisting of functioning groups that are more likely to be used in future behavior. Neurons in neuronal groups are populations, and repertoires form higher-order populations. (Ibid, p. 7)

Well and good. We want to know, of course, how repertoires are related to perceptual categorization. Edelman says, "A central assumption of the theory is that perceptual categorization must both precede and accompany learning" (Ibid, p. 5). If it precedes learning, perceptual categorization must be in some sense innate. If so, is the innateness associated with the primary or with the secondary repertoires? Edelman doesn't clarify innateness or specify precisely where it occurs; he seems to point to the primary repertoire, and says the local anatomy of those neuronal groups, "is determined by genetic factors regulating cell shape and by epigenetic events regulating the primary developmental processes of cell division, movement, death, adhesion, and differentiation" (Ibid, p. 7).

Are we to understand that because of the local anatomy of the neuronal groups of the primary repertoire our perceptions of certain objects will result in their categorization? How? He doesn't say. He continues:

One of the fundamental tasks of the nervous system is to carry on adaptive perceptual categorization in an "unlabeled" world---one in which the macroscopic order and arrangement of objects and events (and their definition or discrimination) cannot be prefigured for an organism, despite the fact that such objects and events obey the laws of physics. (Ibid, pp. 8-9)

We, of course, agree that the world is unlabeled. The question that is of concern to us is how the brain affixes its labels to that world and the validity of that process. Edelman says, "An individual animal endowed with a richly structured brain must also adapt without instruction to a complex environment to form perceptual categories or an internal taxonomy governing its further responses to its world" (Ibid, pp. 7-8).

Alright. The need to categorize is viewed as urgent. What is it that the brain sees (via its optic nerves) that makes it form a category? The need to form perceptual categories and the implication that they are formed by the brain is Lamarckian. But we will be patient. "A necessary condition for such perceptual categorization is assumed to be reentry between separate parallel systems of local maps serving different modalities, each of which is capable of independent disjunctive sampling of a stimulus domain" (Ibid, p. 18).

Perhaps we are getting somewhere now. Disjunctive sampling of a stimulus domain is about all we ever do: seeing different objects on different occasions. As for the stimulus and what it stimulates, Edelman says:

the nature of the stimulus is dynamic and polymorphous, that there are two initially independent domains of variation (the world of potential stimuli and collections of neuronal groups), and that the fundamental and prior basis upon which learning rests is perceptual categorization. (Ibid, p. 8)

The world and the brain-cells are variants in dynamic change. If we are to learn, there must be some foundation, not out there in the world bombarding us with dynamic and polymorphous stimuli, but inside the brain in those neuronal groups where perceptual categorization occurs. Indeed, but how does it occur? Edelman's intention is, as he says, to, "show how neuronal group selection and reentry in mapped systems can operate together in a self-consistent fashion to yield perceptual categorization" (Ibid, p. 26). Alright. He goes on, "The self-consistency of the theory of neuronal selection in providing a basis for categorization has been demonstrated by constructing a recognition automaton embedding the assumptions of the theory" (Ibid).

That is not good news. We had hoped that his theory of perceptual categorization could be demonstrated by his work with actual brains. However, we must follow where he leads. If the basis for categorization has been demonstrated by a recognition automaton we must find out how it was done. If the machine and the brain are sufficiently analogous in the matter of perceptual categorization, then Edelman may make a case of some sort after all. He says, "selection upon degenerate repertoires of reentrantly connected neuronal groups in this automaton can result in effective categorization without a preexisting explicit program describing the objects to be categorized" (Ibid, p. 31).

It is time to ask what Edelman understands categorization to be. Perhaps we can obtain that understanding from these remarks:

Perception may be provisionally defined as the discrimination of an object or an event through one or more sensory modalities, separating them from the background or from other objects or events. ...Categorization, a process by which an individual may treat nonidentical objects or events as equivalent. (Ibid)

We have no quarrel with his notion of perception. His notion of categorization recalls Rosch's definition in which the term equivalent was also used. We pointed out that to posit the equivalence of things that are not identical---and Edelman emphasizes their non-identity---undermines the quest for understanding whether or not the brain can operate categorically without our socially acquired posits. If most of us already treat some non-identical objects or events as equivalent---because we are told, like Kuhn's Johnny, that they are---why do we need a machine to demonstrate that fact? The issue is: how does our brain, in viewing non-identical objects and events, actually see something which enables it, indeed requires it, to form a category which is presumably valid by that neuronal in-sight?

Further insight into perceptual categorization is pursued by Edelman by a switch from psychology to philosophy:

If one considers the problem of categorization from a philosophical point of view, the data suggest that the classical summary description of a class defined by singly necessary and jointly sufficient conditions does not hold. Membership is more like family

196

resemblance... This is one of the major issues considered by Wittgenstein in his philosophical investigations. Wittgenstein's considerations led to the idea that categorizations are in fact polymorphous even when language is used to define categories. (Ibid, pp. 31-32)

We have already signaled the importance of Wittgenstein's family resemblance notion for cognitive psychologists. Edelman uses this notion too. We note that Edelman holds that while perceptual categorization is in some sense prior to learning as well as accompanying learning, there is a disjunctive sampling of a stimulus domain. We and other animals need to classify things in their environments.

Edelman has not shown us how anything other than language is used in obtaining categories. In fact, he is quite knowledgeable about it: he believes that, with the exception of natural categories, categories are polymorphous sets. This means that membership in a category can be defined so as to disjunctively permit any m out of n possible properties; he says:

A classical [m]realist would have insisted conjunctively upon n properties out of n, each singly necessary and all jointly sufficient to define a set. A nominalist would have insisted upon the unique disjunction, that is, members of sets have nothing in common except that you may choose to name any one of them in a certain way (one set out of n). (Ibid, p. 32)

197

It is clear that Edelman agrees with Smith and Medin when he says humans, "employ statistical or disjunctive combinations of attributes or scaled variables, or they use exemplars...or employ both strategies" (Ibid). As we saw, Smith and Medin accept the fundamentals of Rosch's work, but so does Edelman, who says this work is related, "mainly to conceptual issues that are strongly language-bound and, to some extent, culture-bound" (Ibid).

The question for Edelman is, "What properties of its nervous system allow an animal to deal adaptively with polymorphous sets" (Ibid)? We are to remember that, "because of evolutionary selection, certain recurrent objects or relatively constant features of objects in a niche may be consistently and recurrently recognized by animals in a given species" (Ibid, pp. 18-19).

Those features of objects that are consistently and recurrently recognized by animals comprise natural categories; all other categories are polymorphous. The natural categories, says Edelman, fit the classical view of defined, hence closed classes or sets. Polymorphous sets are more open, having some common features necessary for membership. The categories assembled out of polymorphous sets are simply Wittgensteinian classes. That is, they are based on the notion of family resemblance. Edelman accepts the notion, but does not inquire into its validity.

We should recall that Edelman was concerned in his studies not only with perceptual categorization, but also with generalization. The two notions are closely related. I promised, above, that we would pursue generalization for it is a metaphysical activity. We will interrupt our discussion to turn to his theory of how we and other animals are able to generalize.

> In realizing the importance of generalizations to problem solving and learning, and therefore the need to provide a neural substrate for generalization, the theory emphasizes the fundamental role of degeneracy of neuronal groups in repertoires and of reentrant anatomy and function among the parallel systems....Animals can...generalize; that is, an individual organism can encounter a few instances of a category under learning conditions and then recognize a very great number of related but novel instances. (Ibid, p. 27)

The brain's neural machinery, of course, is intimately involved, "This ability of individuals in a species to categorize novel objects in classes is a stunning reflection of what might be called the idiosyncratic (i.e., self-adaptive) generalizing power of neural networks" (Ibid, p. 30). What is rather remarkable is that Edelman assures us that animals without language can carry out perceptual categorization and also generalization. He refers to work with pigeons that, he says, have clearly shown that pigeons are capable of generalization. For example, After receiving three or four rewards when faced with an image of a leaf from quercus alba, the pigeon could generalize and distinguish patterns of oak leaves of every genus presented from patterns of all other kinds of leaves.

That is impressive. We are reminded of Berlin's preliterate folk. The pigeon's behavior, its success in recognizing patterns of oak leaves of every genus presented from patterns of all other kinds of leaves demonstrates something! What is it? Edelman infers perceptual categorization and generalization. I infer something else; it is one thing to recognize that one leaf differs from another, or that oak leaves differ less from one another throughout the genus than they do from, say, maple leaves. But it is quite another thing to turn those recognitions of differences into generalizations or categories. Are we to believe that a pigeon can recognize a given leaf as an instance of a class? I would rather think that the experimenter is adding that interpretation to the pigeon's responses. We cannot say that a pigeon can perceive sameness or identity of two or more objects, for neither can be seen. As with humans, we can say that the pigeon may ignore differences, especially minor ones, and that leaves with the least differences will be accounted as those which should be placed in this area, while those with greater differences will be placed in that area. It is the experimenter who must infer that leaves in one area constitute a category and that the placement of leaves proceeds according to some neural substrate for generalization. Why Edelman, and the cognitive psychologists, want to make pigeons m-realists is clear; they are delighted to have company. The pigeons I know have brains that enable them to discriminate some measures of difference, while ignoring, or not registering, more detailed differences. However, these experiments suggest that pigeons are more clever than I thought; they manage to get rewarded for their inability to do what the experimenter believes they are doing: categorizing, and generalizing on the basis of similarity.

In criticizing these studies involving human and pigeon brains, I am not saying that we don't generalize, or believe that we can form categories, only that there is no valid basis for doing so. Categorization and generalization are so important for the purposes of Western logic and science that philosophers, cognitive psychologists, and now a neuroscientist, try to tie them to neuronal machinery and substrates in the brain. M-realists, in other words, insist on the a priori nature of categories and resemblance or similarity. They try to make them innate. They believe that Darwin proved that our brains are the outcome of a host of adaptive responses by our ancestors, and that perceptual categorization and generalization and the recognition of similarity are evolved abilities of those brains. All that, of course, is required to make us rational, reasonable! But Darwin is not on the side of the philosophers, the cognitive psychologists, and the neuroscientists. That makes all the more ironic Edelman's label for his theory: Neural Darwinism. Darwin's brain and perceptions told him that there is no such entity as a species. His brain and his perceptions told him that each and every organism is a variant. Not a variant of something which does not vary, just ontologically other and different from every other. If things cannot be perceived as, or formed into, a species, then what likelihood is there that there are any natural categories? And if there are no valid categories, then generalization is a process which has no rational basis. Edelman's Neural Darwinism makes sense in brain development and some functioning, but not on the issues under consideration here. I rather believe that we and pigeons recognize each thing as other and different, but not altogether different from others;

that is, some things don't differ too greatly and we can ignore whatever difference there is if we are rewarded for doing so. The training of pigeons in leaf-recognition and the education of young people proceeds precisely on that basis. Ignoring differences for logical purposes is the basis for rationalism. However, our ignoring differences (or otherness) of two or more objects cannot be interpreted as class inclusion. Our brains cannot form classes or categories from differing objects, for we cannot perceive anything which would unite them into a class or category. We do, of course, learn our categories, and we do learn to generalize out of our ignorance, but the categories are false groupings and the generalizations are erroneous activities resulting from social conditioning and superficial perceptions of particulars. Surely our brains have not evolved neural substrates and repertoires generating classes and categories from stimuli that are particulars, each of which is other than and different from every other. If Nature has made us that way, then Nature requires us to falsify her very nature. Nature is odd, indeed, but malicious?

We will not understand our nervous systems until we understand that all particulars are unique, that there are no recurrences, and that is the nature of Nature. In other words, things don't have a nature (an essence, a metaphysical being). Our nervous systems are selectively designed to detect what Nature is and can only present to us: otherness and differences. Each nervous system is an unavoidable variant, precisely as Edelman has shown, but it is selectively designed and functions to detect differences and adapt the individual to ranges of differences, if we do not interfere and cut the processes short. In my view, tying perceptual processes to a fixed substrate which generates fixed categories is to promote non-adaptation to the environment. Nature is more Heraclitean than we are willing to admit. In fact, Cratylus was correct about the nature of Nature, not Heraclitus. It would behoove us to get the cognitive interplay of Nature and brain right. An education in m-realism maladapts.

Let us turn to Edelman's views on learning. The existence or non-existence of a cognitive foundation for learning is, indeed, important. Edelman says:

> Such [adaptive] behavior in a phenotype requires initial categorization of salient aspects of the environment so that learning can occur on the basis of the resultant categories. A fundamental task of neuroscience is thus to show how, in a particular species, the structure and function of the nervous system permit perceptual categorization to occur as a basis for learning and meaningful adaptive behavior. (Ibid, p. 260)

We have not been shown how...the structure and function of the nervous system permit perceptual categorization to occur. The basis for learning, which depends on its occurrence, is absent. But, we do learn. If Edelman, and others we have discussed, views learning as occurring only after we have formed the necessary categories through perceptions then, if we cannot form the categories, we must not be able to learn. Nominalists don't form those categories. Are they able to learn or not? They certainly learn what m-realists (who can't form the categories either but say they do) learn. Does it matter, then, how we learn? Indeed it does. If we cannot form categories and concepts, then they cannot be entities on which learning can be based. If we pretend we can form them, then our learning is also pretense.

Edelman agrees with Rosch and others concerning the way people form concepts and categories. "We have seen that studies of conceptual categorization show evidence that subjects use both probabilistic feature ensembles and exemplars" (Ibid, p. 261). He continues:

> there is no closed definition either of a universal or of a universal in absence ("a memory") by the nervous system; in confronting stimuli, there is no definition in terms of singly necessary and jointly sufficient features. Instead, the choices mimic Wittgenstein's family resemblances or his definition of games...it is clear that games do not necessarily have anything in common except that they are games. (Translation: if n is the size of an arbitrarily long list of attributes of games, a list that is not closed, any m out of the n attributes would suffice to make a particular activity a game.) (Ibid)

What are we to make of those remarks? Is he giving up universals? No, but he is giving up on defining them in the classical manner. That still leaves exemplars and probabilistic feature ensembles and Wittgensteinian family resemblances, all of which can, for m-realists, yield universals. Still, is Edelman an m-realist or a nominalist? As with others we have discussed, it seems that Edelman forswears Platonism, essentialism, typology---all labels for m-realism---and opts for open classes and open categories which are held together by open family resemblances. Recall that games do not necessarily have anything in common except that they are games. Is that nominalism? Realism? Neither? I think it is trying to have it both ways without clearly declaring for either side. I think nominalism is an incomplete, but entirely defensible, position regarding the rejection of universals and real entities etc. Edelman exhibits this incomplete nominalism in his remark that games do not necessarily have anything in common except that they are games. If the word *necessarily* is left out, the statement would be one leveled against nominalists by m-realists. Does Edelman mean that games don't necessarily have anything in common but they do have something in common? He doesn't say. It is time to turn to Wittgenstein and his commentators and examine the doctrine of family resemblances but before we do we must say something about the innateness claim.

Chapter 18 Are Concepts Innate?

Fodor and Carburetors

Along with Chomsky's longstanding claim that the rules of grammar are innate (that humans have a preset language organ in their brains), is Fodor's claim that concepts are innate. His defense of this claim parallels Chomsky's in longevity. Steven Pinker's book, *The Stuff of Thought,* makes a stab at undermining Fodor's innatist view of concepts. He believes that Fodor's claim that all concepts are innate (that even carburetor is in the brains of humans before cars were on earth) is at best partially true; some concepts Pinker believes are not innate, others may be. I will forego giving his argument opposing Fodor's universal innatism claim because having thought about Fodor's views and his defense of innate concepts for some time, I have a quick answer.

The claim that there are innate concepts is false. Fodor claims that we cannot have learned our concepts, whether dog, cat, carburetor, or whatever and, therefore, they are innate. We can forget why he makes this claim, because we don't need it for our discussion. We might remind ourselves that Fodor has never given us a proof that learning cannot be involved in obtaining so-called concepts, it's just that he cannot see how this is possible. Even without a proof, his argument has stood its ground because learning theorists have not come up with a clear presentation of facts to counter Fodor's claim that we do not learn our concepts. Fodor's notorious carburetor concept refers to all particulars of a kind, all carburetors. This concept in the mind is a metaphysical carburetor). For Fodor the m-real carburetor is in the brain and we will become mentally aware and know it as a concept when stimuli from outside (i.e., particular carburetors) activate our brain circuits. We can believe this fairytale or, following Ockham, we might take a more believable and parsimonious route to a solution of the origin of concepts. However, if we claim that we see carburetors first, then have the concept of these automotive parts, then we are claiming that we learn our concepts. Seeing a many, then forming a one (concept) of them. This is rejected by Fodor. I also reject it, for it is not the solution to the problem of concepts. Why? Well, and here is my solution to the problem of concepts. We can't form a concept at all. Why? Because of the nature of things, including carburetors: each is other and different from every other. There is no concept of them to be had, no way to get these diverse particulars into a mental oneness that is a concept. If that is the case, then Fodor cannot claim that all concepts are already in the brain as innate entities. There simply are no concepts, so we no longer need to worry about what they are, where they are, or how we obtain them. That being the case, Nature has either made a terrible mistake by implanting all those concepts in our brains or Fodor has blinded himself to the possibility of a critique which will put an end to his view of concepts as innate.

To learn the language is to internalize the potential to generate concepts, for they are implied by all those common nouns parents force their children to hear and pay attention to. This internalizing of the common nouns and images in language-learning outfits the neural circuitry for remembering, producing, and reproducing those linguistic elements. And more, it outfits the neural circuitry for learning the one-over-many notions and the generating of the concepts implied by the common nouns. Thus, it is not some mysterious organ produced by genes that innately controls the learning of language and the production of concepts, but ordinary language-learning itself. Ordinary language-learning sets up the neuronal circuitry which generate Chomsky's grammar and Fodor's concepts. The brain is pre-set to function in a mode that is metaphysical realism because that is the default position of ordinary language function. There is nothing innate about the whole affair, it is precisely what one would expect if we pour nouns into a child's brain and point to their references. Words are learned by ostension. Recall Kuhn's walk with Johnny who was told how to recognize ducks and geese and swans. We marvel at the rapidity of linguistic development, but it is not the result of some innate language organ. Given the default position of m-realism, metaphysics issues from the mouths of babes as if they were born m-realists. They may equally be viewed as born nominalists or born conceptualists. Correcting one's linguistic orientation from the default position of m-realism is to become a nominalist or nominalistic conceptualist. All of these linguistic positions must give way to one which is in accord with the actual nature of the things of our universe. There is no name for this position. Since communication requires names, and since metaphysical or real entities are fictions generated by ordinary language, we need a word for our new point of view which correctly labels it.

PART IV   The Role of Resemblance/ Similarity in Modern Philosophy and Science (Holding World, Self, and Logic Together)

Chapter 19 Wittgenstein's family resemblances

Bambrough and Thorpe

All the roads we have traveled thus far bring us to the lane leading to the *Philosophical Investigations* and a brief remark there by Wittgenstein which is viewed by many as the solution to the problem of universals and the solution to the problems of concept and category formation. The brief remark is this:

> Consider for example the proceedings that we call "games." I mean board-games, card-games, Olympic games, and so on. What is common to them all?--Don't say: "there must be something common, or they would not be called 'games'"--but look and see whether there is anything common to all---For if you look at them you will not see something that is common to all, but similarities, relationships, and a whole series of them at that. (Wittgenstein, 1953, p. 31)

In Wittgenstein's *Blue Book*, we find:

We are inclined to think that there must be something in common to all games, say, and that this common property is the justification for applying the general term "game" to the various games; whereas games form a family the members of which have family likenesses. Some of them have the same nose, others the same eyebrows and others again the same way of walking; and these likenesses overlap. (Wittengenstein, 1965, p. 17)

What, then, is our justification for applying the general term game to the activities we call by that name? Wittgenstein did not deny that some common names are justified by the commonality perceived among the particulars comprehended by the name. In which case he would be an m-realist. He did say that with regard to some plurality of particulars, we do not see their commonality, but we do see similarities and relationships. Games, he says, form a family the members of which have family likenesses. Surely, seeing a similarity with regard to some number of particulars is on a par with seeing their commonality. To see either one is to see what holds them together or unites them into a oneness of kind. Is that m-realism? Indeed it is. Others have differing opinions about Wittgenstein's remarks. Bambrough says, "I believe that Wittgenstein solved what is known as "the problem of universals." ...In seeking for Wittgenstein's solution we must look mainly to his remarks about "family resemblances" and to his use of the example of games" (Bambrough, 1961, p. 207). He continues, "...according to Wittgenstein, games have nothing in common except that they are games, and red things have nothing in common except that they are red" (Ibid, p. 214).

Ayer is quoted by Bambrough as objecting to that view, "It is correct, though not at all enlightening, to say that what games have in common is their being games" (Ibid, p. 215). Bambrough believes that while it may be trivially and platitudinously true, it is significant. He points out:

> the platitude that all games have in common that they are games is denied by the nominalist, who says that all games have nothing in common except that they are called games... The very terms of the nominalist's challenge require only that the realist should point out something that games have in common apart from being called games, and this onus is fully discharged by saying that they are games. (Ibid)

We might interject an observation and a comment. It appears that Bambrough is an m- realist; he meets the nominalist's challenge by claiming that what games have in common is that they are games. Does this meet the challenge of the nominalist who, as Bambrough put it, believes that all games have nothing in common except that they are called games? If nominalists believe that sharing a term is the *in common* that some number of particulars have, then we must be told how this sharing comes about. For example: in watching three sets of people playing games, we remark, "that is chess," "that is chess," and "that is chess." Three different pairs are playing three different games of chess. We must agree that they are not playing the same game; each pair is playing its own particular game, a game which is other and different from the other two games. How, then, can the word chess (presumably spoken to describe the three activities) be shared? Actually, it cannot. My use of a word, uttered or written, say "share," is sound or marks and ontologically unsharable. The in common that three different chess games have cannot be a word, chess. In truth, those games have nothing in common, not even the sharing of a word which, presumably, designates them. That every game of chess is other and different and called by a word, chess, which is not shared by any is the way it is and we understand, without a commonality or a sharing. As to Bambrough's belief that games are, indeed, called games, but have nothing in common except that they are games, requires us to believe that areness conveys, if not commonality, then some ontological identity. Evidently we just see, or intuit, that however diverse the activities we call games, each shares the name because each is a game...and we see or intuit the sameness or identity in their differences. We have already discussed the short-comings of the notion of identity as well as the emptiness of being, i.e., is and areness. Bambrough continues:

> It is assumed as obvious by both the nominalist and the realist that there can be no objective justification for the application of a general term to its instances unless its instances have something in common over and above their having in common that they are its instances. The nominalist rightly holds that there is no such additional common element, and he therefore wrongly concludes that there is no objective

justification for the application of any general term. The realist rightly holds that there is an objective justification for the application of general terms, and he therefore wrongly concludes that there must be some additional common element. (Ibid, p. 217)

Since Wittgenstein, according to Bambrough, denied the assumption that is common to nominalism and realism, Bambrough can write, "...that is why I say that he solved the problem of universals" (Ibid).

We have indicated that Bambrough's unexpressed identity notion places him on the side of m-realism. He believes, as do m-realists, that there is an objective justification for the application of general terms, a justification stemming from his interpretation of Wittgenstein and not seen before in the battle between nominalists and m-realists. In his view, the m-realists go wrong in pointing to commonalities; the nominalists are right that there are no commonalities. Commonalities are out for Bambrough, but he must tell us about that areness that games have (i.e., the ontological identity notion lurking in areness), for each game may be viewed as other and different, hence having no connection, no identity, with any other. Bambrough doesn't tell us about the areness, so we will push on and deal with Wittgenstein who may or may not have agreed with Bambrough.

Examining what Wittgenstein said in the above quotes, we may wonder, when he thought about, or looked at, a number of activities, why does he give the name game to some of them? When he looks at all those activities, actually or in his mind, that he has given the name game, calling them games, why does he say that they form a family? Is he simply following linguistic convention or does he have an a priori notion or concept respecting them? He doesn't say. Does he intuit something about them, in spite of the fact that not all have something in common? Did he hold, as Bambrough seems to believe, that games are called games because they are games? He never said that. He did say, as we quoted above, that games form a family the members of which have family likenesses, and that if you look at them you will not see something that is common to them all, but similarities. Clearly, what he is emphasizing is the absence of commonality (at least in some cases) and the presence of similarities and likenesses. He says we can see similarities.

Thorp responded to Bambrough's essay and lectured him on having gone wrong in his understanding of the Problem of Universals as the medieval schools of Nominalism and Realism understood it. He has this to say:

> The Nominalists held not that there is no criterion for the application of a universal term to a series of individuals where such a term is applied, but rather that there is a criterion---the criterion of a common feature or common features---but that the universal term is a name referring to a merely derived conceptual entity. For the Nominalist, individuals were ontically fundamental and their features ontically dependent. Therefore, the concepts to which such universal terms refer are abstract constructions with low ontic dignity. Aristotle tried to be a Nominalist. (Thorp, 1961, pp. 567-68)

He continues:

> The Realists held not merely that there is some
> criterion for the application of a universal term to a
> series of individuals where such a term is applied,
> but also that the universal term designated an entity
> of high ontic dignity which "preceded" and founded
> the individual thing, which was therefore dependent
> and of lower ontic dignity. Plato was a Realist. (Ibid)

And, "...Arbitrarianism is an extreme form of
Nominalism which may have been held by one important
medieval philosopher, Roscellinus, but our only evidence for
this possibility is the testimony of his adversaries" (Ibid, p.
568). So:

> One can understand how [Bambrough] confuses
> Nominalists with Arbitrarians: Nominalists ascribed
> low ontic dignity---dependent status---to what is
> denoted by a universal term; Bambrough takes this to
> mean that they ascribed it no ontic dignity, that they
> ascribed non-existence to what is denoted by a
> universal term, and hence that they thought there to
> be no criterion for the use of such a term, nothing to
> which it might apply. But something which is mere
> machination of the human brain is nonetheless
> something. (Ibid)

Thorp accuses Bambrough's debilitated notion of the
Realist claim as being generated by opposition to his
exaggerated notion of the Nominalist claim. We can enjoy

the little lecture on the sides taken in the war of universals and note his view that ontology comes in degrees of dignity. If one can be a little bit pregnant, then ontology can come in degrees. This is not to say that Thorp's view doesn't make sense; it does, but it widens the discussion and does not resolve the problem of universals.

Thorp's criticism of Bambrough's interpretation of what has come to be called the Theory of Family Resemblances should be noted:

> For surely Wittgenstein is not telling us merely that all individuals called games or called brothers are in a family (and hence called by the family-name), but also that they deserve to be in a family (and hence deserve to be called by the family name). And the grounds of this desert are resemblances in respect of features. (Ibid)

And,

> Thus neither in the case of perplexing universal terms like "games", nor in the case of simple universal terms like "red", nor in the case of straightforward universal terms like "brothers" is Wittgenstein to be read as saying that family members have in common only that they are members of the family---they have in common also grounds for desert to be members of the family and called by the family name. (Ibid, pp. 569-70)

There we have the *in respect of* which seems to be

implied by Wittgenstein's pronouncements on resemblances without commonality. This leads to the search for the resemblance entity which brings the resembling particulars together, unites them, into a concept or kind or whole or family.

Is Thorp an m-realist? He rejects the traditional way of explaining concepts, ultimately, in terms of necessary and sufficient conditions, for it leads to infinite regress. Concepts and such definitions remain open. But he does not reject all ways of defining. He says:

> To define a thing is not to say, as Bambrough objects, something over and above the thing, but rather something under and beneath---something underpropping and explaining the fact that the thing is whatever it is. Brothers have in common something slightly more telling than simply that they are brothers: that they are male and that they are siblings. (Ibid, p. 569)

It seems that Thorpe is an m-realist, for he believes that brothers have something in common...an essence, perhaps, as Aristotle said...and that something is the foundation for the universal term brother.

Bambrough has failed to convince us that Wittgenstein solved the problem of universals. Resemblance without commonality, however, was quickly seized by the cognitive psychologists, and at least one neuroscientist, as a legitimate way to form concepts and categories. Our inability to see a resemblance that two or more particulars have or share undermines concept and category formation and the learning theory based on those concepts and categories. We indeed know and learn, but we do not know the entities presumed to form their bases and we ought not believe that we learn by the processes described by cognitive psychologists and pointed to in neuroscience. There are only particulars, including those comprising the brain and its processes, and all are unique, dynamic, changing, more or less. Those particulars present to us their otherness and their differences, more or less. Cognitive stability was desired by Plato and Aristotle, and the hosts of m-realist philosophers and scientists and psychologists who followed, so they started inventing entities that did not change, entities that we could hang on to, use in logic and science and so obtain increasingly comprehensive and stabilizing concepts and categories and laws that kept the world from the chaos of change. The world is no more and no less chaotic for not having, or presenting to us, those pretend-entities. It will not hurt us to discover the truth and tell it.

Chapter 20 Similarity and Resemblance in Berkeley and Hume

Berkeley

Although much of Berkeley's energy was spent in destroying the prevailing philosophic notion of matter, his most endearing critique is of Locke's abstract ideas which we described earlier. Hume also appreciated that critique, so we will look into it. "...I do not deny absolutely there are general ideas, but only that there are any abstract general ideas: for in the passages [of Locke], wherein there is mention of general ideas, it is always supposed that they are formed by abstraction" (Berkeley, 1975, p. 69). Berkeley ridicules Locke's---and for that matter, the Scholastic and Aristotelian---process of abstraction which, he believes cannot, and need not, be done either by children or grown men or in order to carry on communication. We heartily agree. He continues, "...I believe we shall acknowledge, that an idea, which considered in itself is particular, becomes general, by being made to represent or stand for all other particular ideas of the same sort" (Ibid, p. 70).

Since, for Berkeley, all ideas are particular, even if complex, and all are concrete, not abstract, what makes a concrete particular idea general is its alleged ability to represent. We may call this the notion of the *representative particular* or *exemplar*. Rosch and other cognitive psychologists inherit the non-classical way of forming categories and concepts from Berkeley. The question is, how can any concrete particular represent other concrete particulars? Berkeley says it is because the other particulars are of the same sort. But what is it about the other particulars that makes us aware of them as of the same sort? If we know they are the same sort, then we know the representative particular, the exemplar, is representative or exemplary. But this is circular reasoning. Berkeley, in criticizing Locke's way of creating generals by abstracting, has simply introduced another problem, the problem of representation.

Before going further into Berkeley's way of creating general ideas, we will see how he demolishes Locke's way of generalizing or creating universals:

> It is I know a point much insisted on, that all knowledge and demonstration are about universal notions, to which I fully agree: but then it doth not appear to me that those notions are formed by abstraction in the manner premised [by Locke]; universality, so far as I can comprehend, not consisting in the absolute, positive nature or conception of anything, but in the relation it bears to the particulars signified or represented by it: by virtue where-of it is that things, names, or notions, being in their own nature particular, are rendered universal. (Ibid, p. 71)

The words are mindful of Hobbes' nominalism, but Berkeley is subscribing to the m- realist doctrine that knowledge and demonstration (logic) require universals. He simply disagrees with Locke on how to obtain them. He believes that the representation of particulars by a particular creates no real entity, only a functional universality by the particular's representational relation to them. This is mindful, too, of Ockham's way of obtaining logical universality. It is m-realism without real entities; instead of real entities, there are real relations. The shift is significant and was heralded by Empiricists in their battle with rationalists, but m-realism abides.

We must understand that Berkeley's way with obtaining universality by representation also does away with the process of conceptualization. He said, "...*universality*, so far as I can comprehend, not consisting in the absolute, positive nature or *conception* [my emphasis] of anything..." (Ibid).

If we cannot create, or abstract, a general particular, for all ideas for Berkeley are particular, then we are left with particular ideas of sorts or kinds but without the realist's abstractive glue to make the particulars of those sorts or kinds one. We have the representative particular which is not a concept, for it was not formed by gathering together by perceived or innate means. Conceptualism is thus thrown out the window by Berkeley when he rejects abstraction as a legitimate mental process.

Berkeley lays the blame for the false principles generating abstract general ideas on language controlled by reason. He maintains that abstract ideas are made in order to name, but that a general name has no one precise and definite signification; it signifies indifferently a great number of particulars, that is, ideas. These are his words:

> ...a triangle is defined to be a plane surface comprehended by three right lines; by which that name is limited to denote one certain idea and no other. To which I answer, that in the definition it is not said whether the sides are long or short, equal or unequal, nor with what angles they are inclined to each other; in all which there may be great variety, and consequently there is no one settled idea which limits the signification of the word triangle. 'Tis one thing for to keep a name constantly to the same definition, and another to make it stand everywhere for the same idea: the one is necessary, the other useless and impracticable. (Ibid, p. 73)

If there were one settled idea limiting the signification of the word triangle, that idea would be an abstract general idea, which is to say, a concept. And while triangle and "plane surface comprehended by three right lines" is relating a name to its definition, we note that, for Berkeley, no concrete thing, or particular idea, has been defined. If there is "no settled idea which limits the signification of the word triangle," then the process of actual definition is open; an open definition is no definition at all, just as an open concept is no concept at all, and an open idea no idea at all. The bonding glue of m-realism has come apart.

Berkeley must be given credit for putting the heat on reason and so dissolving its power of forming concepts, definitions, and abstract ideas. We can only admire his rejection of abstract general ideas and his emphasis on viewing particulars (ideas) as they are:

> Since therefore words are so apt to impose on the understanding, whatever ideas I consider, I shall endeavor to take them bare and naked into my view, keeping out of my thoughts, so far as I am able, those names which long and constant use hath so strictly united with them. (Ibid, p. 75)

And,

> He that knows he has no other than particular ideas, will not puzzle himself in vain to find out and conceive the abstract idea, annexed to any name. And he that knows names do not always stand for ideas, will spare himself the labor of looking for ideas, where there are none to be had. (Ibid, pp. 75-76)

Lastly, "...we need only draw the curtain of words, to behold the fairest tree of knowledge, whose fruit is excellent, and within the reach of our hand" (Ibid, p. 76).

What a pity Berkeley did not turn his gaze from the ideas that held him in thrall and behold actual particulars as they are and can become.

Berkeley brings us as far as philosophers are able to go in dissolving reason and its ways with particular things. Particulars, whether ideas or the actualities out there, were fundamental to Empiricists who, however, remained m-realists on the matter of universals. We will turn to the last of the three great British Empiricists and see how he deals with the problem of universals.

Hume: The Father of Resemblance without Commonality

Hume agrees with Berkeley's view of generality, the notion of the Representative Particular. Berkeley held that the *sort* that the Representative Particular represents can be represented by it because it and the sort are *similar*, not because they and it have something in common. Hume agrees, but goes on to make observations that end in a somewhat different view, a view we might call resemblance without commonalty, the view attributed to Wittgenstein. What Hume said is this:

> 'Tis evident, that even different simple ideas may have a similarity or resemblance to each other; nor is it necessary, that the point or circumstance of resemblance should be distinct or separable from that in which they differ. Blue and green are different simple ideas, but are more resembling than blue and scarlet; tho' their perfect simplicity excludes all possibility of separation or distinction. (Hume, 1969, p. 67)

What is it that Hume sees when looking at things which he labels simple green, simple blue, and simple scarlet? If, as he believes, simple green and simple blue are more resembling than simple blue and simple scarlet, is he seeing resemblances? Is he not seeing differences? For, if he sees that the blue-green pair differ less, the one from the other, than the blue-scarlet pair differ, the one from the other, he has seen things (differences) which he can tell truths about. Risking overkill, I say again, we cannot see anything that is a similarity of two or more things. Hume's vocabulary, as Berkeley would have said, gets him into trouble, for it is based on an unexamined assumption! Hume was the master of examining unexamined assumptions; he broke the logical tie assumed to necessarily exist in the cause-effect relation. He dissolved the substance assumed to exist as the mental stuff (Self) in which impressions and ideas have their existence. As a critic of rationalism, he was without peer. His empiricism would have prevailed had he grappled with the notion of resemblance or similarity. Unable to get rid of this notion, he made it fundamental in his thinking, just as John Stuart Mill did. So important is this notion for Hume that we will see that he is convinced that we cannot think (reason) without it. I will try to show that Hume is half correct. We can think without the notion of similarity, but without it, and the notion of identity, we cannot reason. I am not trying to destroy all reasoning, just metaphysical reason, the tyrant of thinking, and its pretensions. We will see how Hume ultimately incorporates the tyrant rather than turning him out.

Hume was able to undermine abstract or real entities by a principle he insisted on, a principle which becomes the foundation of his empiricism. As we saw, in the section on Zeno and the application of pure mathematics, mathematical realism buries itself deep in the psyche and generates real entities as if they were actualities in nature. Hume was aware of this:

'Tis usual with mathematicians, to pretend, that those ideas, which are their objects, are of so refin'd and spiritual a nature, that they fall not under the conception of the fancy, but must be comprehended by a pure and intellectual view, of which the superior faculties of the soul are alone capable. The same notion runs thro' most parts of philosophy, and is principally made use of to explain our abstract ideas, and to show how we can form an idea of a triangle, for instance, which shall neither be an isosceles nor scalenum, nor be confin'd to any particular length and proportion of sides. 'Tis easy to see, why philosophers are so fond of this notion of some spiritual and refin'd perceptions; since by that means they cover many of their absurdities, and may refuse to submit to the decisions of clear ideas, by appealing to such as are obscure and uncertain. But to destroy this artifice, we need but reflect on that principle so oft insisted on, that all our ideas are copy'd from our impressions. (Ibid, p. 120)

From particular things (impressions) we don't get abstractions, and particular things (impressions) are all we have to base our ideas on. Ideas are particulars. Hume is ridiculing the notion that mathematicians have ideas which are not derived from impressions (of actual things). His principle of empiricism is intended to keep people honest, and sober. But, what kind of ideas does Hume allow that we have? For if only particulars (impressions of them) exist and we can know them, what do we need ideas for? Quite simply, Hume believed that impressions were thought about and related in terms of ideas. In fact, thinking was the relating of ideas. Four of those relations were fundamental and secure; the relations of ideas he called: resemblance, proportion in quantity or number, degrees in any quality, and contrariety. These were the foundation of science. Three other relations involved matters of fact: identity, the situations in time and place, and causation. Of concern to us is his notion of resemblance, for it is the one which he tried to reduce all the other relations to. *"...Resemblance...is a relation, without which no philosophical relation can exist; since no objects will admit of comparison, but what have some degree of resemblance"* (Ibid, p. 61).

If objects do not "admit of comparison," they cannot be reasoned about. Reason follows resemblance and its degrees.

We must note what Hume says after describing the seven relations:

It might naturally be expected, that I should join difference to the other relations. But that I consider rather as a negation of relation, than as anything real or positive. Differences of two kinds as oppos'd either to identity or resemblances. The first is call'd a difference of number; the other of kind. (Ibid, pp. 62-63)

There is where Hume fails to complete his critique of rationalism! Difference is nothing real or positive, but resemblance is! Difference is not a relation, and indeed it is not, but the negation of relation...and indeed it is. Clearly, the reader at this point may at last understand that if difference is actual, and particulars are each other and different, then there are no (m-real) relations at all. Hume destroyed the real relation (logical necessity) presumed to exist between cause and effect, and it caused him considerable distress:

> The intense view of these manifold contradictions and imperfections in human reason has so wrought upon me, and heated my brain, that I am ready to reject all belief and reasoning, and can look upon no opinion even as more probable or likely than another. Where am I, or what? From what causes do I derive my existence, and to what condition shall I return? Whose favour shall I court, and whose anger must I dread? What beings surround me? and on whom have I any influence, or who have any influence on me? I am confounded with all these questions, and begin to fancy myself in the most deplorable condition imaginable, inviron'd with the deepest darkness, and utterly depriv'd of the use of every member and faculty. (Ibid, p. 316)

The glue of rational necessity is coming undone in the world that is Hume's mind. Fortunately, a bit of backgammon and conversation with friends helped to dispel Hume's philosophic melancholy. Destroying the logical necessity presumed to exist between cause and effect was not only personally destabilizing, it caused philosophers for the next two hundred years to seek refuge either in Idealism or the mathematics of probability. What if Hume had gone one step further and examined the remaining relation of all philosophic relations: resemblance? We must examine his thoughts and feelings about that, but to set the stage we must recall where Hume finally stood in his beliefs. If he allows difference to be something positive, then since it is a negation of relation, there will be no relations whatever. Difference, he says, is of two kinds: "as oppos'd either to identity or resemblances." That is, if we allow difference to be applied to identity, then number falls; if we allow difference to be applied to resemblances, then kind falls. Since Hume is not willing to allow number and kind to dissolve, as he had allowed the necessity between cause and effect to dissolve, he stops short of critiquing those notions (ideas). If, however, particulars do not resemble and things are not members of kinds, then we can have no ideas of resemblances and kinds. Recall Hume's principle: all our ideas are copied from impressions. If philosophers write books with ideas not derived from impressions, then, says Hume, they are worthless. Hume believed he had ideas of resemblances and kinds. Why did he stop short of inquiring where he got the idea of resemblance, an idea he made absolutely fundamental in philosophic thinking? (Bertrand Russell was willing to sacrifice all metaphysical relations except similarity.) Since that idea is still fundamental in both philosophy and science, I will focus on its centrality in Hume's philosophy; this will not only illuminate its importance, but also explain why it was passed on to modern and contemporary empirical thinkers, some of whom we have discussed.

Chapter 21 Thinking and Thinking about Self: Resemblance is the Cement of Self and the World

Hume's Dilemma

Little David Hume did not impress his mother as having abilities out of the ordinary, but his thinking amounted to unnerving the philosophic world. By focusing his critical attention, he realized that he could break the necessary, or rational, connection presumed to exist between the past and the future. In logical terms, he broke the back of Induction, the reasoning which carries us from a cause, for example, to its effect. The humpty dumpty that is induction can never be put together again, although tons of paper carry the marks of such attempts. We may believe otherwise, but there is no way to secure a tie between the premise and conclusion of inductive inference. One's expectations for tomorrow, or the next second, may not be realized. The problem stems not from some defect in the use or paraphernalia of logic, but from the way the world is: its diverse particulars and their changes.

I mention Hume's achievement regarding Induction, for it demonstrates his critical dissolution of a real element in rationalism, the element of logical necessity presumed to exist as part of the world's furniture. So unsettling was that critique that philosophers had to begin shoring up the damage to reason. Kant got a wake-up call and began work immediately. Probability theorists are still honing mathematical mechanisms to narrow the inductive gap. Hume could have dissolved more real elements, but he was, after all, a Rationalist.

He divided what could be thought about philosophically into Inductive areas on one side and Deductive areas on the other. He never intended to undermine his own rationalist presumptions of the truth of deduction:

> All the objects of human reason or inquiry may naturally be divided into two kinds, to wit, "Relations of Ideas," and "Matters of Fact." Of the first kind are the sciences of Geometry, Algebra, and Arithmetic, and, in short, every affirmation which is either intuitively or demonstratively certain. That the square of the hypotenuse is equal to the square of the two sides is a proposition which expresses a relation between these figures. That three times five is equal to the half of thirty expresses a relation between these numbers. Propositions of this kind are discoverable by the mere operation of thought, without dependence on what is anywhere existent in the universe. Though there never were a circle or triangle in nature, the truths demonstrated by Euclid would forever retain their certainty and evidence. (Hume, 1962, p. 47)

The division did not appear at all arbitrary to Hume. It was already a matter of tradition, and he did not question it. The "intuitively or demonstratively certain" was as firmly set in his personal world of ideas as the firmament was for Aristotle. So, he turned away from deductive procedures of logic itself and of mathematics---excepting a few swipes at geometry---and focused his gaze on the relations presumed to connect ideas involving matters of fact. Note, however, that all these ideas are, of course, in his head. We may wonder about the world outside his head, but Hume, like Quine, begins with impressions, impingements on his sensory surface. Philosophically, Hume operates totally within the psychological or subjective half of the Cartesian World, the half filled with ideas generated from impressions which, he-knows-not-how, are connected with things out there, the stubbornly material world of Descartes. That material world will disappear, as with Berkeley, because his only philosophic materials for inquiry and understanding are ideas and their association, for ideas cannot represent anything, but are themselves a kind of perceptions. The world lost to Psychology! Indeed, we have not yet recovered the actual world.

Hume's ideas are not Platonic, for each and every one is in us and is particular. Three of the relations of ideas are ideal:

> These are the uniting principles in the ideal world, and without them every distinct object is separable by the mind, and may be separately considered, and appears not to have any more connection with any

237

other object than if disjoined by the greatest difference and remoteness. It is therefore on some of these three relations of resemblance, contiguity, and causation that identity depends... (Hume, 1969, pp. 307-08)

The uniting principles are resemblance, contiguity, and causation. Identity also unites, but is not a separate and independent relation; it is dependent on the other three. Hume is saying that without these uniting principles, the glue of rationalism, each and every particular is simply other, unconnected. He looked closely at causation and dissolved the glue between cause and effect. When contiguity failed to hold up as an independent principle, that left resemblance, with identity dependent on it. Let us see how this dependence was established. In the treatise, Hume says, "Two objects, though perfectly resembling each other, and even appearing in the same place at different times, may be numerically different..." (Ibid, p. 117).

And:

We readily suppose an object may continue individually the same, though several times absent from and present to the senses; and ascribe to it an identity, notwithstanding the interruption of the perception, whenever we conclude, that if we had kept our eye or hand constantly upon it, it would have conveyed an invariable and uninterrupted perception. (Ibid, p. 122)

And:

When both objects are present to the senses along with the relation, we call this perception rather than reasoning; nor is there in this case any exercise of the thought, or any action, properly speaking, but a mere passive admission of the impressions through the organs of sensation. According to this way of thinking, we ought not to receive as reasoning any of the observations we make concerning identity... (Ibid, p. 121)

In the first passage, Hume seems to be admitting that two different objects, however resembling, are numerically different. They therefore cannot be the same or identical, ontologically, actually. We agree. In the second passage, he is giving his opinion of an object which is "several times absent and present to the senses." Is it the same (i.e., identical) object? Does it continue individually the same during its absence from our perception of it? He concludes that if "it would have conveyed an invariable and uninterrupted perception," we would have no reason to think it not "individually the same." Although we did not always perceive it (i.e., during its absence), we are allowed to say that it is the same or identical object if we are sure that during its absence it would have "conveyed an invariable and uninterrupted perception." As with the principle of Induction, so, too, in perception, no such certainty is available. Of course, no perception endures as "the same one" between any object and perceiver, so the notion of "invariable and uninterrupted perception" is mistaken, and, especially, as a means to establishing the validity of identity of an object over its (and the perceiver's) changes. The third passage is of great interest. In it, Hume is speaking of two objects, present to the senses along with the relation (i.e. of resemblance). If the relation of resemblance is present with respect to the two objects (numerically non-identical), we don't reason about the resembling identity of the two, we just passively perceive it there with the two objects. Is it? If pressed, Hume would have to admit that perceived resemblance (i.e., identity dependent on resemblance) is an assumption of his rationalism. We can say two things resemble, but we cannot see (or otherwise perceive) the resemblance of two (or more) things unless we see (or otherwise perceive) the respect in which they resemble, and that requires that we see (or otherwise perceive) something, the thing, whereby they resemble (and which for Hume, makes them one or identical in that respect). Denying that resemblance is a relation is a step in the right direction, for it makes alleged resemblance a particular thing, not still another real entity or universal. Since contiguity is dropped by Hume, and causality as a necessary relation drops out because of his critique, we have left only perceived resemblance which identity can depend on. With our critique, resemblance drops out, and identity, too, for it has nothing to depend on.

Hume failed to pursue a critique of resemblance. Why? Perhaps we can answer that question by pursuing his thinking about personal identity.

In the section, "Of Personal Identity," Hume says:

> There are some philosophers who imagine we are every moment intimately conscious of what we call our self; that we feel its existence and its continuance

in existence; and are certain, beyond the evidence of a demonstration, both of its perfect identity and simplicity. (Ibid, pp. 299-300)

And:

But self or person is not any one impression, but that to which our several impressions and ideas are supposed to have a reference. If any impression gives rise to the idea of self, that impression must continue invariably the same, through the whole course of our lives; since self is supposed to exist after that manner. But there is no impression constant and invariable. (Ibid, pp. 299-300)

And, "I may venture to affirm [that the self is] nothing but a bundle or collection of different perceptions, which succeed each other with an inconceivable rapidity, and are in a perpetual flux and movement" (Ibid, p. 300). And:

The mind is a kind of theater, where several perceptions successively make their appearance; pass, repass, glide away, and mingle in an infinite variety of postures and situations. There is properly no simplicity in it at one time, nor identity in different [times], whatever natural propension we may have to imagine that simplicity and identity. (Ibid, p. 301)

Hume goes on for several pages in the above fashion, piling Pelion on Ossa: the self is no one thing existing over time; there is no simplicity, no unity, no identity with respect to it. Yet, as he proceeds, he seems to begin doubting what he is saying, and in his Appendix he backs away from the notion of self that he is putting forth as a conclusion; that personal self is a changingly diverse and disconnected plurality. In giving the reasons why others hold to a belief in a self which is both simple and identical, he asks, "What then gives us so great a propension to ascribe an identity to these successive perceptions, and to suppose ourselves possessed of an invariable and uninterrupted existence through the whole course of our lives" (Ibid)? His explanation leads him on to the notions of resemblance and causation. But first he repeats his view that the notions of identity, and sameness are equivalent. "We have a distinct idea of an object that remains invariable and uninterrupted through a supposed variation of time and this idea we call that of identity or sameness" (Ibid).

We have pointed out that Hume could not have gotten a distinct idea of identity or sameness from any of his impressions of resembling particulars, for resemblance is not a particular thing which two or more particulars can have in common. And, he is adamant that successive perceptions are distinct, not the same ones. "'Tis still true that every distinct perception which enters into the composition of the mind, is a distinct existence, and is different, and distinguishable, and separable from every other perception, either contemporary or successive" (Ibid, p. 307). Hume says the notions of diversity and identity become confounded with each other by the notion of resemblance:

That action of the imagination, by which we consider

the uninterrupted and invariable object [i.e., its "identity"], and that by which we reflect on the succession of related objects [i.e., a "diversity"] are almost the same to the feeling... This resemblance is the cause of the confusion and mistake, and makes us substitute the notion of identity instead of that of related objects [i.e., "diversity"]. However at one instant we may consider the related succession as invariable or interrupted, we are sure the next to ascribe to it a perfect identity, and regard it as invariable and uninterrupted. Our propensity to this mistake is so great from the resemblance above mentioned, that we fall into it before we are aware; and though we incessantly correct ourselves by reflection, and return to a more accurate method of thinking, yet we cannot long sustain our philosophy, or take off this bias from the imagination. (Ibid, pp. 301-02)

Hume is holding firm to the skeptical results of his analysis. He believes he can have a distinct perception of identity, but it does not apply to personal self. the self is diverse, a congeries of perceptions, each distinctly other and different. Still, we slip back all too easily into our old belief. But that slipping back is understandable; from the resemblance of diverse perceptions, our imagination then attributes identity to them.

Can Hume see a resemblance? He calls resemblance a relation and says, "upon the appearance of the picture of an absent friend our idea of him is evidently enlivened by the resemblance... In producing this effect there concur both a relation and a present impression" (Ibid, p. 148). He would have us believe that the impression stemming from the picture resembles our stored impression (memory) of our friend. We may believe it, but we are not seeing something called resemblance. Nor do we have an impression of a relation.

In the treatise, he says, "every simple idea has a simple impression, which resembles it, and every simple impression a correspondent idea. That the idea of red, which we form in the dark, and that impression which strikes our eyes in sunshine, differ only in degree, not in nature" (Ibid, p. 51). If resemblance were a simple impression, we could have an idea of it. If we examined, somehow, the impression and the idea we might also see the resemblance of the two. Since there is no simple impression of resemblance there is no way to complete the examination. From the conclusion to his abstract of the treatise, Hume says:

> Through this whole book there are great pretensions to new discoveries in philosophy; but if anything can entitle the author to so glorious a name as that of an "inventor," it is the use he makes of the principle of the association of ideas, which enters into most of his philosophy. Our imagination has a great authority over our ideas, and there are no ideas that are different from each other which it cannot separate and join and compose into all the varieties of fiction. But notwithstanding the empire of the imagination, *there is a secret tie or union among particular ideas which causes the mind to conjoin them more frequently together and makes the one, upon its appearance, introduce the*

other. [my emphasis] ...These principles of association are reduced to three..."resemblance"---a picture naturally makes us think of the man it was drawn for; "contiguity"---when St. Dennis is mentioned, the idea of Paris naturally occurs; "causation"---when we think of the son we are apt to carry our attention to the father. It will be easy to conceive of what vast consequences these principles must be in the science of human nature if we consider that so far as regards the mind these are the only links that bind the parts of the universe together or connect us with any person or object exterior to ourselves. For as it is by means of thought only that anything operates upon our passions, and as these are the only ties of our thoughts, they are really to us the cement of the universe, and all the operations of the mind must, in a great measure, depend on them. (Ibid, p. 302)

Imagination, admittedly, has great authority over our ideas. This was also true for Kant who gave it even greater authority after he read Hume. What is especially noteworthy in that long passage is Hume's claim that there is a secret tie or union among particular ideas that causes the mind to conjoin them more frequently together, and that one such tie---the fundamental one for him---is the principle of association which he calls resemblance. It is pretty important: "the cement of the universe."

As a fundamental principle of association, or cement of the universe, resemblance is admittedly obscure. He says it falls, "more properly under the province of intuition than demonstration. When any objects resemble each other, the resemblance will at first strike the eye, or rather the mind; and seldom requires a second examination" (Ibid, p. 118). Well, there is a backing away from resemblance as an unquestioned perception. An intuition of resemblance is certainly an obscure sort of apprehension, and he admits that resemblance is not a distinct something which can be demonstrated. Quine, without doubt, read Hume, for he agrees that resemblance is indeed opaque.

That something so important to thought should be so unavailable leaves a dark hole in the center of rationalism. It would seem that we can neither know nor be certain about an object called resemblance, although it is required in order to have rationalism!

Since Hume was a rationalist, we will see how it urges him to draw conclusions about personal identity which are at odds with his empirical analyses:

> The whole of this doctrine leads us to a conclusion, which is of great importance in the present affair, viz. that all the nice and subtle questions concerning personal identity can never possibly be decided, and are to be regarded as *grammatical* [my emphasis] than as philosophical. (Ibid, p. 310)

A new school of philosophy was founded late last century on the word I emphasized in that passage. If philosophy is mostly a matter of grammatical blunders, then the cure is making it properly grammatical. This is a wrong turn for philosophy. It turns philosophy over to English departments, and we have seen how that fares. A correct view of the nature of actual things was needed. This could not be generated until the truths about categories and concepts and their formation were available.

Hume's analyses of claims that the self was a simple, identical, unified thing enduring over time resulted in his view of self as a bundle of disconnected perceptions; the self was diverse, changing, and non-substantial. Now he is saying that "all the nice and subtle questions concerning personal identity can never possibly be decided, and are to be regarded as grammatical." His philosophical analyses are put aside. Add to the above passage this one:

> But as the relations, and the easiness of the transition may diminish by insensible degrees, we have no just standard by which we can decide any dispute concerning the time when they acquire or lose a title to the name of identity. All the disputes concerning *the identity of connected objects* are merely *verbal* [my emphases]. (Ibid)

If the identity of connected objects is merely verbal, then why has he spent so much time trying to persuade us that identity is based on resemblance, and the latter is perceived, or, later, perhaps only intuited. It is quite a pull-back to make identity a problem (grammatical or verbal) in our use of language! But several philosophers blossomed, Wittgenstein among them, as a result of these remarks by Hume.

My question is: has Hume precipitated a dilemma for himself? Further, is he unable to come up with the idea of resemblance while still requiring it (even if only verbally) as a principle of association? The notion of resemblance, of which he has no idea, is the only thing which can prevent his world of ideas, the only world he knows, from falling into uncontrollable disconnectedness. If we return to the Appendix to the treatise, we find Hume despairing, "I had entertained some hopes, that however deficient our theory of the intellectual world might be, it would be free from those contradictions and absurdities which seem to attend every explication that human reason can give of the material world" (Ibid, p. 675). However, "But upon a more strict review of the section concerning personal identity, I find myself involved in such a labyrinth that, I must confess, I neither know how to correct my former opinions, nor how to render them consistent" (Ibid). What troubles Hume? He is unsure of his conclusion about the self. So, he reviews the arguments he has used on both sides of the issue. He concludes:

> In short, there are two principles which I cannot render consistent, nor is it in my power to renounce either of them, viz. that all our distinct perceptions are distinct existences, and that the mind never perceives any real connection among distinct existences. Did our perceptions either inhere in something simple and individual, or did the mind perceive some real connection among them, there would be no difficulty in the case. For my part, I must plead the privilege of a sceptic, and confess that this difficulty is too hard for my understanding. I pretend not, however, to pronounce it absolutely insuperable. Others, perhaps, or myself, upon more mature reflections, may discover some hypothesis

that will reconcile those contradictions. (Ibid, p. 578)

Hume clearly admits to the dilemma. If, however, we look closely at the two principles (emphasized, above), there is no inconsistency. Whence comes the dilemma? He thinks there is an insuperable difficulty because firstly, he cannot perceive the simple substance which our perceptions are supposed to inhere in; secondly, he cannot perceive some real connection among his perceptions. Why doesn't he celebrate? Quite simply, if Hume accepts his analyses, he cannot think! That is the contradiction lurking behind his careful and correct analyses. There is simply no inconsistency in his view that perceptions are both distinct existences and unconnected, i.e., by some real connection. Thinking, which is to say reasoning, requires the real connection of ideas. Hume succeeded in spite of himself. Others believed that his skepticism was avoidable; just believe that identity and resemblance are real connectors, otherwise the cement that holds together the whole that is rationalism dissolves. Hume's Rational World is falling into empiricism. He could not let it go. He should have. The mind needs some respite from the illusions it creates to prop itself up and prevent its falling into actualities.

Chapter 22 Rationalism Cannot Validate its Logic

We have presented some of the history of the use of similarity (or resemblance) and shown its importance for m-realists, who also are rationalists. Resemblance generates m-real entities and relations and, as Hume believed, is the *cement* holding together the world of ideas thus making it rational. It is time to focus on the logic, the ultimate weapon in rationalism's armory used in defense of itself and its ways. We must understand where logic gets its authority to reign supreme. This authority must come from its hold on inference, for inference is all that logic can accomplish. Inference is deductive and inductive. The validity of these activities, then, will be our focus.

The certainty of inductive inference was shattered by Hume, as we indicated. It has been reduced to a logic of probabilism, as in statistics. We have undermined the notion of generalization in forming classes or kinds, for it is a falsification of actual particulars and their natures. Statistics is the attempt to apply m-mathematical realities to the actual world, as we saw in our discussion of Zeno; it creates problems. Induction at bottom is guessing, no matter how sophisticated the mathematics or reasoning used. To ask about its validity, in a logical sense, is simply non-sense. Inductive inference isn't logically valid. But since in living it is important to guess, we make the guesses as to outcomes as likely as we can. Our successes do not validate induction, they simply keep us interested in trying harder to close a gap that can never be closed: the gap between the changes of dynamic particulars in a uniquely changing world. Newell puts the problem with induction this way:

> Since induction justifies conclusions by pointing to regularities, prior to inductive generalizing it must be decided whether to regard an array of instances as being instances of similar or of different sorts. But regularity presupposes similarity and the perception of differences, so decisions about whether a given number of cases constitute a regular sequence, on the basis of which we might predict, cannot themselves be justified inductively. (Newell, 1986, p. 88)

Generalizing, indeed, requires deciding on the nature of the particulars one is generalizing over. If particulars are viewed as candidates for *sorts*, they will be viewed as instances of some sort, based on similarity. regularity presupposes similarity, so decisions about whether a given number of cases constitute a regular sequence cannot themselves be justified inductively. Induction cannot be logically validated.

What of the claim of validity for deductive inference? Again, Newell has something interesting to say, and he refers to wisdom:

In the case of deductive inference, we must push back in two dimensions, Wisdom thinks. First...the fact that a conclusion follows by deduction from the premises cannot be an ultimate ground for asserting or denying the conclusion. Second, when we push back the claim that the conclusion follows by deduction from the premises, the claim itself emerges as being parasitic on reasoning of a non-deductive kind. We standardly test the validity of an argument by an inspection procedure to determine whether it has the same form as some valid argument; thus, we take an argument to be valid if it is a substitution instance, or reducible to a substitution instance, of a logical truth. (Ibid)

And, most importantly, "as Wisdom points out, the thesis that an argument is valid when it is an instance of some valid form is not itself formally valid or a rule of any logical system, but expresses a practice underwritten by non-demonstrative inference from parallel cases" (Ibid, pp. 88-89).

Although not surprising to logicians, these are very important observations. An argument is valid "if it is a substitution instance, or reducible to a substitution instance, of a logical truth." Logical truths are true by their form; they don't say anything about the world. Newell gives this example, "given a valid sentence built only of logical particles and blanks 'Every F that is G is F' one consequently assents to, or is in some sense constrained to assent to, the validity of the sentence 'Every man who is bald is a man'" (Ibid, p. 89).

Focusing on the two sentences, the first a logical

sentence, the second a substitution instance of the first, Newell continues:

> One sees them as like each other, as subjects for the same symbolic generalization. We test validity by inspection as a final check on our formulas; and inspection is no more than inspection for parity in relevant respects, that is, parity by our lights. It seems to follow that the ascription of validity, thus pushed back, is ultimately non-deductive and rests on the discernment of parallel cases, or as Kuhn would say, "on the assimilation of similar exemplars without answering the question, similar in respect of what?" (Ibid)

This passage points out what logicians well know: "the ascription of validity is ultimately non-deductive and rests on the discernment of parallel cases or the assimilation of similar exemplars without answering the question, similar in respect of what?" Briefly: deductive validity rests on our seeing similarities! But we cannot see them. We cannot see the similarity of the two sentences in the above example, for each is other and different. We can say that they are similar, as logicians (who are m-realists) do, but we cannot see any thing the two sentences have in common and which we could name a similarity. The "discernment of parallel cases," required for validity, fails for we cannot see the similarity implied in parallel cases. If we go the alternative route suggested, Kuhn's "assimilation of similar exemplars without answering the question, similar in respect of what?" validity falters when we fail to see the similarity of similar exemplars.

We have already pointed out that Kuhn's refusal to answer the question "similar in respect of what?" was a strategy to avoid re-introducing criteria and correspondence rules, the positivists' way of attaching symbolic expressions to nature. Such rules were taken to be operational definitions of scientific terms or else a set of necessary and sufficient conditions for a term's applicability. The strategy isn't needed; we cannot see similarities anyway. We have already pointed out the incompleteness and incoherence of the Humean-Wittgensteinian notion of sorts, games, or families resembling, but without regard to any respect.

The conclusion of our endeavors, thus far, is a simple one: if we remove the cement that is similarity (and identity) from the logical structure that is m-realism-rationalism it comes unglued.

PART V The Role of "Species" in Contemporary Biology and Philosophy of Science

Chapter 23 Resolving the Species Problem

The long-standing problem of species was not solved by biologists or philosophers during the last decades of the 20th century nor was there a definitive solution to the problem of *race* by the decoding of the so-called human genome at the beginning of the 21st century. We entered the 21st century still speaking of species as if they were the undeniable actual entities, the basic units, involved in the processes of evolution. Ernst Mayr's definition of species was granted truth-status by consensus as if that settled a major question in ontology as well as the one-many problem in philosophy. The need for a unit called species in evolutionary theory was overwhelming and outweighed the obvious difficulties felt by many in accepting such a unit. Some evolutionists (e.g., Gould and colleagues) with decidedly metaphysical dreams of units higher than organisms and species went on to build hierarchical castles in the air. Others (Gareth Nelson at the Museum of Natural History in New York City and his colleagues), almost to the point of shunning species altogether, sought actual relationships of living things in the transmitted characters of organisms and focused their efforts on a more reliable method (Cladism) for generating information for taxonomic and evolutionary consideration.

We will take up the story of species as that notion was modified for theoretical acceptability in the last half of the 20th century. Darwin's own view will be given and a final resolution to the species problem will be offered. To get there, we must give analytic consideration to the metaphysics in the part-whole notion, for it will be used in reconceptualizing species along m-realism lines. This reconceptualization became tolerable, if not completely acceptable, to a majority of evolutionary theorists and is central in current evolutionary studies. We will begin by clearing the field of misguided notions surrounding the species problem.

The Part-Whole Relation: David Lewis and Mereology

David Lewis believes that part and whole apply to classes. His book, *Parts of Classes*, centers on set theory as the foundation for mathematics. Finding that the notion of classes is troublesome, he believes that part-whole and not membership is the way to go in explaining set theory.

Of interest to us is not set theory and its relation to logic or mathematics but the use of the set-theoretical notion of part-whole in biology. Specifically, its use to solve the species problem.

Lewis defines *mereology* as "the theory of the relation of part to whole, and kindred notions."(1991, p. 1) Lewis finds mereology, and its part-whole relation, unproblematic and capable of replacing the notion of class and its membership relation.

The part-whole relation goes back to the very beginning of the Sceptic tradition. Sextus Empiricus commented on it. We are right to suspect that a whole and its parts are an alternative to the metaphysical one many problem. Lewis is aware that many philosophers view mereology with the gravest suspicion and he addresses some of their complaints. The heart of the matter, however, is the very notion part-whole and especially the alleged relation of a whole to its parts. Lewis uses this example to illustrate part-whole:

> Suppose it turned out that the three quarks of a proton are exactly superimposed, each one just where the others are and just where the proton is. (And suppose the three quarks last just as long as the proton.) Still the quarks are parts of the proton, but the proton is not part of the quarks and the quarks are not part of each other. (Ibid, p. 75)

Lewis is in trouble in the very attempt to state the relation of a whole (a proton) to its parts (the 3 quarks). Is there an entity called a proton and 3 other entities, called quarks? In other words, can scientists distinguish an entity called a proton and three other entities called quarks? Are the three wheels of a particular tricycle parts of something called the tricycle? If so, there are three wheels and the tricycle, which by common understanding must already have three wheels! Accordingly, there is no proton and its three quarks, for a proton already is its contents, the three quarks, much as a pizza is the dough, sauce, cheese, etc. We will return to Lewis and summarize all this.

The three quarks (two ups and a down) of a proton give us the distinction: 3 individual quarks and 1 proton. The quarks, says Lewis, are parts of the proton, but the proton is not part of the quarks and the quarks are not part of each other. The assertion that the proton is not part of the quarks makes it a distinct entity all its own, but also claiming the quarks are parts of the proton denies the assertion and confuses what a proton is. He wants the proton to be a whole which can be distinguished from its parts which, in physical fact, are necessarily parts of it. We certainly cannot actually distinguish a proton and three quarks in the same proton. If we could, we would have a whole and its parts. The three quarks and their interactions are the plurality we call a proton. There is no distinguishable whole (i.e., separable proton) and its parts (i.e., three quarks). A little m-mereological creationism is at work in Lewis's account and, unfortunately, it is carried over into biology. But let us go on. "Suppose a material thing occupies a region of substantial space-time; it does not follow (though is just might be true) that the region is part of the thing" (Ibid).

One may wonder, here, how it just might be true that space-time, now thought of as a substance, could be part of the thing in which it is, especially since neither space (nothingness or void) nor time is a substance. D.M. Armstrong has contended that space-time location adds particularity to things, so Lewis may be bowing in his direction. We will see, shortly, that Lewis agrees with Armstrong on the matter of mereology. Lewis continues, "So I claim that mereology is legitimate, unproblematic, fully and precisely understood. All suspicions against it are mistaken. But I claim more still. Mereology is ontologically innocent" (Ibid, p. 81).

Lewis quotes D.M. Armstrong about two adjoining

terrace houses that share a common wall. They:

> are not identical, but they are not completely distinct
> from each other either. They are partially, and this
> partial identity takes the form of having a common
> part. Australia and New South Wales are not
> identical, but they are not completely distinct from
> each other. They are partially identical, and this
> partial identity takes the form of the whole-part
> 'relation'... Begin with New South Wales and then
> take larger and larger portions of Australia. One is
> approaching closer and closer to complete identity
> with Australia. (Ibid, pp. 82-83)

Lewis also quotes Donald Baxter:

> The whole is the many parts counted as one thing.
> On this view there is no one thing distinct from each
> of the parts which is the whole. Rather, the whole is
> simply the many parts with their distinctness from
> each other not mattering. This is not to deny the
> existence of the whole. It is merely to deny the
> additional existence of the whole... (Ibid, p. 83)

He then gives this example:

> Suppose a man owned some land which he divides
> into six parcels. Overcome with enthusiasm...he
> might try to perpetrate the following scam. He sells
> off the six parcels while retaining ownership of the
> whole. That way he gets some cash while hanging on

to his land. Suppose the six buyers of the parcels argue that they jointly own the whole and the original owner now owns nothing. Their argument seems right. But it suggests that the whole was not a seventh thing. (Ibid)

All of this requires comment. I will address three claims. First, regarding the first quote, Lewis claims that "mereology is ontologically innocent." Secondly, the claims about the two adjoining terrace houses that share a common wall and their partial identity as well as the partial identity of New South Wales and Australia. Thirdly, the six parcels of land and Baxter's claim that the whole is not an additional something which exists along with the parts, but is the parts without their distinction from one another.

Is mereology ontologically innocent? Lewis argues that the whole that is a proton is an existence separable from the quarks, but it does not add to the furniture of the universe; we get it free, ontologically. Just as the fusion of all cats doesn't add anything ontological to all the cats, their fusion carries no existential weight. What is added by the whole, here, is a metaphysical entity. It may be free and carry no existential weight but it does considerable theoretical work and clutters the mind. It is anything but innocent.

In Baxter's example of the six parcels of land the separate existence of the whole is denied. The whole, for Baxter is "the many parts counted as one thing." He says:

There is no one thing distinct from each of the parts which is the whole; the whole is simply the many parts with their distinctness from each other not mattering. This is not to deny the existence of the whole, it is merely to deny the additional existence of the whole. (Ibid)

All that is interesting, but it won't wash. Baxter says that he won't deny the existence of the whole, he just doesn't want us to think of the whole as an additional existence. But he talks about the whole and the parts of that whole. This is the very framework which is in dispute! It generates a metaphysical entity, namely the whole. Baxter may not worry about his whole not having an additional existence because he enjoys metaphysical entities. Ontologically, it matters. A proton has two up quarks and a down quark, and their distinctness from each other makes all the difference! Are we to believe that in Baxter's example of the six parcels of land the parcels are identical (which would be untrue) or that their actual differences make no difference? Baxter's whole which is many parts counted as one thing is the tired attempt to solve the one-many problem by declaration and without the exertion of analytic effort. Not at all strange, for Baxter is a metaphysical realist. Lastly, the two terrace houses which share a common wall aren't two houses, as asserted in the beginning statement. Nor is partial identity involved. Again, identity is an incoherent expression whether the alleged identity is full or partial. So, too, with the partial identity of New South Wales and Australia. Australia is the wonderful land bounded by the Pacific Ocean. New South Wales does not overlap Australia. It is continental Australian territory given the right to place the label *New South Wales* to refer to the land within its mapped borders.

The very use of the notion of part-whole outside mathematics and logic should make us aware that metaphysics is involved. In the sciences, especially biology, the part-whole relation is no relation of things called parts to something called a whole. The whole in the above examples is a non-existent, m-real (i.e., metaphysical) entity. No whole is related to its parts by partial identity because identity is not something which is actual and can be seen or recorded. That does not mean it can exist unseen. It means that there are no identities to be seen. An identity is still another way m-realists obtain entities to keep their metaphysics going. We will see in the so-called radical solution of Ghiselin, below, an attempt to keep species alive in evolutionary theory by means of the part-whole relation.

Chapter 24 What Darwin Said Concerning Species in On the Origin of Species by Means of Natural Selection

Three of the first five chapters deal with variation. The notion of species as fixed entities must be destroyed. The weapon of destruction is the perceptual one of pointing out that all individuals (i.e., organisms) vary, more or less. If no two individuals are identical, if no two are the same,---if all individuals are modified by descent and change as they live---then they cannot be a fixed entity in nature, nor can they be the basis for the concept of a fixed entity, whatever you would call it. If we cannot put individuals into a category or class, then we have no concept of species and we cannot define it.

Darwin is not writing a philosophic tract. He is telling us about living creatures, organisms, which descend with modification from others and either adapt to their circumstances and live and reproduce or die and are forgotten.

The other two of the first five chapters show us the struggle for existence and how successful variations promote survival.

Now, it will be well to keep in mind that, from the

first chapter on, a dilemma confronts Darwin in his exposition. First, the evidence is presented which will undermine the reigning notion of species as fixed. Second, evidence presented is intended to persuade us that not only are species not fixed, there are no such entities in nature. Third, given that there are no such entities, is he, in the end, talking about them and their origin? No. But he must talk about what naturalists call species. He must use the term species knowing it is confusing and knowing that everybody will think he believes that even if there are no fixed species he is proposing mutable species. Even a mutable species is an entity, one that changes. But recall, Darwin emphasized that there are no species entities, mutable or immutable.

There are, then, two opposing tensions in Darwin's discussion, tensions that he is fully aware of: first his aim, which is to establish individuals as variants which give rise to other variants; and second, the language of metaphysical realism which was unavoidable in his day (and in ours) in speaking about individual organisms. M-realism, with its implied m-real entities, is simply the categorical, and metaphysical, way of thinking and speaking.

In the first chapter, "Variation Under Domestication," Darwin establishes, without question, the variability of those individuals which breeders use in their experiments, especially cattle, horses, sheep, dogs, and pigeons. That he is talking
about individual organisms and their differences is clear from the first sentence:

When we look to the individuals of the same variety or sub-variety of our older cultivated plants and animals, one of the first points which strikes us, is, that they generally differ much more from each other, than do the individuals of any one species or variety in a state of nature. (Darwin, 1964, p. 7)

The weight of his observations falls on individuals. That he cannot avoid the categorical way of speaking about those individuals as variety, sub-variety, and species, is also obvious. The crucial terms variety and species are used knowingly in two senses by Darwin from the beginning: what his peers understand by those terms and his understanding of them, which will emerge as his discussion proceeds.

Individuals which vary from a parent stock or species comprise a variety or a race. Darwin noted that the more numerous and widespread the parent stock, the more numerous the variations, hence the greater number of varieties. Pigeons, which had been bred into a bewildering number of varieties, were a special study of his:

> Great as the differences are between the breeds of pigeons, I am fully convinced that the common opinion of naturalists is correct, namely, that all have descended from the rock-pigeon (Columba livia), including under this term several geographical races or sub-species, which differ from each other in the most trifling respects. (Ibid, p. 23)

Again, the intent here is the exhibition of variation, not that the variants are validly placed in breeds, races, sub-species, or that the rock-pigeon's genus and species are actualities in nature.

As for Dogs:

> if, for instance, it could be shown that the greyhound,
> bloodhound, terrier, spaniel, and bull-dog, which we
> all know propagate their kind so truly, were the
> offspring of any single species, then such facts would
> have great weight in making us doubt about the
> immutability of the many very closely allied and
> natural species---for instances, of the many foxes---
> inhabiting different quarters of the world. (Ibid, pp.
> 16-17)

The doctrine of immutability is under attack. Finally, this observation:

> One circumstance has struck me much; namely, that
> all the breeders of the various domestic animals and
> the other cultivators of plants, with whom I have ever
> conversed, or whose treatises I have read, are firmly
> convinced that the several breeds to which each has
> attended, are descended from so many aboriginally
> distinct species....The explanation, I think, is simple:
> from long-continued study they are strongly
> impressed with the differences between the several
> races; and though they well know that each race
> varies slightly, for they win their prizes by selecting
> such slight differences, yet they ignore all general
> arguments, and refuse to sum up in their minds
> slight differences accumulated during many
> successive generations. May not those naturalists

who, knowing far less of the laws of inheritance than does the breeder, and knowing no more than he does of the intermediate links in the long lines of descent, yet admit that many of our domestic races have descended from the same parents---may they not learn a lesson of caution, when they deride the idea of species in a state of nature being lineal descendants of other species? (Ibid, pp. 28-29)

Surely, here, Darwin is to be read: breeding variants (i.e., species) in a state of nature can be lineal descendants of other breeding variants (i.e., species). Clearly, if we use our imaginations, "differences accumulated during many successive generations" sum up to a collection of individuals quite different from those earlier on. Individuals can be bred to differ little from one another or depart from that difference. If individuals breed true, their offspring differ little from them; if they do not breed true, the offspring differ in those ways they in fact differ. All this was common knowledge. The question was, given a stock (species) could it produce variants whose descendants would be quite different from that parent stock? Could stocks produce differences (varieties) and could those differences (variations) eventually produce stocks (species) significantly different from earlier ones? Darwin's peers, especially Lyell and Hooker, whose opinions he most respected, believed species were immutable, although they granted some variations within species---an obvious contradiction calling attention to the term 'immutable' as being related to an m-real entity or concept and not to individuals they could see. In a letter to Hooker on 11 January 1844---about 8 years after he had opened his notebook on the question of species---Darwin let the cat out of the bag. "At last gleams of light have come, and I am almost convinced (quite contrary to the opinion I started with) that species are not (it is like confessing a murder) immutable" (De Beer, 1964, p. 135).

Another letter to Hooker, on 13 June 1849---after Darwin was well into his work on barnacles---reads:

> I have been struck with the variability of every part in some slight degree of every species. Systematic work would be easy were it not for this confounded variation, which, however, is pleasant to me as a speculatist, though odious to me as a systematist. (Ibid, pp. 136-37)

Darwin is referring to individuals in every species; their parts, each and every one, vary in some slight degree from the parts in every other. The result? Classification becomes a nightmare (impossible?). Still, seeing those variations is *pleasant*. Why? They are the evidence he needs to destroy the claim that there is a fixed species-entity in nature. Had Darwin's notion of species not been rattled in looking at those individual variations, he would have been just another naturalist, taking his cues from philosophy. Strange. Mayr waxes eloquent over Darwin's research; each and every individual he examined was a variant; each was unique. Rather than understanding, as Darwin did, that such determinations wreak havoc with classification, Mayr and his colleagues, Ghiselin and Hull and Eldredge ignore those observations and re-create a metaphysical species-entity! And other metaphysical entities besides. The sine qua non of systematic work has been to ignore difference, at some point, as Darwin learned, and allow the notion of similarity to suggest cohesion and a boundary. However, the eight years he spent on barnacles provided him the evidence on variation he was searching for in closely related individuals. After publishing the four barnacle volumes, Darwin was at work on his great book. Lyell had encouraged him to make haste, and on 25 July 1856 Lyell wrote to Hooker, "Whether Darwin persuades you and me to renounce our faith in species or not, I foresee that many will go over to the indefinite modifiability doctrine" (Ibid, pp. 147-48)

What a nice way to put it! "Indefinite modifiability." (Isn't that what is occurring in each of us because our genomes are changing all the time, for good or not?) For Darwin, species in their descent with modification become inexact, unclear, indefinable. In fact, their boundaries disappear, leaving a clear Darwinian view of just variant organisms changing over geological time. Hooker came over to Darwin's way of thinking two years later. Lyell came over six years after the publication of *On The Origin*. They must have been impressed with Darwin's evidence on variation and the divergence of descendants from parental stocks.

In chapter two, Darwin begins his discussion with these remarks, "Nor shall I here discuss the various definitions which have been given of the term species. No one definition has as yet satisfied all naturalists; yet every naturalist knows vaguely what he means when he speaks of a species" (Darwin, 1964, p. 44). Indeed, we all know, vaguely, what is meant by species, those closely related individuals that don't differ to much one from another as for variety, "The term "variety" is almost equally difficult to define; but here community of descent is almost universally implied, though it can rarely be proved" (Ibid). Then Darwin launches into the fact of individual differences:

> Again, we have many slight differences which may be called individual differences, such as are known frequently to appear in the offspring from the same parents...No one supposes that all the individuals of the same species are cast in the very same mold. These individual differences are highly important for us, as they afford materials for natural selection to accumulate, in the same manner as man can accumulate in any given direction individual differences in his domesticated productions.... I could show by a long catalogue of facts, that parts which must be called important, whether viewed under a physiological or classificatory point of view, sometimes vary in the individuals of the very same species. (Ibid, p. 45)

And, "I should never have expected that the branching of the main nerves close to the great central ganglion of an insect would have been variable in the same insect..." (Ibid, p. 91).

Why are all those individual differences he is emphasizing important? They "afford materials for natural selection to accumulate." Where are those materials (i.e., differences) accumulating? In entities called species? No, in organisms. In their egg and sperm cells.

Darwin then alludes to the well-known cases of so-called *polymorphic species* in which the individual differences run wild:

> I refer to those genera...in which the species present an inordinate amount of variation; and hardly two naturalists can agree which forms to rank as species and which as varieties. We may instance Rubus, Rosa, and Hieracium amongst plants, several genera of insects, and several genera of Brachiopod shells. (Ibid, p. 92)

As to ranking, it is quite arbitrary, "in determining whether a form should be ranked as a species or a variety, the opinion of naturalists having sound judgment and wide experience seems the only guide to follow" (Ibid, p. 93). Indeed, Darwin follows that statement with a number of doubtful varieties in plants and birds. Highly competent judges simply cannot agree on what to call them, "But to discuss whether they are rightly called species or varieties, before any definition of these terms has been generally accepted, is vainly to beat the air" (Ibid, p. 94).

Darwin knew no definition would be forthcoming. Who can define the indefinable? Nor are there lines of demarcation separating variant individuals from varieties, varieties from sub-species and sub-species from species:

> Certainly no clear line of demarcation has as yet been drawn between species and sub-species---that is, the forms which in the opinion of some naturalists come very near to, but do not quite arrive at the rank of species; or, again, between sub-species and well-marked varieties, or between lesser varieties and

individual differences. (Ibid, p. 95)

With all boundaries gone, Darwin now outlines his view of how variant individual organisms, in their descent, lead us to view them, correctly, as proceeding from one stage of difference to another. This is the climax of his argument on variation, and in getting there he has destroyed the notion of fixed species in nature. This he did by showing that every individual is a variant and that variants do not provide us any means for drawing demarcations. Without boundaries, there can be no category, and no concept. Without a category or a concept there can be no definition. What his peers had been calling a species was no entity at all.

> I look at individual differences, though of small interest to the systematist, as of high importance for us, as being the first step towards such slight varieties as are barely thought worth recording in works on natural history. And I look at varieties which are in any degree more distinct and permanent, as steps leading to more strongly marked and more permanent varieties; and at these latter, as leading to sub-species, and to species. *the passage from one stage of difference to another...*" [my emphasis] (Ibid, p. 96)

This is, in my opinion, the most important claim in Darwin's great book, and it is based on empirical evidence. The descents with modification are undeniable (if one cares to look closely at each individual); you can begin anywhere, with any variant, and all roads of descent are but passages from one stage of difference to another. Differences, the bane of systematists, are the very stuff of natural selection.

> If a variety were to flourish so as to exceed in numbers the parent species, it would then rank as the species, and the species as the variety; or it might come to supplant and exterminate the parent species; or both might co-exist, and both rank as independent species....From these remarks it will be seen that I look at the term species, as one arbitrarily given for the sake of convenience to a set of individuals closely resembling each other, and that it does not essentially differ from the term variety, which is given to less distinct and more fluctuating forms. The term variety, again, in comparison with mere individual differences, is also applied arbitrarily, and for mere convenience sake....The amount of difference is one very important criterion in settling whether two forms should be ranked as species or varieties.... The species of the larger generally resemble varieties, more than do the species of the smaller genera....Finally, then, varieties have the same general characters as species, for they cannot be distinguished from species---except, firstly, by the discovery of intermediate linking forms, and the occurrence of such links cannot affect the actual characters of the forms which they connect; and except, secondly, by a certain amount of difference, for two forms, if differing very little, are generally ranked as varieties, notwithstanding that intermediate linking forms have not been discovered;

but the amount of difference considered necessary to give to two forms the rank of species is quite indefinite. (Ibid, pp. 97-101)

For those who believed in species as fixed forms, varieties were simply slight departures from their types. Darwin has not only removed the boundaries around variant individuals, he has also erased the lines of demarcation between populations of them. Populations of variant individuals have no known essence and while the terms variety and species may be used for them interchangeably, those terms are not definable. Otherness separates individuals, all of which differ, more or less, from one another. Mayr would say that the reproductive gap is the specific difference, the separator, that which defines populations as species. But, Darwin was quite aware of the reproductive gap. He knew that the reproductive barrier could not be used to create the means for defining any group of individuals as a species. Varietal individuals afford no basis for definition, nor does interbreeding or the absence of it. Nor does a metaphorical gene pool create a definable essence or commonality. Darwin made clear that neither sterility nor fertility could be a measure to determine a species. Organisms that breed together are likely to differ less among themselves and more from others, but that activity and its products can only be viewed as a succession of kinds by imagining and imposing a oneness that is kind on the variant individuals. Darwin would have found Mayr's definition laughable, along with the others he had told Hooker about. How could the mating of some number of adult males and females make the associated infants, the adolescents, the infertile, the aged and the non-mating adults of a population all one kind? In fact, how can a male and a female, even if producing offspring be one or same kind?

Darwin went to great lengths to destroy the notion of fixed species in nature. It is unexpected, then, when we read the concluding words of his work:

> There is grandeur in this view of life, with its several powers, having been originally breathed into a few forms or into one; and that, whilst this planet has gone cycling on according to the fixed law of gravity, from so simple a beginning endless forms most beautiful and most wonderful have been, and are being evolved. (Ibid, p. 102)

What are we to think of, "a few forms... endless forms...have been, and are being evolved?" Are those forms species? Are they entities, after all, which evolve? The word evolution has not been used once in the entire work; only that last word, evolved. Are we being asked to believe that species are mutable? I believe not. After having labored to show that the word species is an arbitrary label placed on changing individuals, he is not at long last reversing himself and claiming that species are forms, actual entities, above and beyond those changing individuals. In this rather religiously poetic conclusion, he is bowing to his peers who believe that species are forms, are entities, but he knows that they must now take into account what he has said about species for those alleged fixed forms now lie in shambles in his pages.

In the end, perhaps Darwin felt guilty, felt like a

murderer, as he had confessed to Hooker, for he had delivered the deadly blow to one of the most sacred of his friends' beliefs. Out of respect for them, and others, he used the biblical breath and their metaphor, forms, through which they will try to glimpse the myriad actual descents he has passed before their eyes. Those descents give us the impression of movement, of variant individuals changing over the eons. But, of course, there is no movement of some one thing, one plurality, being changed into some other plural thing. Particulars modified by descent are all there are. The changing of variants is all we have. Evolution as scientifically conceived---of a species-entity changing into another species-entity over time---is an illusion. Darwin knows that systematists will continue classifying individuals (in their search for actual connections) and that such classifications can be reified into forms alleged to exist in nature. But he also knows that the only bond between individuals which allows us to bring them together to be connected in a natural way is that of descent, and descent is always with modification. For Darwin, the fact of descent, with its differences, makes classing possible.

> We use the element of descent in classing the individuals of both sexes and of all ages, although having few characters in common, under one species; we use descent in classing acknowledged varieties, however different they may be from their parent; and I believe this element of descent is the hidden bond of connection which naturalists have sought under the term of the Natural System. On this idea of the natural system being, in so far as it has been

perfected, genealogical in its arrangement, with the *grades of difference* between the descendants from a common parent expressed by the terms genera, families, orders, &c., we can understand the rules which we are compelled to follow in our classification. We can understand why we value *certain resemblances* far more than others... [my emphases] (Ibid, p. 103)

I want to point out that Darwin's view, here, of a systematics which would be *natural* would involve three things: that continuing descents with modification occur as stages of difference; that natural classification should be based on grades of difference between the descendants of a common parent; and certain resemblances (i.e., relative absence of difference) are to be valued over others. I ask, what resemblances is he referring to? Surely not morphological ones, for he rejects morphology as a criterion for classifying, but not for determining relationship. What, then? I suggest that he is talking about those resemblances systematic biologists call homologies. They are most often structures, parts of organisms; they are evidences for relationships of descent. Resemblance, in the superficial sense of visual appearance is not what Darwin is valuing here. I am suggesting that Darwin's understanding of variation not only undermined the prevailing notion of species but it also undermined the traditional notion of the criteria for classifying; it is no longer similarities and differences; it is differences and grades of difference. Homologies, crucial in suggesting relationships, are not similarities, but differences, or grades of difference, in the comparative anatomy or genetics or physiology or behavior of variant organisms. Our learned notion of similarity (i.e., lack of difference) at best, suggests homology, and homology for Gareth Nelson is the Cladist's synapomorphy, the focal point for determining relationship. If this is so, then, metaphysical realism drops out of systematics and out of biology. Darwin thought his way to the door through which we must pass to leave m-realism behind. We needn't go back to the Pre-Darwinian thinking of Ghiselin, Hull, Mayr, Eldredge, and Gould with his metaphysical capstone of species-individuals to top off Darwin's organisms descending with modifications.

Chapter 25 Metaphysical Realism takes an Active Role in Evolutionary Theory

The Radical Solution to the Species Problem

Michael Ghiselin announced his radical solution to the species problem in the journal Systematic Zoology in 1974, "...species are individuals, not classes" (Ghiselin, 1974, p. 536).

The terseness of the declaration is commendable. It was printed in a technical journal addressed to experts who knew that a species, a class-like notion, was a problem from the standpoint of empirical fact as well as demarcating and defining it. Biologists were in no doubt that organisms were individuals, but readers of the journal also knew that collections of organisms called species were not classes. They also knew that each such collection, a plurality of distinct organisms, was not an individual. Was Ghiselin asking these readers to play some kind of semantic game? Surely, they might say to themselves, he is not morphing a plurality of organisms into one thing! An individual has rather distinct boundaries enclosing itself and which mark it off from other things. But when we think of what we have always understood as species some plurality of whales or lions or oak trees or humans, we wonder how the declaration makes sense. How can some number of actual individuals, this and that human and all the others (taxonomically described), be declared an individual? What kind of an individual is such a collection? Indeed, what did Ghiselin have in mind when he declared species to be individuals? An individual is usually one thing. If a plurality of differing individuals we call a species has become one thing, we want to know how Ghiselin discovered their oneness. Since in his declaration he is saying that each species, as a whole, is an individual, not a class, he must either be able to perceive something about organisms or have something heretofore unknown in mind as the basis for his solution to the species problem.

Traditionally, the word 'species' has been viewed as roughly equivalent to the word 'class.' Ghiselin, however, is not making declarations about semantics; he is not declaring that individual is a better word than class in dealing with actual Darwinian variants. He is saying that the organisms we call, collectively, a species is an individual. What we call a species is a thing, one thing! That is some declaration.

What, for Ghiselin, are individuals? We learn that they are wholes with organisms as parts. We have examined the part-whole relation above, and will now pursue its relevance to the species problem. That relation, as we saw, is a very old one in the history of philosophy. David Lewis, some twenty years after Ghiselin's declaration, saw the wisdom of replacing the troublesome notion of classes with the mereological notion of whole-part in his treatment of set theory (which I critiqued above), is a context quite different from evolutionary theory and biological systematics. Nelson Goodman, prior to Ghiselin's declaration, rejected the notion of classes and used whole-part for his own philosophic purposes.

David Hull, a philosopher of science specializing in biological systematics and evolutionary theory, accepted the radical solution in 1975 and forcefully argued its merits in journals over the next half-dozen years; he made it central in his major work, Science as a Process, published in 1988. "One of the main messages of this book is that species, if they are to play the roles assigned to them in evolutionary theory, must be treated as historical entities" (Hull, 1988, p. 79).

A living, or once alive, entity such as an organism is or was, of course, an actual thing. The question of what a species is has provoked the production of more paper than almost any other question in biology. Notions of species are almost too numerous to mention, but Nelson and Platnick list a few. "there are biological species, evolutionary species, morphological species, polytypic species, phenetic species, ecological species, paleontological species, essentialistic species, nominalistic species, and doubtless many others" (Nelson, 1994, pp. 10-11).

Proposed definitions are clarifications, usually stemming from field and taxonomic work, and amount to redefinitions or, in Ghiselin's case, a move to the reconceptualization of species using Mayr's definition of biological species as a
base.

Some quiet has prevailed in the biological community from the time Ernst Mayr announced his redefinition, in l969, updated from a 1942 formulation, "A species is a reproductive community of populations (reproductively isolated from others) that occupies a specific niche in nature"

(Mayr, 1982, p. 273). The definition, here, carries the usual, and unremarkable, ontological claim that organisms, or populations of them, actually exist. Mayr is not, here, claiming that the reproductive community, isolated from others by a reproductive gap, is an ontological or actual one, an individual, but he will, later, when he accepts Ghiselin's radical solution.

George Gaylord Simpson jumped on the biological definition's shortcomings and offered his own evolutionary definition, "a lineage (ancestral-descendant sequence of populations) evolving separately from others and with its own unitary evolutionary role and tendencies" (Ibid, p. 294).

Other biologists were unhappy with Mayr's definition; botanists, especially, noted its failure to guide them in demarcating species from among the great diversity of breeding systems found in plants. Zoologists also had problems with borderline cases and especially incipient species, which seemed to violate the criterion of reproductive isolation. Since it did not cover all organisms, only the sexually reproducing ones, it fell short of universal utility. Many field biologists were supportive for, like Ray in the 17th century and Buffon in the 18th, they already thought of species as reproductive communities. Mayr did not claim that he had solved the hoary philosophical problem of species by redefining the word, species Ghiselin did make that claim.

Ghiselin accepted Mayr's biological definition and managed to convince him that his own preconception, which incorporated the core notion of sexual-cohesion was more suitable for ontological reasons connected to the construction of evolutionary theory. Mayr saw the value of the reasoning and accepted this philosophical maneuver in 1976.

Biology and Philosophical Notions

Scientists are quite aware that their several disciplines had their beginnings in that larger domain that is philosophy. The sciences have increasingly gained their autonomy and now scientists themselves, and especially physicists, largely create the philosophy (i.e., the principles and methodologies) of their disciplines. Physics was first to achieve autonomy. Chemistry followed. Biology has been looked upon as a dependent science, dependent on principles established in physics and chemistry, but is increasingly manifesting its uniqueness, especially with the break-through deciphering of the genetic material in a number of genomes. Biology encompasses a number of sub-disciplines which are more (genetics) or less (psychology and sociology) *scientific*, where scientific refers to methodologies tied firmly to experiment and mathematical quantification.

Writings in biology have always included philosophical notions, many deriving from Aristotle, including his metaphysical realism and essentialism. But there is also idealism, deriving from Plato, including his methodological typology. Some biologists are also conceptualists, after the fashion of Ockham or Kant, others are nominalists, after the fashion of Locke. And of course there has always been the oscillation between rationalist and empiricist methodologies. However, shortly after the modern synthesis of genetics and evolutionary thinking in the 1940's, philosophical metaphysics entered biology and took on an active role, moving evolutionary theory into a working consciousness grounded in metaphysical realism. Some thought that injecting an evolutionary bias into biological systematics, a discipline already embroiled in debates concerning the best methodology for determining relationship among organisms and their parts, was not wise. Gareth Nelson, a leader in the search and development of a better methodology (i.e., cladistics) came to object to the use of partisan philosophical perspectives in determining actual relationships. The methodology proposed by the evolutionary systematists, which included Mayr, Hull, and Ghiselin saw systematics not as a neutral science but as a hand-maiden to an activist evolutionary biology. Phonetics, a mathematical methodology, could remain neutral with respect to evolutionary theory, but not with respect to a typology generated by the use of a notion of overall similarity. Cladistics, in the methodology ultimately honed by Nelson, directed its attention to determining actual relationships irrespective of the philosophical or theoretical claims as to how they came to exist. In fact, Nelson's inclination to keep philosophy at bay was evident, according to Hull, who noted the fewest number of articles with philosophical content in the journal, *Systematic Zoology*, during Nelson's tenure as its president.

The ongoing search for a definition of species to suit the needs of both researchers and theoreticians was thus confounded when Ghiselin and Hull injected the philosophy of metaphysical realism into the debate and gave it the dominant role over other philosophical perspectives, such as nominalism or a logical conceptualism (a la Ockham). What each had done was, in effect, resolve the longstanding dispute over species in favor of m-realism, using Ghiselin's notion of what a species is. What a species is declared to be and whether such an entity exists was crucial to evolutionary theory as Hull and Ghiselin and most biologists saw it..

To better understand the philosophic content, in biology, connected with the species problem, and especially Ghiselin's radical solution, we can begin with some of Mayr's comments in his major work, *The Growth of Biological Thought*, published in 1982. We will look briefly, first, at his view of m-realism and then at his reasons for rejecting nominalism; then we will inquire into his connection with conceptualism, the philosophical perspective he does not discuss but takes for granted.

What is remarkable is that so long-standing an issue as the philosophical problem of universals was not dealt with at all by Mayr, Ghiselin, and Hull and that its sub-issue, the species problem, should have been dealt with so shallowly by them. Shallow because the issue was settled by a simple declaration: "species are individuals." (Ghiselin, 1974, p. 536) What argument there was by Ghiselin and Hull proceeded by the use of metaphor and analogy. The result? M-realism is the winner if it is not driven from the contest. And it was not. Among others, some of the more nominalistically-minded scientists did object, but they could not settle the issue. The issue, which includes both problems, universals and species, cannot be settled until the question of the validity of categorizing is settled, and that cannot be settled until we understand the nature of particulars. If the very character of each and every actuality prohibits the imposition of categories then we have the basis for a thorough examination of m-realism and its underpinning of rationalism and their critique. In other words, we have the basis for solving the long-standing problems of universals and species (as well as the noxious notion of race).

Since, as Darwin remarked, workers in the field know vaguely what they are calling a species, the turmoil surrounding the species problem would appear to be a tempest in the biological teapot. It is more. Stephen J. Gould, in the section to follow, stakes his intellectual career as a macro-evolutionary theorist on the notion of species as individuals.

Realism Dismissed, Almost

We can begin with this observation by Mayr:

The dominant philosophy of scholasticism was the Thomistic one believed by Aquinas to have been mainly derived from Aristotle. This philosophy is known under the strangely misleading name of realism. Its most characteristic aspect, as it appears to a modern biologist, is its total support of essentialism. Nominalism, the only other powerful school of scholastic philosophy, stressed that only individuals exist, bracketed together into classes by name. (Mayr, 1982, p. 92)

Mayr makes it clear in his book that Platonic forms have no place in biological thinking; they are responsible for typology, and that is viewing organisms in terms of fixed forms. He also makes it clear that essences, stemming from Aristotle's discerning them in actual, particular biological individuals, also have no place in biological thinking.

Typology and essentialism are part of the philosophical doctrine, metaphysical realism. Mayr, in the quote, above, rejects (metaphysical) realism, a philosophy known under that strangely misleading name, realism. He doesn't tell us why he finds it misleading. We can guess; he is aware that Platonic forms and Aristotelian essences are not actual, but somehow real nonetheless. Misleading indeed!

Mayr characterizes nominalism as the only other powerful school of scholastic philosophy; it stresses that only individuals exist and are bracketed by a class name. Individuals, for the nominalists, were actual particulars. Conceptualism and nominalism were both operative in the Middle Ages. Ockham was nominalist and conceptualist. But nominalism, stressing that only particulars exist, was a greater threat to church theologians.

It is strange that Mayr did not understand that Ghiselin's *individual* is at least a questionable construct if not still another m-real entity in the basket of metaphysical realism. It is perhaps not so strange, when we learn of his insistence on finding an objective entity out there in nature which could carry the name species and evolve. That was philosophically paramount for him.

Mayr recognized that Buffon "had gone a long way toward the biological species concept [when he said,] a species is a constant succession of similar individuals that can reproduce together" (Ibid, p. 262). Mayr commented that, "one can always recognize a species by characteristics of its life history. A species is something natural and real" (Ibid).

Whoa! "Natural and real?" Mayr has forgotten that real is an ambiguous term, a term which misleads because, unknown to him, it is a conflation of the actual and the metaphysical. Should he have said *natural and actual* (for he means that a species is both natural and something that exists) and avoid the ambiguity of real? He could have, but he clearly knows that to say that some reproducing populations of organisms are natural and actual is hardly newsworthy; it is redundant and quite different from saying that a species is actual. Biologists might wonder what, besides the organisms, is Mayr saying is actual, for they know that they are natural. For Mayr, his concept of species must denote an actual unit in space-time, for that, as Ghiselin and Hull would have it, was required by evolutionary theory; it is species that evolve, not one or another organism. Of course, Hull and Ghiselin and Mayr could be wrong not only about the requirements of evolutionary theory but also about what actually is naturally selected and evolves.

To understand the depth of Mayr's standing in the philosophical doctrine of metaphysical realism, with its built-in ambiguity and tendency to mislead when it is not prefaced with M or metaphysical, we will look at what Mayr calls the nominalistic species concept. First, however, we must mention that nominalists did not have a concept of something called a species. Conceptualists did. Strict nominalists, as Roscelin may have been, did not construct concepts. It was conceptualists who, in saying they could abstract from particulars, constructed a concept that which the particulars had, allegedly in common, and could be called by a common noun. Roscelin apparently held that universals or common nouns, such as *robin*, were breaths of hot air, vocis flatus, when uttered. The particulars called robins were simply covered by that name and the name denoted no real entity either inside the head or outside it.

Conceptualists, of course, held that the concept was either a real or a logical entity, but not that that real or logical entity also existed out there with the robins. Ghiselin would have us believe it does exist out there with the robins. A conceptualist, in the minimal sense of entertaining a concept as a logical sign in the head for a plurality out there, has advanced one step too far for the nominalist and one step short of being a full m-realist. Mayr is both a conceptualist and an objective m-realist; he believes his concept of a species denotes a real (i.e., actual) object in space-time. No object is both (metaphysically) real and actual. If scientists require m-real entities in space-time, they are trying to populate space-time with strange objects which do not exist. Ockham was offended by those who would multiply objects beyond necessity and became a logical conceptualist.

Nominalism Dismissed, Not Quite

Mayr says:

The two philosophers who exercised the greatest influence in the early and middle eighteenth century, Leibniz and Locke, were both uncomfortable with the concept of a well-defined, sharply separated species. Locke did not necessarily deny the existence of species, but said: "I think it nevertheless true that the boundaries of species whereby men sort them, are made by men." He exclaimed that he was unable to see why two breeds of dogs "are not as distinct species as a spaniel and an elephant...so uncertain are the boundaries of species of animals to us." (Ibid, pp.

263-64)

Mayr had mentioned, earlier, that in Leibniz' theory of monads there was "a potential for population thinking, [for each monad was] individualistically different from every other monad, a major departure from essentialism" (Ibid, p. 46) With such a notion, firmly held, Leibniz should be more than uncomfortable with the concept of a well-defined, sharply separated species. If each monad were, as he imagined, other and different, ontologically, then no plurality of them could constitute a unit sharply separated and so subject to being well-defined. As for Locke, who believed in both real and *nominal* essences, hence in real and nominal definitions, he saw no sharp boundaries setting off actual living things, hence a nominal definition with its vagueness and uncertainty must suffice; real definitions can be used for the real essence of things, but these are hard, if not impossible, to come by in actual things. For Locke, the essences of mathematical objects such as the triangle could be determined and real definitions given. Darwin saw both Leibnizian uniqueness with respect to each living thing and Lockean uncertainty with respect to the boundaries of populations of them. With such knowledge of living things, Darwin could hardly entertain a unifying concept of them; he was neither an m- realist nor a conceptualist. Whether, or to what extent, he was a nominalist will be discussed later.

Mayr refers to the nominalistic concept of species: only individuals exist and all that classes of similar individuals share is a name; species are classes, man-made constructs. The notion was held, more or less, by Lamarck and Buffon as well as by Schleiden. Mayr notes that his own

294

biological species concept has, at last, caused the decline of the nominalistic concept which is no longer "in vogue, at least not among biologists." (Mayr, 1982, p. 265)

Given their claim that living particulars or individuals have no shared essence, nominalists cannot be said to have, as Mayr puts it, a concept, a mental entity which in the obtaining of it somehow unifies the individuals. Mayr claims that he has such a concept (of biological species) and that the unifying factor is the sexual or reproductive activity, the interbreeding, of the individuals. Given that he insists that population thinking is about unique individuals, we may wonder how he can manage to unify the individuals in his head or see their unity out there in nature (i.e., see the unity as an object)?

Mayr also refers to Darwin's species concept and discusses it. Again, given Darwin's assertions about the uniqueness (variation) of each and every living thing, Mayr is incorrect in claiming that Darwin had a concept of something out there called a species.

In a chapter heading (Concepts in the Biological Sciences), Mayr uses the word concept but we are never told how he comes to have one. Their importance, however, is emphasized:

> Instead of formulating laws, biologists usually organize their generalizations into a framework of concepts....Progress in biological science is, perhaps, largely a matter of the development of these concepts or principles. The progress of systematics was characterized by the crystallization and refinement of such concepts as classification, species, category,

taxon and so on...Scientific progress consists in the development of new concepts, like selection or biological species, and the repeated refinements of definitions by which these concepts are articulated....It is strange how little attention the philosophy of science has paid to the overwhelming importance of concepts. (Ibid, p. 43)

And:

...definitions are temporary verbalizations of concepts, and concepts---particularly difficult concepts---are usually revised repeatedly as our knowledge and understanding grows. This is well illustrated by the definitions of such concepts as species... (Ibid, p. 45)

Coming as the result of an alleged process of abstraction from some number of particulars, a concept is said to be a mental object, an in re object or universal as the philosophers in the Middle Ages would put it. Mayr does not relate his use of the word concept to an origin in the psychological arena; he does relate its use to the outer arena of nature, maintaining that the organisms out there exhibit a oneness of kind called a species. He also notes the relation of concept and definition, the latter being a temporary verbalization of the former. This implies that when the concept such as what a species is, becomes firmly established, its definition is also more firmly fixed.

Is Mayr a conceptualist? I believe he is, and more. He

is an objective m-realist, for he believes that a species is a real (i.e., actual) entity, a species-individual, out there in nature and that he has a concept of it (i.e., his biological definition.)

Chapter 26 Ghiselin's Radical Solution

As far back as 1966, Ghiselin had tried to cut the Gordian knot that is the species problem by casually remarking that, "in the logical sense, species are individuals.... In logic, 'individual' is not a synonym for 'organism.' Rather, it means a particular thing" (Ghiselin, 1974, p. 536).

Right off, we wonder how some number of organisms can be "a particular thing." However, Ghiselin continues with examples of individuals (and we are told they need not be physically continuous): a human being is continuous and The United States of America is not. The latter is an individual in the class of national states, and California is a part of that individual. (Alaska and Hawaii, although disconnected, are also parts of the whole that is the United States). Further, "It is characteristic of individuals that there cannot be instances of them" (Ibid).

Classes, of course, can have instances (and members) and whereas the names of classes are universals the names of individuals are proper. Answering the question of what a species-individual is composed of also brings him to accepting Mayr's view of species:

One answer is individual populations---in the sense

of genetical populations (syngamea). These are breeding communities---composite wholes---not to be confused with classes of organisms sharing certain intrinsic genetical properties. Of course one has to add...that they are reproductively isolated, to differentiate "species" from "subspecies" and other populational categories. This, the biological species definition, is adequate... (Ibid, p. 539)

Accepting the biological species definition of Mayr, Ghiselin says:

The morphological, genetical, and physiological species concepts suffer from a common fault. They treat composite wholes as if they were classes defined in terms of the intrinsic properties of their members. If one were to define "craftsman" in terms of the properties of cells in certain organisms, it might seem odd. Likewise, we are not interested in the properties of employees when we define "firm," but rather in the properties common to firms generally. The attributes of organisms are not defining of the names of social groups, in spite of the fact that social groups must have constituent organisms. That John Doe has a particular set of genes is about as relevant to his being a specimen of Homo Sapiensis as it is to his working for the manufactures of Brand X. (Ibid)

And, "The species and the firm are real in the sense that they designate entities which exist: particular species and firms" (Ibid). Further emphasizing their ontological status, Ghiselin says, "Species are individuals, and they are real. They are as real as American Motors, Chrysler, Ford and General Motors" (Ibid, p. 538). Finally, having argued that species are ontological individuals, distinguishable from their parts, Ghiselin asks, "Are the taxa ranked at categorical levels higher than the species merely conceptual" (Ibid, p. 540)? He answers, "The economic analogy here seems rather remote. Is the automobile industry real? One's answer depends upon his metaphysics, but at least industries have not the same ontological status as firms" (Ibid).

The conceptual door to higher levels is there for whomever has the metaphysical urge to open it. Eldredge, as we shall see, walked through it.

A comment on the above quotes is in order. Note the use of "real." It is abundantly clear that Ghiselin's use of the ambiguous term (i.e., metaphysical and actual) stands to gain advocates by such usage. Also, Ghiselin is clearly, and admittedly, doing metaphysics. Eldredge will, down the line, scold all of us, including scientists, for neglecting the queen of the sciences, Metaphysics.

The Arguments for Individuals: Analogy

The following comments focus on Ghiselin's appeals to logic and metaphysics and then his use of analogy and metaphor to argue his ontological claim that "species are individuals" and real (i.e. actualities).

First, the logic. Why are species individuals in a logical sense? Indeed, in logic individual is not a synonym for organism, but biologists believe that organisms are individuals, singular things (or particulars, as opposed to universals). Some number of organisms (call them a species) are not an individual logically---logic has not the power to confer oneness on such a plurality! Oneness is an empirical matter, a matter of possible fact. Ghiselin is trying to transmute a linguistic expression, species, into an ontological entity!

The metaphysics of species as individuals is pointed up in his remarks comparing species with firms such as Chrysler, Ford, and General Motors while keeping the constituents of both species and firms distinct from species and firms. The following quote is clear on the matter:

> Species are units, and they have evolutionary importance, but the same may be said of organisms. Doubtless both organisms and species specialize. And probably organisms become adapted but species do not, except in so far as they consist of adapted organisms. Such ambiguities represent a transitional stage in our growing appreciation of what the two levels mean. We are experiencing a rapid and fundamental restructuring of our basic concepts. (Ibid, p. 543)

Ghiselin speaks of two levels; organisms on one level, species on another. It is the higher, species-level, that is metaphysical. Philosophers who enjoy non-sense revel in metaphysical levels; it is questionable that scientists should rise to folly even if Ghiselin invites them, along with evolutionary and cognitive psychologists, as well as neuroscientists (Edelman), to do just that.

Third, Ghiselin, and his main defender, Hull, engage in the use of analogy, along with metaphor, to argue the ontological existence of Ghiselin's species-individual. First the metaphor: species are individuals. Given their disconnectedness, to say that distinct organisms (e.g., humans on the surface of the globe) are an individual, a particular entity, is simply false, and one shouldn't have to respond to such a nonsensical claim. Are all the buildings on the surface of the globe an individual? We sometimes say, metaphorically, that all people are one. The intent, perhaps, is to make us feel good, not to get us to believe that all people are one. To say that species are like Ford or Chrysler or General Motors is to hope to trade on the notion, in legalese, that such firms are corporate individuals. Ford and Chrysler and General Motors are no more individuals, actually, than are species so the analogy more than fails.

Responses to the Radical Solution: 7 years later

To better understand the import of his solution and the variety of responses to it, we will turn to focus on Ghiselin's article published in 1981. Seven years had elapsed, a period sufficient for biologists and philosophers to understand his original metaphysical claim about species.

In his opening remarks, Ghiselin notes that he had been thinking that species were not classes as far back as 1966. He says, ironically, "This thesis was so obviously 'wrong' that it was casually dismissed by the few philosophers who paid any attention to it" (Ghiselin, 1981, p. 270). Toulmin appears to have been the exception because, as Ghiselin remarks, "Toulmin's evolutionary metaphysics is

303

not all that different from my own" (Ibid). It was a decade before his views were endorsed, but he complains, "it is still being studiously ignored by philosophers" (Ibid).

Ghiselin's bibliography lists no journals of philosophy to which he submitted his views on species as individuals. Referring to the original essay, he mentions six biologists who were *competent to judge*, and either converted or judged it favorably, between 1975 and 1980: Mayr, Platnick, Patterson, Wiley, Eldredge, Cracraft. Gareth Nelson is notably absent. Still, Ghiselin remarks, "Why philosophers should have had so much difficulty realizing that species are individuals is also a puzzle. It is not just a matter of lack of acquaintance with modern biology, for we are dealing with an old problem in metaphysics" (Ibid).

Mark one up for Ghiselin. He is philosophically correct. In one way or another, as I have tried to show, the old problem in metaphysics had been addressed by the best philosophical minds in the history of philosophy. It was passed on to Ghiselin unsolved. There was thus no assurance that even with a strong philosophical background a scientist would find it easy to fully understand the problem and evaluate Ghiselin's solution.

Of the 17 respondents to the target article we are considering, seven are philosophers and competent to judge. What did they think of the article? First, the two extremes: Hull, who endorsed the solution a year after it was published, aims to help scientists who are philosophically challenged to understand it and its implications. On the other end, Michael Ruse says, "I think Ghiselin is dead wrong." (Ibid) Ruse found the notion of species as individuals logically, biologically, and philosophically unacceptable. Strange. Hull had found the notion acceptable for just those reasons. Perhaps philosophical disagreements are just a matter of taste, a matter of metaphysics. But the metaphysics of Ghiselin and Hull carries a science label; one might have thought science not just a matter of taste. Nobel laureate Weinberg, we recall, is offended by such a notion. Of the five remaining philosophers, Mario Bunge notes that the species problem is:

> the construal of the term species and [Ghiselin's] proposed solution that of conceiving of species as individual things, not as sets or classes. Nobody doubts that the notion of a species is genuinely problematic. Thus if a species is a set, it cannot possibly evolve, for sets are concepts, not things. The question is whether Ghiselin's thesis...does work. I submit that it does not, and that there is an alternative correct solution. (Ibid, p. 284)

I will omit consideration of Bunge's alternative solution, one of dozens advanced in the literature on the problem, but a brief comment is called for. Bunge remarks, "if a species is a set, it cannot possibly evolve, for sets are concepts, not things" (Ibid, p. 285) Ghiselin, of course, emphasizes that a class is also unable to evolve. We thus have sets, concepts, and classes unable to evolve because they are not *things* which can evolve. My question, which no one in the literature on this topic seems either courageous, or foolish, enough to ask, is: Is there anyone, anywhere, now...or was there ever anyone who claimed that sets or classes or concepts could evolve? Is the claim that sets and classes and concepts cannot evolve, a profound claim? Is it possible that it is utter nonsense, and no one wants to say it out of fear of offending against someone's first amendment rights to utter nonsense? My view is that Ghiselin knows that philosophers talk nonsense, more or less, a good bit of the time and that he can pull a bit of philosophic wool over the eyes of scientists for most are under-educated in its ways. Surely, they say to themselves, Ghiselin cannot be saying that I once believed that a set or class or concept or metaphysical whole could evolve! Surely, it is no news that a class cannot and does not evolve. Aren't we all talking about the plurality of things we assign to a class? Ghiselin, as an m-realist, would not be helpful in his answer; yes and no, for he has endowed the whole that is a species with a thingness distinguishable from whatever things or parts it contains. He wants and must have it, as an m- realist, both ways; the whole is real (i.e., actual) and the parts are real (i.e., actual). Simply put, he requires both a whole...and its parts; you get the whole free---as we saw with David Lewis and his mereology---a gift from Ghiselin, whether you want it or not. If you take it, you live in the embrace of m- realism's ambiguity. But you make it possible for a metaphysically real entity, a species, to actually evolve.

Arthur Caplan begins his comments:

> Species, on Ghiselin's view, are best viewed as integrated wholes. They evolve as units and persist over time. Species are composite wholes with causal powers that are unique and distinctive. The relationship between organism and species is to be understood on the order of parts and wholes, not

members or instances of classes. (Ibid, p. 285)

Caplan asks a crucial question. Why is it:

> that a class-based interpretation of species cannot do
> the work Ghiselin feels the term species must do in
> evolutionary biology...why class-based definitions of
> species taxa based upon cluster concept definitions
> could not accommodate the very distinctions to
> which Ghiselin draws attention in citing his criteria...
> Nothing Ghiselin says in any way demonstrates the
> link between static, essentialistic, or typological
> notions of species and cluster concept definitions.
> (Ibid)

Cluster concept definitions stem from Wittgenstein's notion of family resemblance and have become important, as we saw, in cognitive psychology. Caplan points out, as I did earlier, that there is a philosophical literature on the notion of individuals. He says, "The question of the ontological and explanatory status of classes and individuals has been discussed by philosophers, but not in the literature that Ghiselin cites" (Ibid).

Caplan may also be questioning Ghiselin's claim of originality respecting the notion of individual and its use as ontological replacement for classes. I do not know who all Caplan has in mind, but I would emphasize that the philosopher who used the notion of individuals as the nominalistic counter to Platonism is Nelson Goodman, whom we discussed earlier. His book, *The Structure of Appearance*, was published in 1951. In Part One, Chapter One,

Section 5: "On Systems of Predicates of Individuals," Goodman says, "I shall confine myself as far as I can to language that speaks of no entities other than individuals...such language must be free of bindable variables construed as taking classes or any other nonindividuals as values..." (p. 29). Further on Goodman says:

> In foregoing all use of variables having nonindividuals as values, we give ourselves the task of retranslating a great many everyday statements that are customarily construed as pertaining to classes.... The problem of dealing with a sentence like "Every species of dog is exhibited" is a little more difficult, but in such cases we may often speak of wholes rather than classes. The species of dog may be regarded as certain discontinuous wholes composed of dogs. (Ibid, p. 40)

Goodman taught at Harvard for years and his works were known by everyone who would presume to know philosophy. Goodman showed how it is possible to avoid an ontology of classes, platonic metaphysics, and replace it with a nominalistic approach using individuals. I cannot account for Ghiselin's failure to refer to his work. I can imagine that philosophers who knew Goodman's work would not have found Ghiselin's radical use of individual philosophically remarkable. They evidently did not find his *solution* an answer to the species problem.

Caplan makes an important final observation; Ghiselin contends that a composite whole, such as his species is other and more than the sum of its parts. As Caplan puts it, "it is an integrated entity that acts and reacts in distinctive and unique ways in the course of time" (Ghiselin, 1981, p. 285). In other words, Caplan is worried about the individualizing or personalizing of social classes, national groups, religious organizations---as was Isaiah Berlin---who warned against the irrational and dangerous consequences that flow from "the treatment of state, race, history, epoch, for example, as super-persons exercising influence" (Ibid) Says Caplan, of Ghiselin's selling his solution to other disciplines, "reification and the multiplication of entities beyond necessity have costs ..." (Ibid). Ghiselin's fears of typology in biology are one thing, the reification that gives us active wholes, as individuals or super-individuals, is another. We will see, later, what Eldredge thinks of reification and multiplication. Ghiselin's response to Caplan's and Berlin's fears is:

> Time and again the doctrine that societies are "superorganisms" has been used to justify despotism. Species can be abused in this way too. It is all too readily forgotten that species do not possess those properties of organisms that would qualify them as worthy of our moral sentiments. Unlike human beings and other organisms, they do not love, hate, fear, or suffer pain. (Ibid, p. 309)

What is too readily forgotten is that reifying collectivities gives us the means to make illusory identifications that have considerable practical consequences. The error of a species-whole and its parts is carried over into the error of a nation-whole and its parts, a religious-whole and its parts, an ethnic-whole and its parts, a racial-whole and its parts. Indeed, Ghiselin is not to be faulted for what others may do with his particular identification of living parts to their wholes and the individuals that arise from such a notion. The 20th century had more than enough of those super-organic totalitarian entities, fascistic states. Helen Heise begins her response, "It may be that Ghiselin has someone like me in mind when he expresses puzzlement, and perhaps annoyance, at philosophers who casually dismiss his thesis that "species are not classes: they are individuals" (Ibid, p. 289). She goes on to remind Ghiselin, "In philosophy the issues regarding the classification of any entities whatsoever are grouped together under the traditional label 'the problem of universals'" (Ibid). She explicates universal and particular and says, "As early as Plato the discussions reached a high level of sophistication. It would not be wrong to say that nearly every problem can be included under the problem of universals, since so many kinds of issues were dealt with under that rubric" (Ibid). Heise concludes with a comment which I find most cutting, "But Ghiselin's labeling species differently has changed nothing in the world. So, if species seemed artificial before, they will seem artificial now" (Ibid, p. 290). This is a clear denial of the ontological relevance of Ghiselin's "species-individuals." As early as 1968, Heise, a philosopher, and Starr, a bacterial taxonomist, wrote:

> One might want to say that a species is an individual and the species' name is consequently a proper name... But if one says that a species is an individual

one must make some accommodation or other. The ones occurring to us do not seem attractive. Either one must say that a species is complete (in order to qualify it as an individual) thereby precluding new members, or one must revise the concept of individual such that an individual does not have to be complete. This matter requires a fuller treatment, but our opinion now is that treating a species as an individual requires too serious revisions of the present conceptual scheme. (Ibid)

She continues:

But if we look at Homo sapiens not being able to be pointed to in the same way that a person can be pointed to and further, not being able to be perceived as a whole, in the way that a person can, we think that a species is not an individual, and so, rather, a class. In each case, the judgment is based on what we take to be real properties, but they do not all work together to give us a single concept by means of which we unite the plural entities. (Ibid)

Of some importance is Ghiselin's response to Heise's comment, above, that Homo sapiens cannot be pointed to in the same way that a person can. Ghiselin says:

she tries to make a case for species not being individuals on the basis of their not being observable. Is observability an accident here? As a scientist I deal with unobserved things---such as ions---routinely.

Why not a species or a corporation? If I wanted to observe a species I could. I would only need to find a very small localized one, perhaps consisting of but a single organism. (Ibid, p. 305)

First, let us wonder about a single organism which Ghiselin can observe as a species. If his claim is that a species is a whole with parts, what can we see when we look at a single organism? Certainly we cannot see the whole of which it is assumed to be a part. We cannot see its potential for being a part of a whole, and it surely is not, itself, that whole. A single organism simply cannot be seen as a species or a species-individual. Secondly, the analogy Ghiselin uses is invalid: ions, even if not directly visible, are not analogous to an organism's species simply because we can never observe a species or the individual a species is declared to be! Ions are observable indirectly. We learn of things called ions by using devices which tell us they exist. Gareth Nelson told a story at a meeting of biological systematists that he and a companion came upon water out West and unexpectedly saw some fish, but could not see their species. However, all this is not about eyesight.

Alexander Rosenberg tells us right off that: "I write as one converted" (Ibid, p. 302), having announced it in 1980. He thinks Ghiselin's categorical breakthrough is even more important than he knows. I immediately looked up Ghiselin's comments on Rosenberg and found that Ghiselin not only knew, but told Rosenberg how much more.

Rosenberg and Ghiselin, along with many others in biology and sociology, still smart at the remarks of positivists, including Campbell, who laid out the criteria for

312

what is a scientific theory and what is a scientific law. Before they descended into the great quietude, positivists rejected most of biology and all of sociology for falling short of scientific theory and law. Biology, it was said, was largely a historical science and lacked a reach of generality necessary to form laws. Mendel's gene work and Darwin's natural selection remarks helped to remove some of the stigma of being historical. Rosenberg writes that Ghiselin's conceptual breakthrough of species as individuals is not only a step up for biology from the historical, but viewing species-individuals from above the species-level, a class level, species-individuals can enter theory and the theory can achieve a breadth of generality no less than any true science, e.g., physics. Homo sapiens, along with countless other species-individuals, can become entities in theories and laws. I must ask, shouldn't it be clear that such *entities* exist before they become crucial elements in theories and laws? Do Ghiselin and Rosenberg (and Hull and Eldredge) feel safe in making such entities parts of theories and laws? They apparently do, for no one has proven that such entities do not exist, and no alternative theory is likely to come up with such a claim. And, we are reminded of Heise's remarks, above; Ghiselin has changed nothing in the actual world by changing the labels from class to individual. Why, she asks, along with Caplan, can't Homo sapiens as a class enter a theory? Truth is it can and does, without the categorical breakthrough suggested by Rosenberg.

Stephen P. Schwartz thinks a slightly less radical view than species are individuals is closer to the truth. He has in mind that "species are natural kinds whose names are rigid designators that gather their extensions by underlying traits." (Ibid) We take this opportunity to understand and critique another small dogma of m-realism, rigid designation:

> Suppose now that these beings on the distant planet not only superficially resemble Homo sapiens, but by some highly improbable evolutionary parallelism are genetically indistinguishable from us (assuming now also that genetics provides the underlying trait of Homo sapiens). It seems likely to me that we would grant that these organisms are Homo sapiens even though they do not share a lineage in common with us. Indeed, I would say that spatially distant beings that are genetically identical to us are Homo sapiens even if they don't superficially resemble us. They are Homo sapiens because they have the underlying trait of Homo sapiens. Also, it seems to me that members of a species could be created artificially in the laboratory. Such artificial members would not share a lineage with natural creatures, but would belong to the species nevertheless if and only if they had the appropriate genetic code. If any of these are possible outcomes, as I think they are, then Homo sapiens is not an individual but a kind whose members belong because they share an underlying trait. (Ibid, p. 302)

Schwartz is enunciating the new theory of reference, due to Kripke, Putnam, and Donnellan, the claim that proper names and natural kind terms (like tiger, gold, and water) are rigid designators. A designator is rigid if it refers to the same thing or things in every possible world in which it has a

314

reference. Schwartz says, "If it is correct that natural kind terms are rigid designators, then the mechanism of reference cannot be conventional definitions" (Ibid). Why are conventional definitions disallowed? Schwartz says that, for example, we might discover that tigers don't satisfy the conventional definition:

> The upshot is that it is up to scientists and experts on the kind in question to tell us its necessary features...[which] are part of, or follow from, the underlying trait of the kind in question. We presume that tigers have an underlying trait that makes them tigers and not giraffes or turtles, just as there is an underlying trait that makes gold gold or water water. (Ibid)

Sounds like gold and water have essences. Well, says Schwartz:

> Underlying traits may be essences of kinds, but there is nothing metaphysical about them. They are discovered by empirical research, not by rational insight or by language analysis. In the case of tigers, the underlying trait is probably a genetic code, the underlying trait of gold is probably its atomic number, of water its chemical composition. Our beliefs about the underlying trait of some kind do not get incorporated in definitions because we are always ready to change our minds about the underlying trait on the basis of further research. (Ibid)

Species then (e.g., tigers), are natural kinds (along with gold and water) whose names are rigid designators. The name refers to whatever has the underlying trait of the kind (e.g., genetic code, atomic number, or chemical compound), and the kind is not restricted in time and space. This is where Ghiselin's individual differs from a natural kind; it is restricted in time and space. Classes, as well as kinds, are not restricted. In giving up classes, he gives up natural kinds.

In rigid designation we seem to have another solution to the species problem. Is it? It tries to avoid going the customary route of definition. Does it? That a species is a natural kind is either a description or a definition or both. Is there additional information? Yes. The underlying traits. So, we have, a species is a natural kind because of the underlying traits of each of its members. The underlying traits are determined by specialists, hence the definitions are scientific or, perhaps, technical. Definitions all the same. The underlying traits are, admittedly, each member's essence (metaphysical or not) and an essence defines what it is the essence of. Thus each tiger (and there are different particular tigers) has a genetic code specific to it, and the traits generated by this code is the essence of the natural kind of all the tigers that have that specific code. The universal or species name of these tigers is fixed in its reference and rigidly designates each one. The possession of the specific genetic code places the individual tiger in a kind, a natural kind. So, too, with any and all living individuals. To know its genetic code is to know its kind. Sounds like the species problem has been solved, along with the problem of universals. No abstracting from particulars has been used to obtain the universal or kind. We (i.e., experts) simply determine the genetic code of each living thing, and all the individuals with the same or identical genetic code are a species, a kind. And there's the rub. No two humans (even so-called identical twins), or tigers, whose genomes have been examined have the same or identical genomes. The genomes of all the humans so far examined vary. No two are the same or identical. Ditto for tigers and a host of other animals. The reply that human genomes and tiger genomes, etc., are mostly the same or alike, is not to the point. Differences in those genomes destroys the claim of their oneness of kind. The result of a study published in the March, 2008 issue of *American Journal of Human Genetics* is to the point. The article (see also "Scientific American," May 2008) was authored by Jan Dumanski and Carl Bruder, both at the University of Alabama at Birmingham. Human genomes are apparently dynamically changing entities. As Bruder says: "[the genome even of monozygotic twins] is changing all the time, for good or for not" (p. 26). Where, then, are the individuals with the same or identical genetic code? There aren't any! Codes change and so vary, one from another. But that means there are no kinds, hence, no way to rigidly designate them. That makes Schwartz's attempt to save metaphysical natural kinds a failed attempt.

That leaves the m-real experts examining the phenotypic traits of particular humans and particular tigers to determine how similar the traits are: hair, eyes, immune systems, etc. etc. To say that the traits of humans or particular tigers are sufficiently similar to be assigned species names is a claim that can be made (and it is invalid), but we are now far removed from rigid designation. If the genomes of particular humans and particular tigers differ, human and tiger can't rigidly designate. That just may be the way the natural world is.

Kripke claims that water is a natural kind and is rigidly designated by its chemical composition: H2O. Whatever molecules are H2O are water. And water molecules comprise a natural kind. Water molecules are natural, but they do not comprise a kind. Our critique of kinds is that the individuals comprising them allegedly share an identity, resemblance, or some commonality. Kripke claims that two hydrogen atoms and one oxygen atom is what water molecules have in common. Indeed, water molecules each have two hydrogen atoms and one oxygen atom, but they are not held in common. Each water molecule has its own hydrogen and oxygen atoms. Since each water molecule is ontologically other and ontologically different, we cannot assign them to a single category or kind. Each water molecule does not resemble any other nor is it identical to any other for no resemblance-entity or identity-entity can be seen. We may say, however, that while water molecules are other and different ones, their difference one from another is significantly slight, given our instruments of measurement. That slightness of difference seems to be characteristic of things on the molecular, atomic, and sub-atomic levels. Differences increase as we ascend from the micro-levels to macro-levels.

Kripke didn't deal with the problem of kind, the problem of essences, the problem of definition, the problem of universals, the problem of identity, the problem of similarity. Given the nature of things on the genetic and micro-levels, his rigid designation fails. What of personal names such as *Nixon*, which Kripke used as an example in his notion of rigid designation? Nixon was not rigidly designated in this world, let alone in all possible worlds. Nixon, the name, differs every time it is uttered or written; Nixon, the man, changed throughout his life, and is changing now. How rigid can Nixon (my utterance or the remains in a casket) be? Does this reduce naming to absurdity? Indeed, not. We can, and must, use names, but not as rigid designators. Nixon is ok, even if uttered non-rigidly, for pointing to the physical entity, Nixon, but only if he does not change too much; the point beyond which we would with-hold Nixon is unclear. And that is because any thing is only viewable along lines of change which present lesser or greater differences.

The problem with kinds, then is that they are dependent on our ability to see identities (or similarities) in numerically, and ontologically, different individuals when those individuals are, in fact, unique. Kinds don't exist in nature, nor can we construct them as concepts, for how can we unite ontologically unique individuals even in our minds?

We began this section with Ghiselin's announcement of the radical solution: species are not classes but individuals. I would like to point out that, since no one has ever demonstrated that a species is anything other than some number of actual variant (different and differing) organisms, neither Ghiselin nor his respondents could actually make sense of his claim of individuality respecting species. Still it is believed by some and continues to distort biological science. Nature has no such entities as Ghiselin's individuals. Nor can we form valid concepts of them, given the natures of actual organisms and all other particulars.

Hull's Philosophic Support of the Radical Solution

Hull's essay "Are Species Really Individuals?" was published in the journal *Systematic Zoology* in 1976. Scientists reading the article were treated to a defense of Ghiselin's claim. In the abstract of his essay, Hull (1976) makes this remark, "The processes which contribute to the evolution of biological species take place at a variety of levels of organization; e.g., genes give rise to other genes, organisms give rise to other organisms, and species give rise to other species..." (p. 174).

"Species give rise to other species?" Is this believable? Even non-scientists have seen chromosomes giving rise to other chromosomes when they viewed a cell undergoing mitosis in a high school biology lab; they have even seen cats or dogs or mice giving rise to cats or dogs or mice, but a species giving rise to a species?

Hull continues, with the quote that follows, and tries to make the case that what he is calling a species is an actuality possessing sufficient unity to be a unit which can evolve. This unit, recall, is on a level above organisms:

> In addition to spatiotemporal continuity, species must also possess a certain degree of unity to function as units of evolution. Gene exchange is one means by which such unity can be promoted....However, if species are chunks of the genealogical nexus, they cannot be viewed as classes. Instead they possess all the characteristics of individuals---that is, if organisms are taken to be

paradigm individuals. (Ibid)

The gene exchange, the reproductive criterion of Mayr, is said to promote the unity of a species. One wonders if this exchange is accomplished with or without the organisms on the level below. In addition, we hear again (Ghiselin said it first) that "species are chunks of the genealogical nexus." We meet, again, the use of metaphor to suggest solidity of a non-existent, metaphysical entity. The materializing power of metaphor.

Following the use of the chunk-metaphor, Hull uses analogy to argue that what he and Ghiselin are calling a species is an individual like those paradigm individuals, organisms. Organisms are individuals because they are entities that are reasonably discrete, develop continuously in space and time, are spatiotemporally localized, and are unique. Gould will repeat all this. The metaphysical realism is apparent in the two final quotes of Hull's "Are Species Really Individuals?" "The relation which an organ has to an organism is the same as the relation which an organism has to its species" (Ibid, p. 176). This, again, is the use of analogy. We can understand the relation of an organ to an organism. Can we actually understand that that relation is the same as the relation which an organism has to its species? Is there not a feeling that the relation between an organism and a species is empty on the species end? Finally, Hull says:

> Two organisms can be identical to each other in every respect save spatiotemporal location without thereby becoming the same organism. No matter how identical twins might be, they are still two

individuals and not one. In short, organisms on the common-sense level are individuated on the basis of spatiotemporal location and continuity. (Ibid, p. 181)

I disagree with Hull's view of identity. Two, or more, organisms cannot be asserted to be identical unless the identity-factor (the shared respect in terms of which they are declared identical is seen). All this was discussed above. The claims Hull is making here involve the notions: identity, space-time location, and continuity. That spatiotemporal location has a crucial role in individuating two identical organisms is an interesting philosophical claim. I don't believe biologists would have come up with it, and I don't believe anything important will be missing from their lives or their science if they do not understand how space-time location (and Hull does not mean the particular environment and its effects on an organism) can have a role in the individuation of organisms. Two organisms that are "identical to each other in every respect" would be the same organism were it not for their space-time locations according to Hull, following D.M. Armstrong's contention. Hull admits that no matter how identical twins might be, they are still two individuals, not one. We can agree that such twins are two in number, not that they are identical in any way. Since the identity of two or more things is not perceived because the alleged identity-factor is metaphysical and their individual characters are ontologically other than those of others, we may safely believe that the otherness of each individual thing is surety for its difference. That belief, in any case, is superior to the factual falsity that individual things are identical, or resemble, or have something in common.

Ontological otherness and difference would appear to characterize the things of the universe if we remove the metaphysical scales from our eyes.

Mayr, following Darwin's observation that each living thing varies from others, insists that biological organisms are unique. I believe Darwin and Mayr are correct. If so, living things are not identical. Mayr has told us that it is the uniqueness of living things, each and every one, that sets biology off from the physical sciences, where atoms and electrons, etc., are, he says, identical. Aristotle needed the notion of identity, and philosophers ever after have used it, especially as part of the paraphernalia of metaphysical realism. Things can be said to be identical (as Hull has said of two organisms) and a thing can be said to be identical with itself. But these claims fall apart when we apply the foregoing critique. To repeat, 1) two things cannot be claimed to be identical for, ontologically, each is other than the other and hence are different ones with different characters however much they resemble or appear identical. Surely, the fact that all particulars (particles, molecules, organisms) are acted on differently in their environments by internal and external forces accounts for difference. Clearly those actual particulars cannot be acted on identically or the same. 2) A thing cannot be said to be identical with itself for a thing doesn't have a self (even a past self) to be identical with; there is no thing and that thing's self. 3) Most importantly, in order to say that two things are identical, or that a thing is identical with its self, we must see that something with respect to which we can validly say the two are identical. We cannot see such a something for there is no something to be seen. Of two things said to be identical, we should look for

323

differences and degrees of difference, for they can be seen. Our brains were naturally evolved to tell us of differences (i.e., truths), not identities and sameness (i.e., illusions of metaphysics).

Chapter 27 Eldredge and Biological Hierarchies in Nature

Niles Eldredge endorsed Ghiselin's radical solution of the species problem early on---and taking note of Ghiselin's open-door offer and Hull's claim about the requirements for a scientific theory---proceeded to climb the metaphysical ladder in the name of evolutionary theory. We must not forget Hull's claim, "At the very least, populations and species evolve. ... A gene or an organism cannot evolve because not enough change can take place before they cease to exist, either terminally or by replication" (Ibid, p. 282). We must not forget this claim because if organisms don't evolve, and species and populations (as metaphysical wholes with parts) are non-existent entities, what can Hull and Ghiselin be talking about in their great concern for biological evolution? Dawkins has something to say about Hull's denying genes the power of evolutionary change, but we cannot pursue that here.

Eldredge's book, *Unfinished Synthesis: Biological Hierarchies and Modern Evolutionary Thought*, was published in l985. Ghiselin's open-door offer came after he had argued, analogically and metaphorically, that species are individuals and real like all those automobile companies. Are the taxa ranked at categorical levels higher than the species merely conceptual? "One's answer depends upon his metaphysics..." Hull's purpose is, "...to show that evolutionary theory requires a...shift in the ontological status of species as units of evolution. Instead of being classes, they are individuals" (Hull, 1976, p. 175).

So, enter Eldredge with the belief that taxa ranked higher than the species level are not just conceptual. They are real and individuals to boot. Theory legislates that species are real and individuals so, *zap*, they are real and individuals and capable of carrying those changes that amount to evolution. Wand in hand, Eldredge waves it toward nested sets and, *zap*, the higher levels become real individuals. Eldredge puts it this way, "Viewing species...as individuals---following the lead of Ghiselin and Hull---enlarges the range of entities that take part in the evolutionary process. What we need, it seems, is a revised ontology of evolutionary entities" (Eldredge, 1985, p. 7).

The actual evolutionary process in which humble variant organisms descend with modification and either struggle, adapt, and survive or die is being transcended. We are about to witness *evolutionary drama* in the *big hierarchical tent*, with species and other higher class actors strutting their real imaginary stuff. Is this going too far? Perhaps. Perhaps Ghiselin, Hull, and now Eldredge, have gone too far. Ghiselin and Hull, focusing on species have told us species are a level above organisms and they are real (i.e., actual). I have trouble with that, perhaps others do too. Now, Eldredge wants to make actual the category which nests species and even those higher up:

This revised ontology, I will argue, automatically forces us to consider an alternative approach to the very structure of evolutionary theory---simply because it presents us with an alternative description of the organization of biological nature. That structure is hierarchical. Genes, organisms, demes, species, and monophyletic taxa form one nested hierarchical system of individuals that is concerned with the development, retention, and modification of information ensconced, at the base, in the genome. But there is at the same time a parallel hierarchy of nested ecological individuals--- proteins, organisms, populations, communities, and regional biotas systems, that reflects the economic organization and integration of living systems. The processes within each of these two process hierarchies, plus the interactions between the two hierarchies, seems to me to produce the events and patterns that we call evolution. (Ibid)

Eldredge's two hierarchies interact causally, "producing those events and patterns that we call evolution." We understand cause in its use for the interactions of genes, chromosomes, and organisms, but is it clear that monophyletic taxa, communities, ecosystems, and regional biotas are individuals that causally interact? Isn't this carrying entification too far? Where are the arguments as to the facts? Are there such higher-level individuals? Isn't this still another arbitrary declaration that such is simply the case? And those hierarchies? Are they biological facts discernible in nature?

327

It is incorrect, however, to call them nested sets. Sets obviously are classes. The trick in seeing these biological hierarchies correctly is to view them as nested but not to think of the higher levels merely as aggregates of lower-level individuals; that is, as sets. The higher-level units are themselves individuals though not ipso facto, as the ontological status of each putative individual needs to be independently established. Thus, for each hierarchy broached in the following pages I present a formal argument for the view that at all the levels (classes) of entities included in the hierarchy, the entities that occupy those levels are, in each particular instance, to be construed as individuals. (Ibid, p. 141)

Eldredge has not made the case that those putative individuals are, in fact, actual. Only actual entities can be causal in nature. We already suspect that they are not, and will not, become actual (i.e. ontological) individuals. Why not? Where is the boundedness that configures, for example, mammals into an individual which is actual and which gives it the agency of causality? Where is the boundedness of a community or ecosystem or regional biota that can configure each of them into individuals, causal agents? Ontology is not a matter of fiat. As to that, Eldredge says:

It is fashionable nowadays (see Sober and Lewonton 1982) to warn against the perils of "reification" and "entification," that is, falling prey to the error of seeing some phenomenon or other as real where in fact it is only apparent. ...The potential error of reification is saying something is there when it "really" isn't. I am concerned with the converse: treating real things as if they don't exist---to my mind the more serious source of error in the actual practice of contemporary evolutionary biology. (Ibid, p. 174)

If you fail to make your favorite ghost materialize, tell those who can't see it that they are committing the error of treating ghosts as if they don't exist---a serious error, the failure to reify and entify. The failure, of course, is not to be worried over; it is the failure to be an objective m-realist. To my mind, treating m-real things as if they don't exist is the proper way to treat them. If those m-real things are in the actual practice of contemporary evolutionary biology, then evolutionary biology is voodoo science.

There is a long tradition in taxonomy of placing organisms in groups on the basis of characters or shared descent and then representing those groups or classes on a chart as nested sets. The result is a hierarchy of categories the most inclusive of which is labeled: living things. We could, of course, imagine the category, living things, as a unit, an individual, capable of bumping up against the non-living category, imaginable as another individual, and the two individuals interacting causally. Entification and reification, in an imaginative mind need have no limits. But what scientific purpose would it serve?

Ghiselin was aware that, if species are individuals" then the next higher level includes them and is a class, and so on up the nested sets. Eldredge, in making individuals of the higher classes or sets goes through the ceiling. Where does one stop turning classes into individuals? Darwin said naturalists know, vaguely, what they are calling species. We all know, vaguely, that different organisms, for scientific reasons are called species. What, we will ask, did Mayr, Ghiselin, and Hull think Darwin meant when he used the word species? After all, Darwin presumably wrote a book about them and their origin, or did he?

Chapter 28 Three Evolutionists on Darwin's View of Species

Hull

"Throughout the history of Western thought, species have been a constant source of controversy" (Hull, 1988, p. 213). Amen. David Hull notes that for most of that history, species have been viewed as universals, secondary substances, or classes. Ghiselin brought this history to a close when he "turned his gaze on a fundamental problem, the metaphysical status of species" (Ibid). Darwin, of course, was confronted with a class-notion in which species are fixed, unchanging, a belief as Hull put it, "that an organism might change its species or that certain species might cease to be exemplified, but not that species themselves change" (Ibid, pp. 213-14). Thus:

> One reason why Darwin's theory was so threatening was that it implied that species themselves evolve. The only way that new species can come into existence is from preexisting ancestral species... On the traditional view, one species evolving into another was as incomprehensible as one element

evolving into another. (Ibid, p. 214)

Hull then makes the following observation:

If species are classes, then they should be definable in terms of sets of characteristics that only and all the organisms belonging to that species possess; but if species evolve as gradually as Darwin claimed, then such definitions are necessarily impossible. (Ibid)

Hull is saying that on the one hand, Darwin believed that "species themselves evolve" i.e., from one into another--- and on the other, that if "species...evolve gradually" their class-boundaries become indistinct and "definitions of them are necessarily impossible." We will examine Darwin's view of species-definition later. However, that Darwin believed that "species themselves evolve," (i.e., are mutable) is, I shall try to show, false. That he believed that species were entities which evolve
gradually is also false. False because Hull entifies species, Darwin did not. Nor did Darwin believe that the reason species could not be defined was because they evolve gradually. Darwin did believe that organisms are variants, they change in descent, more gradually than not, and are not subject to class-definition because the lines or boundaries of demarcation are impossible to discern. Darwin's alleged belief that species themselves evolve implies that species are actual, mutable entities of some sort, not classes. It was the class-notion of species as real entities that he undermined in his great work, but he did not proceed to a radical solution in which fixed entities move and change. Hull, of course, is not

saying that the entity that Darwin must have had in mind and which he thought of as evolving was an individual. But he does seem to think of a Darwinian species as an incipient individual. For Hull, not to be an individual is not to be a candidate for selection.

Eldredge

Eldredge repeats the question of Ghiselin and Hull and then gives his view of Darwin's notion of species:

> Are species real? A brief summary of the history of the problem would go something like this: The pre-Darwinian majority saw species as both real and fixed. William Whewell (1837...) perhaps said it best: "Species have a real existence in nature, and a transition from one to another does not exist." Darwin, seeing that characterization of species as antithetical to the very notion of evolution, developed a picture of adaptive fluidity in which species are seen as class-like stages in a passing stream of anatomical transformations. (Eldredge, 1985, pp. 153-54)

Darwin is viewed as having made it possible for species to make transitions from one to another, but in doing so, they become "class-like stages in a passing stream of anatomical transformations." Species either as actual entities or classes have disappeared! The disappearance of species for Eldredge, is unacceptable. Metaphysical realists need them.

Whewell was a realist and conceptualist, so his saying

"species have a real existence in nature" comes as no surprise. Agreeing with him on that account, Eldredge is happy to quote him. "Real existence in nature," we are reminded, contains the old contradiction; m-real existences are no part of nature.

One of the major aims of this essay is to show that Eldredge, along with Mayr, Ghiselin, and Hull (and, later, Gould) rejected Darwin's (anti-metaphysical) understanding of species and continue the pre-Darwinian tradition that species are m-real-actual (i.e., objectively real) entities, the tradition of metaphysical realism, of which Whewell is obviously a part. Pre-Darwinians and Post-Darwinians have joined hands.

Mayr

Ernst Mayr is an elder statesman of biology, a contemporary evolutionary theorist, an ornithologist by trade, a historian of biology, and a founding father when it comes to the notion of species In fact, Mayr has become Mr. Species: "'If you want to discuss species,' he says wryly, you must deal with me. I am Mr. Species" (DeBlieu, 1992, p. 44).

Mayr began to think differently about species in 1942, but the process was not completed until the 1960's. Before we ask our question of what Mayr thinks of Darwin's view of species we might enlarge our view of Mayr's thinking about species for many would say his view of them (minus their recent status as individuals) is the dominant one.

Even primitive people have names for kinds of birds, fishes, flowers or trees, and the species recognized by

334

them are usually exactly the same ones recognized by the modern taxonomist...Such naming of kinds is made possible because the diversity of nature is not continuous but consists of discrete entities separated from each other by discontinuities. One finds in nature not merely individuals but also species that is, groups of individuals that share certain characteristics with each other. (Mayr, 1982, p. 252)

The taxonomic instinct, the urge to categorize, survives in all of us, and we can give reasons for our belief that the word kinds suits what we observe in nature. That is understandable. The problem is the basis for saying that those birds, those fish, the plants with those flowers, those trees are each a kind, or a species. And the even deeper problem is the basis for categorizing anything at all; what is it about birds or fish or electrons that makes it valid to group or categorize them? Their appearance? Their behavior? Their decent? Well, then, what is it about appearance or behavior or descent that authorizes us to construct species or kinds or do we simply see them out there in nature? Mayr has just told us that, "One finds in nature not merely individuals [i.e., organisms] but also species" We have already pointed out that his definition of species centers on a reproductive gap. For him, species are necessary units. "The species are the real units of evolution" (Ibid, p. 269). Not only are species necessary units of evolution, they are the units of systematics, ecology, ethology, and more. "In spite of the variability caused by the genetic uniqueness of every individual, there is a species-specific unity to the genetic program (DNA) of nearly every species" (Ibid, p. 297).

With an obvious problem of unifying birds or fish into kinds or species one wonders how Mayr is able to see a species-specific unity to the genetic program (DNA) of nearly every species. No two genetic programs, even of clones or twins, are the same or identical. (Recall the study published in the *American Journal of Human Genetics*, March 2008.) Where is the unity? I rather believe the unity is in the m-realism of Mayr's pronouncements.

In the introduction to his facsimile of the first edition of Darwin's great work, Mayr has this to say. Darwin was, "confused about varieties and species" (Darwin, 1964, p. vii). Why did Mayr think Darwin was confused about varieties and species? Was it because they had disappeared as entities in his book, as Eldredge and Ghiselin and Hull had noticed? But Darwin made it clear that professional scientists (naturalists) have too firmly fixed in their heads that a species is an entity in nature. What could be a clearer denial of the metaphysics of species? Still, Mayr can't believe it. "It is no exaggeration to state that in the 1830s Darwin had what was very close to the modern biological species concept" (Mayr, 1982, p. 266). He adds, "When one goes to the origin of 1859 and reads what it says about species, one cannot help but feel that one is dealing with an altogether different author" (Ibid).

Darwin came close to Mayr's own conception and then wrote about the notion of species in an entirely different way. The man must have been confused when he wrote the work that he entitled *On The Origin of Species*. Mayr even complains that Darwin didn't tell us the origin of species in that work. I wonder why? Could it be that Mayr (and Hull and Ghiselin and Eldredge) missed his point? That Darwin was not telling us about the origin of a non-entity?

Before examining Darwin's work, we might note Mayr's survey of what Darwin said about varieties and species:

> ...I look at the term species, as one arbitrarily given for the sake of convenience to a set of individuals closely resembling each other, and that it does not essentially differ from the term variety, which is given to less distinct and more fluctuating forms....Varieties have the same general characters as species, for they cannot be distinguished from species. (Ibid, p. 267)

We might note that, although Darwin uses resemblance as a marker for attaching the label species to a collection of individuals, he does not say that resemblance is either a necessary or a sufficient condition for defining species He does not, in other words, hold to a morphological concept of species

In a letter to Hooker (December 24, 1856), Darwin says:

> I have just been comparing definitions of species... It is really laughable to see what different ideas are prominent in various naturalists' minds, when they speak of 'species'; in some, resemblance is everything and descent of little weight---in some, resemblance seems to go for nothing, and creation the reigning idea---in some descent is the key---in some, sterility an unfailing test, with others it is not worth a

farthing. It all comes, I believe, from trying to define the indefinable. (Ibid)

Those remarks seem to me carefully considered; not as Mayr would have it, confused. After working on the problem of species for almost 20 years, and before he completed what came to be *On The Origin of Species...*, Darwin might be given credit for knowing whereof he spoke. No one can define the undefinable. Definition, a major item in the m-realist philosopher's tool kit, was rejected by Darwin. Rejected, too, was another item in that tool kit: concepts. Darwin never uses the term in his viewing things in nature; he is not a conceptualist, not a metaphysical realist. He is doing biology, not metaphysics.

Mayr, unable to believe that Darwin could have gone so far astray on the matter of species blames Darwin's reading and listening to botanists!

What could have brought about this complete turn around in Darwin's species concept? His reading as well as his correspondence indicate that after 1840, and particularly from the 1850s on, Darwin was increasingly influenced by the botanical literature and by correspondence with botanist friends. (Ibid)

What Mayr fails to understand is that Darwin is rejecting the traditional way of thinking that Mayr, and Ghiselin and Hull and Eldredge, and every rationalist-realist metaphysician imposes when he or she thinks about living things. Darwin, dumping metaphysics, has come upon a sublime notion of how living things actually change in nature. For the first time in history, Darwin is seeing living things as they are, as variants, each and every one! He knows the vocabulary of conceptualism and m-realism and nominalism. He says in his conclusion to *On The Origin of Species*:

> In short, we shall have to treat species in the same manner as those naturalists treat genera, who admit that genera are merely artificial combinations made for convenience. This may not be a cheering prospect; but we shall at least be freed from the vain search for the undiscovered and undiscoverable essence of the term species. (Darwin, 1964, p. 485)

Does that sound like a man who is ignorant of philosophy and metaphysics? We cannot define the undefinable, we cannot discover an undiscoverable essence. Darwin is rejecting the philosophy of conceptualism and the philosophy of metaphysical realism. Is he, then, a nominalist? If he views species and genera as "merely artificial combinations made for convenience," then, the words 'species' and 'genus' refer to no actual entities in nature, nor to concepts in the head. Is that position nominalism? Yes. But Darwin knew something nominalists and m-realists did not know. He understood for the first time how biological nature worked. That required him to smash the Humpty-Dumpty that is species which can never be put together again, nor can its pieces be transmuted into an individual. Our task is to understand how he did it.

Contemporary Evolutionary Theorists Returned to a Pre-

Darwinian Notion of Species

We know why Mayr, Ghiselin, Hull, and Eldredge, insisted on a metaphysical notion of species, now terming it an individual, a mutable entity, a whole with parts, which can evolve. Hull said it. "One of the main messages of this book is that species, if they are to play the roles assigned to them in evolutionary theory, must be treated as historical entities" (Hull, 1988, p. 79).

A secondary reason which Mayr, Ghiselin, and Eldredge mention for reifying and entifying species is helping science to progress via this new reconceptualization. It would be hard to find evidence that the alleged individual has helped any area of science to progress, but the philosophy of m-realism has unquestionably made a saltational leap forward. If evolutionary theory requires real entities to evolve and there are no such entities in nature, evolutionary theory would seem to have lost its way. All we ever have to judge that evolution has occurred are organisms or parts of them. If they haven't evolved (descended with modification), then what can be the meaning of evolution? Individuals change, and if modification by descent of an individual from parents is an evolutionary step, then the actual decent of each changed individual is evidence that evolution occurs. That evolutionary steps can sum up, as Darwin put it, to some very interesting changes down the lines of changes, gradual or saltative, is obvious: geological strata proclaim them! If, however, some evolutionary scientists continue to focus on species entities and insist that they (the wholes of which organisms are parts) evolve, that they are real entities in nature, then evolutionary scientists are no better than creationists. Please choose between the person who wants you to believe that real entities, called species evolve and the person who wants you to believe that real entities, called species were created by God. Such scientists are guilty of hubris; they listen to the categorical voice of philosophic reason (m-realism). Creationists are guilty of ignorance; they listen to the voices emanating from ancient texts and modern pulpits. People who hear voices need help.

Chapter 29 Steven J. Gould's Capstone for the Darwinian Theory of Evolution: A Critique

As reflected in his *The Structure of Evolutionary Theory*, Gould's drive to expand Darwinian theory proceeds with fearless optimism. His way was prepared by metaphysically-minded scientists and philosophers of science who, over the previous twenty-five years, saw new possibilities for evolutionary theory. The demise of logical positivism and its attempt to discredit and remove metaphysics from philosophy and science, emboldened those enamored of classical and medieval metaphysical realism. Gould's big book, published in 2002, lays out the new program, a very long argument to convince doubters and unbelievers, that it is time to change the conceptual framework which embeds evolutionary theory.

Gould has assembled what he believes are the outstanding components needed to place a macro-evolutionary capstone of interacting hierarchical individuals on Darwin's humbler base: actual organisms descending with modifications in environments where some of those modifications may or may not be helpful and naturally selected. Those organisms that gain advantages in surviving and reproducing and passing the modifications to their offspring demonstrate genealogies involved in evolution. I must emphasize, however, that Darwin never had a "theory of evolution." He did have a theory of "natural selection." They are not the same. If natural selection occurs, evolution is, on hindsight, the result. It was Darwin's discovery of natural selection as a process in nature (akin to Newton's discovery of the universality of gravity) which he held fast, knowing it to be an important contribution to our understanding of living things. What were selected by natural processes were organisms, not mutable species. Darwin was well-informed about theories of evolution, for Lamarck had one and his grandfather had written of evolution. Of Lamarck's theory, Darwin rejected it and his grandfather's views which he said were too speculative, i.e., not sufficiently based on facts.

Gould's base for his expansion of evolutionary theory is something relatively new, a species-individual. Darwin would never have accepted such an entity, for he rejected the notion of entities called species. It is therefore disingenuous of Gould to have us believe that he is building on a Darwinian base. Still, we have Gould's book on the structure of evolution, and we need to understand it as well as his *marrying* his theory to Darwin's own base of variant organisms.

Darwin's focus on organisms as the locus of evolutionary events does not, according to Gould, tell the whole tale of what can be selected and what it is that evolves, especially from his perspective as a paleontologist and geologist. Needed, to begin with, is an entity higher than individual organisms which can be involved in selection

344

processes. To obtain it, a new notion of species is required. Ghiselin had already prepared the way. Rightly re-conceived, each species becomes an individual, a Darwinian individual, according to Gould. Why Darwinian? Because the new entity must not be disconnected from Darwin's theory of natural selection. As Gould puts it:

> David Hull (1976), in the first major philosophical extension of Ghiselin's proposal, firmly linked the concept of species as individuals to the older issue of units (or levels) of selection, thus properly tying the rationale for a causal theory of hierarchical selection to the generalization of Darwin's key insight that *selection can only operate by the differential reproductive success of "individuals."* [my emphasis] (Gould, 2002, p. 600)

He then quotes Hull, "Entities at various levels of organization can function as units of selection if they possess the sort of organization most clearly exhibited by organisms: and such units of selection are individuals, not classes" (Hull, 1976, p. 182). In 1980, Gould notes that Hull added this remark, "Individuality wanders from level to level, and as it does, so too does the level at which selection can occur" (Gould, 2002, p. 315).

Hull's imagination has become fecund, opening new theoretical possibilities for evolution. What Gould is after is some way to validate the notion of hierarchies in nature through which his transformed individuals can interact causally in selection processes. The individuals he has in mind are such as demes, species, and clades, a threesome in which demes are nested in species and species are nested in clades. He says:

> If the rationale for a hierarchical theory of selection resides in the expansion of "individuality" to several levels of biological organization (see Gould and Lloyd, 1999), then we must specify a set of criteria that any material configuration must meet to merit designation as an "individual." (Ibid, p. 600)

Two sets of criteria are specified. The criteria for vernacular individuality are listed as follows, "a discrete and definable beginning, or birth; an equally discrete and definable ending, or death; and sufficient stability (defined as coherence of substance and constancy of form during its lifetime to merit continuous recognition as the same 'thing.'" (Ibid, p. 602) The criteria for evolutionary individuality are as follows, "Inheritance, Variation, Interaction." (Ibid, pp. 609-11)

Gould's vernacular criteria on the issue of individuality are fashioned solely to persuade us that some plurality of organisms can be treated as if they were an organism. Again, the argument is one from analogy and is unlikely to change the minds of those who have observed plants and animals, knows they are organisms, and can tell the difference between one and more than one. Given the language we have inherited, we of course speak of pluralities as if they are one (in kind or class), but we know plants and animals, called species, are not actually one, and certainly not one individual.

Gould's criteria for vernacular individuality of supra-organisms run counter to empirical fact. The organisms of kinds and classes and species have different ongoing births and deaths, and their boundaries, numbers, and locations are, with insignificant exceptions, all but impossible to determine. These analogues of individual organisms do not bump up against selection processes as one thing. (Can any metaphysical entity generated in the brain bump up against natural processes of selection?) Actual organisms are unique and are open, or closed, to selection processes on their own account. The attempt to persuade us that a plurality of living things is an individual like an organism is embarrassing.

The attempt by Gould to transfer criteria applicable to organisms to pluralities of them as if they were individuals asks us to perform a mental task which cannot be done. Gould's notion of evolutionary theory may require it, but not all theorists agree with him. Gould would have it his way, accept nonsense and change theory.

Part of the problem for evolutionists is determining what it is that evolves (i.e., descends with modification). No biologist doubts that organisms with their particular characters are involved in Darwinian descent with modification. Noting the changes of organisms over temporal sequences is what evolution, traditionally, is all about. More recent organisms are compared with individuals who are their ancestors and relatives, near and distant. With the enormous numbers of organisms that have descended, methods honed to best trace lineages and relationships is required. Genetics is a major tool in this effort.

Biologists look at the anatomical characters of organisms (and/or their DNA) in a before and after perspective, establish the fact of change, if such is the case, and conclude that evolution has occurred. If a biologist should say that it is the species that changes (i.e., evolves) over temporal changes, not the individual organisms with their characters, confusion is introduced because we cannot see a species as an entity distinct from organisms. Nor can we see demes or clades as entities distinct from their organisms. The only way to know about change in living things (which is to say, evolution) is to look at particular things, their biological characters, including their DNA. We must look at some organism, its parts (or remains or tracks), and examine its DNA, if available, for that's all there is to look at. If there is no species-individual, no deme-individual, and no clade-individual to look at, then we can't climb Gould's hierarchy of individuals above organisms. And, if there are no such individuals, then there is no selection of them in nature. It's just organisms confronting one another (but not hierarchically) in the environmental circumstances in which they live, reproduce, and die. Still, Gould sees it otherwise. We will listen to his argument.

The species-as-individual tier of the Gouldian capstone came ready-made from Ghiselin and was improved upon by Hull. The major structural elements for expanding the theory are hierarchical levels where selection processes are said to operate on those particular individuals. Gould says:

> I propose, as the central proposition of macroevolution, that species play the same role of fundamental individual that organisms assume in microevolution. Species represent the basic units in theories and mechanisms of macroevolutionary

change. In this formulation, the origins and extinctions of species become strictly analogous to the births and deaths of organisms—and just as natural selection works through differential proliferation based on schedules of organismal births and deaths, so too does species selection operate upon the frequencies and timetables of origins and extinctions. (Ibid, p.703)

We must emphasize, here, and keep in mind what precisely makes it possible for Gould to build his metaphysical hierarchy above the level of Darwinian organisms. It is the acceptance by scientists of species as the units in evolutionary theory. This acceptance came because of the logical structure of scientific theory. A many (e.g., organisms) had to be made one in order to proceed inductively and deductively in theory. Biologists accepted a class notion of organisms as species as the unit for logical purposes. Gould knew that once organisms with their categorical wrappings (species) were in place as the fundamental units in evolutionary theory, all he need do was remove the class label and integrate the metaphysical wrapping into some plurality of organisms. The result of this alchemy is an individual. Scientists are obviously in a bind. How are they to theorize about living things if they don't accept the units (however metaphysical) which make theorizing possible? They can't. We return to Gould and his defense of species as individuals.

We examined the view of species as individuals in the work of Ghiselin, Hull, and Eldredge. Others also examined this view and found it wanting. Gould was obviously not impressed with what critics thought of this questionable notion and, as we shall see, he believes offending criticisms can not only be dismissed, but asserts that his species individuals are better evolutionary individuals than Darwin's organisms.

How important is the notion of species as individuals for Gould? Without that notion there is no macroevolution (of higher-level entities) and, if not, he has no entry to revising evolutionary theory in this respect. Punctuated equilibrium is not, here, under scrutiny, but it is used by Gould to argue for the view of higher individuals in nature. We will examine this use of punctuated equilibrium, below.

We must recall that Darwin, in *On The Origin*, destroyed the notion of an actual evolutionary entity called a species. We may also recall that while nominalists would clearly understand how the word species would henceforth function in the language (i.e., in a vague and non-metaphysical sense), naturalists might have some difficulty understanding the dissolution of a real entity such as species, for its ghost would surely hang around whatever linguistic collectivity of particulars that word might conjure up. That's the way with m-real entities. Darwin's readers were inclined to believe in the reality of taxonomic categories. Aristotle had shown the way with species and genera, and the great Linnaeus devised the system of classification we still use and that bears his name. As a taxonomic system addressed to our understanding of who is related to whom, it is laid out hierarchically. The hierarchy is on paper, not in nature! Darwin's respected confreres believed in the reality of taxonomic categories.

In my examination of Darwin's views on species, I

pointed to the bind Darwin was in when he reached his conclusion of the non-existence of entities called species. He would still have to refer to what all naturalists understood as species (i.e., those individuals that differed less one from another than each did from others) for the term and its alleged reference would not suddenly disappear from scientific discourse. (The notion of race is very much alive and in vogue among some philosophers and geneticists for the same reason. It's hard to kill a metaphysical entity.) The sorting and filing so prevalent in earlier taxonomic work is generated by the categorical thinking that is metaphysical realism. Darwin had to speak and write about species for every naturalist, he said, knew vaguely what was being talked and written about when the word was used. But Darwin did not believe that this taxonomic name referred to actual entities. Gould, with a little help from his friends and wielding the power of the magic that is metaphysics, intends to reverse this view. Species, *zap*, become actual entities, individuals. I say magic, for a metaphysical entity has suddenly been transformed into an actual one. That's called reification, a godly and mystical act of human creationism.

Gould, together with Ghiselin, Hull, and Eldredge, saw the need for revising Darwin's theory upward from the level of organisms, to include the notion of species as actual individuals. Gould was already close to Eldredge (via the theory of punctuated equilibrium which grew out of their examination of data from the Burgess Shale in Canada), and Eldredge was enamored of Ghiselin's notion of species as individuals as well as Dobzhansky's notion of hierarchy. Hull pushed the notion of species as individuals and also backed the notion of hierarchies in nature.

What was missing in all this, of course, was the empirical evidence. Evidence that hierarchies exist in nature, evidence that some collection of particular organisms in nature was one actual entity, and the empirical evidence that selection involves entities above those of organisms. One can say that some plurality is an entity, but one can say anything. One can draw taxonomic circles on the blackboard to represent ranks above organisms, and one can say genes are in cells, cells are in tissues, tissues are in organs, organs are in organisms, organisms are in species, etc., all the way up to kingdom come, but again one can do and say many things.

Among others, R.C. Lewontin aided Gould's cause by entertaining the notion of species selection, but species selection can only operate if there are entities called species. The selection of organisms individually as a result of their characters (anatomy and physiology) is intelligible. The selection of the species-itself, because of its characters, is ruled out as a step into the metaphysical. If Gould could clearly point to a supra-organism-entity, that can itself, independently of its organisms-as-parts, be involved in inheritance, variation, and interaction with selective processes, then evolutionary theory would thereby become more complex and more exciting. Evidence of the existence of such an entity would surely guarantee the expansion of theory. But, not all macro-evolutionary dreams can be realized.

Never did Gould and company worry about the hoary problem that generated philosophy in the beginning: the one-many problem. Never did they confront the philosophic problems of m-realism and nominalism and conceptualism. Never did they deal with the problems involving definition. Never did they examine the notions of identity and difference and similarity. Never was any worry shown about generating and using metaphysical entities as structural elements in scientific theory. In fact, Gould would have us repeat "essence, essence, essence" until we are unafraid of its use in theories, as if all the biologists who had discarded essences were simply unthinking fools. Perhaps we should all repeat "species are individuals" three times and rid ourselves of our disbelief. Still, neither magic nor indoctrination nor metaphysical mind games is what science is all about. Gould's proposed expansion, if not empirically defensible, can do harm to a theory too important to be abused. Gould certainly means no harm. Without question, he loves science, almost as much as baseball. His goal to erect an awesome superstructure, of interacting levels (of nested wholes with parts), on the founding structure that is Darwinism seems architecturally scholastic and medieval.

To attack Darwin's shortcomings, Gould (2002) tells us where he is coming from. Professionally he is a paleontologist and student of macroevolution. He says, "I intend only the purely descriptive definition when I write 'macroevolution'—that is, a designation of evolutionary phenomenology from the origin of species on up, in contrast with evolutionary change within populations of a single species" (p.38).

Gould deals with fossils. He examines things he can perceive with his own senses: fossil imprints, shells of organisms and their parts. What he cannot see in shale or bore-hole samples is a species or its origin. He can see fossil organisms which differ little or not at all from one another, he can see fossil organisms which differ greatly from others.

He cannot see similarities or identities of organisms or their parts. He can estimate geological time by the layers of sediment or rock. He can recognize local trends and patterns of change or stasis in organisms, but not in species. The species attachments to the organisms (their so-called identity, similarity, or commonality with respect to morphology) merely come along for the ride, for they are *read* into the otherwise actual scenario of fossil remains.

When he describes work in macroevolution as the "phenomenology of evolution from the origin of species on up," Gould already has one foot (the up-foot) in metaphysics as a professional given. Strange. Metaphysical entities don't have causal interactions with actual things. That's why Ghiselin, Hull, and Eldredge gave up on species as classes and declared that species are individuals. Although 'phenomenology' in all the philosophical senses I am aware of is about metaphysics, it is unimportant to label Gould a member (or part) of one or another of the many philosophical schools of phenomenology, but we are unlikely to overlook the fact that Gould is a man of words. He would not have used the phrase "phenomenology of evolution" without due, and fearless, consideration. It is clear that Gould relishes mixing science and metaphysics and, in fact, admits as much. He characterized Darwinian gradualism as follows (Gould and Eldredge, 1977), "The General preference that so many of us hold for gradualism is a *metaphysical* [my emphasis] stance embedded in the modern history of Western cultures: it is not a high-order empirical observation, induced from the objective study of nature..." (p. 1017). Knowing that his own theory of punctuated equilibrium would be open to that criticism, he says:

We emphatically do not assert the "truth" of this alternate *metaphysic* [my emphasis] of punctuational change...Nonetheless, we do believe that the punctuational *metaphysic* [my emphasis] may prove to map tempos of change in our world better and more often than any of its competitors—if only because systems in steady state are not only common but also so highly resistant to change. (Ibid, p. 1018 - 19)

Again, I am not passing judgment on the theory of punctuated equilibrium. Rather, I am critiquing Gould's use of it and the incorporation of metaphysics in his structuring of evolutionary theory. Gould's intent is to expand Darwin's unilevel theory of organismal selection into a hierarchical model of selection acting simultaneously on several legitimate levels of Darwinian individuality (genes, cell-lineages, organisms, Demes, species, and clades). (Ibid, p. 21) Or, as he also puts it:

...theoretical development and accumulating data on punctuated equilibrium allowed us to reconceptualize species as genuine Darwinian individuals, fully competent to participate in processes of selection at their own supraorganismic (and suprademal) level—and then to rethink macroevolution as the differential success of species rather than the extended anagenesis of organismal adaptation...This validation of the species-individual aided the transformation of what had begun as a particular argument about group (or interdemic) selection into a fully generalized hierarchical theory, with good cases then documented from the genic to the cladal level. (Ibid, p.26)

Respecting the first quote, we would like to know how genes, cell-lineages, demes, species, and clades became levels of Darwinian individuality. The answer is that he declares them to be so. His defense of them centers on the two kinds of criteria we mentioned above.

Respecting the second quote, we must understand how the data on punctuated equilibrium allows him to reconceptualize species as genuine Darwinian individuals. And, we must examine the claim that selection can occur at levels above organisms (e.g., demes, species and clades). The secret is the notion of *agency*.

Making individuals of pluralities of organisms from lower to higher levels transcends the Darwinian notion of evolution and selection, and it transcends the empirical world of living things perceived by the senses. When we are looking at organisms, we are looking at the obvious. Organisms. When we are looking at so-called species, we are looking at organisms. When we are looking at a deme, we are looking at, yes, organisms. When we are looking at clades, what are we looking at? Organisms. Gould's metaphysical individualizations are acts of mental hubris. He calls it phenomenology. Husserl called it intuition. It requires the suspension of our natural attitude. It allows us to describe the formal (i.e., metaphysical) structures of phenomena. It allows Gould to talk nonsense. Gould sees himself pitted against Darwin:

356

...either Darwin is right and effectively all natural selection occurs at the organismic level (despite the logical conceivability of other levels), or the hierarchical theory is right and several levels make interestingly different and vitally important simultaneous contributions to the overall pattern of evolution....Thus, for Darwin's near exclusivity of organismic selection, we now propose a hierarchical theory with selection acting simultaneously on a rising set of levels, each characterized by distinctive, but equally well-defined, Darwinian individuals within a genealogical hierarchy of gene, cell-lineage, organism, deme, species, and clade. The results of evolution then emerge from complex, but eminently knowable interactions among these potent levels, and do not simply flow out and up from a unique causal locus of organismal selection. (Ibid, pp. 31-32)

Clearly, we need to look closely at the superstructure Gould is erecting. We need evidence that nature has hierarchies, and that selection can and does occur in levels above organisms. Genes and other within-cell entities are not in dispute. The truth is, Gould admits that if there are no individual-entities higher than organisms, then there can be no hierarchical agents causally interacting in selection processes. Hierarchies wilt with the evaporation of his reified individuals.

Still, we must take a close look at those well-defined Darwinian individuals. Even if we should grant that they are well-defined (which we won't), would that make them actual? Gould, of course, wants us to believe that those individuals above organisms (e.g., demes, species, clades) are substantial; like Darwin's organisms. We have already met with this attempt at entification of metaphysical entities in the "chunk of genealogical nexus" analogy of Ghiselin, Hull, and Eldredge.

Gould, we must remember, is making his case before evolutionists as a paleontologist. What species look like in the world of the contemporary biologist, where most of the controversy surrounding the species problem has occurred, may not be what they look like to Gould. In fact, he says of the species-problem, "This supposed problem—more philosophical and definitional than empirical (once one accepts the underlying assumptions about anagenesis as a dominant factual reality)—arises because a true continuum cannot be unambiguously divided into segments with discrete names" (Ibid, p. 775).

He gives an illustration. If a population changes extensively by "anagenesis" so that a population down the line of changes requires a new name, where should the breakpoint between the two populations be placed? Any boundary must be arbitrary, he says, and the problem unresolvable given the assumptions about anagenesis.

> Punctuated equilibrium took a radically different approach by...denying the focal empirical premise that new species usually (or even often) arise by gradualistic anagenesis. Instead, Eldredge and I argued that the vast majority of species originate by splitting, and that the standard tempo of speciation, when expressed in geological time, features origin in

a geological moment followed by a long persistence in stasis. Thus, the classic and endlessly-fretted "species problem in paleontology" disappears because species act as well-defined Darwinian individuals, not as arbitrary subdivisions of a continuum. Species then gain definability because they almost always arise by speciation (that, is by splitting, or geographic isolation of a daughter population followed by genetic differentiation from the parental population), not by anagenesis (or transformation of the entire mass of an ancestral species). (Ibid, p. 776)

In those words, we are directed to the ultimate solution of that "endlessly fretted species problem in paleontology." The solution appears to be that species are not "arbitrary subdivisions of a continuum." That is, they act as do organisms and in Darwinian fashion (i.e. they are involved in inheritance, variation, and interaction. We will look more closely at his solution, for it is important to Gould's argument and to my critique of it.

First, that the "supposed problem" of "species" in paleontology is "more philosophical and definitional than empirical." He calms our nerves: there really is no problem. None, that is, if we understand whence a problem arises: given gradualistic anagenesis in the formation of species rather than splitting, a continuum of organisms is formed which we then cut to form boundaries which are used in defining earlier (parental) and later (daughter) species. The whole process is arbitrary. It is what we might see if we are looking at a roll of geological film of ancestral and descendant species. Separating one species from another in geological time may well be a problem, but that is not the traditional species problem, and that problem resides on the geological film when any two organisms are compared. Paleontologists may have a species problem of their own, but they also have the traditional problem which cannot be resolved by Gould's metaphysical optics: "the classic and endlessly-fretted "species-problem in paleontology" disappears," he says, "because species act as well-defined Darwinian individuals, not as arbitrary subdivisions of a continuum." How can Gould see that some plurality (presumably a totality) of organisms in geological time acts as does one Darwinian organism? And, how is it that he can see, or even infer, that his one Darwinian-like organism (i.e., a species-individual) arose by splitting or geographic isolation of a daughter population? Is that daughter population a half-a-one, a-100th-of a one? Is the species individual by the births and deaths of its parts never one? To end my endless fretting over all this, isn't it the case that examining organisms in deposits over geological time not only cannot solve the traditional species problem (for it is not just philosophical or definitional, but an ontological problem rooted in the categorical attitude toward things), but it also places that problem in a temporal framework which further clouds our ability to deal with it? Far from solving the species problem for paleontology, I would say that paleontology doesn't have a species problem of its own. It cannot distinguish species because there are no species to distinguish, only organisms, their parts, and prints and such. There was never a moment, geological or otherwise, in which a species originated, nor was there ever a speciation of a

360

species. Organisms speciate in the sense of differing from other (prior) organisms which they are related to, and this differentiation may well be promoted by geographic isolation of some from their nearest relatives. Darwin was aware of this process, and it did not result in a continuous amorphous mass in which organisms could not be distinguished one from another. All the metaphysics used by Gould and friends is simply unnecessary. Nature does not take the path of metaphysics to differentiate organism from one another or to get from point A in geological time to a later point B. Darwin may have given the impression that the lives of organisms present us, over time, with a continuum of change which sum to what are called species, but recall that he is the one who said that a species can never be defined. Why? Well, recall that he also said that there are no species entities. Desiring a species he can place in a hierarchical nest and which can speciate, Gould has accepted the Ghiselin proposal of a species individual. Reification is not a good way to expand Darwinian evolution.

To complete our critique of Gould's proposal, some comments are required regarding his dependence on punctuated equilibrium to support his argument for expanding Darwinian theory.

> I have linked my treatments of punctuated equilibrium and the hierarchical theory of natural selection to form the longest section of this book...because I believe that punctuated equilibrium supplies the central argument for viewing species as effective Darwinian individuals at a relative frequency high enough to be regarded as general—

thereby validating the level of species as a domain of evolutionary causality, and establishing the effectiveness and independence of macro-evolution by two of the three criteria featured throughout this book as indispensable foundations of Darwinism. (Ibid, p. 781)

He continues:

First, punctuated equilibrium secures the hierarchical expansion of selection theory to the level of species, thus moving beyond Darwin's preference for restricting causality effectively to the organismic realm alone... Second, by defining species as the basic units or atoms of macroevolution—as stable "things" (Darwinian individuals) rather than as arbitrary segments of continua—punctuated equilibrium precludes the explanation of all evolutionary patterns by extrapolation from mechanisms operating on local populations, at human timescales, and at organismic and lower levels... (Ibid, p. 781)

He concludes:

In other words, PUNCTUATED EQUILIBRIUM MAKES ITS MAJOR CONTRIBUTION TO EVOLUTIONARY THEORY, NOT BY REVISING MICROEVOLUTIONARY MECHANICS BUT BY INDIVIDUATING SPECIES (AND THEREBY ESTABLISHING THE BASIS FOR AN

INDEPENDENT THEORETICAL DOMAIN OF
MACROEVOLUTION). [Gould's emphasis] (Ibid, pp.
781-82)

And there we have it. We must focus on those factors
in Gould's argument which are crucial for him to conclude
that he has established "an independent theoretical domain
of macroevolution." There is in fact only one crucial factor:
the "individuating of species." If this factor is not available,
there can be no "independent theoretical domain," for
without it, there is no hierarchy and thus no higher level for
selection to operate causally. Let us see where and how
things went awry.

First, punctuated equilibrium must secure the
hierarchical expansion of selectionist theory to the level of
species. Nothing observable in the Burgess Shale can create a
hierarchical level above the organisms found in the
geological materials. To get a higher level, he (and all of us)
must view the organisms in the shale as parts of a whole
called a species-individual. Gould knows that all of us won't
(and can't) see his species-individual, so he takes the route of
definition. He defines species as the basic units or atoms of
macroevolution and as stable things (Darwinian individuals).
Well, that is certainly one way to get things on earth up there
in the metaphysical! Gould has solved his species problem
and extended evolutionary theory by defining species so
they can behave as organisms do and also ascend into
hierarchical macro-metaphysical baskets.

It is reasonable to conclude that Gould's theory of
punctuated equilibrium cannot secure the hierarchical
expansion of selectionist theory to the level of species.

Selectionist theory may indeed be expanded, but it must be done by empirical means, not by definition and not by metaphysics.

We will conclude with the following remarks; 1. Gould has not established the actuality of the fundamental stepping stone for his hierarchical theory of selection: "a species-individual."

2. He seems to be aware of metaphysical realism and its entangling embrace of particulars (i.e., organisms), but he doesn't seem to care. Thus, he involves us in ambiguity: when he speaks of "higher level entities," but we ignore metaphysical wrappings and interpret his remark as some number of organisms. While he sees in fossil-bearing rock species-individuals involved in inheritance, variability, and interactions, we see organisms involved in those Darwinian processes. In other words, Gould's observations on the macro-level are thoroughly laden with metaphysics.

3. Lewontin's views on species selection do not escape the ambiguity mentioned in 2, above. Specifically, it is not valid to speak of organisms in a metaphysical wrapper and treat each such collection as a species individual.

A Brief Summing Up

We have answered the question which is the root of the problems we have identified as: universals, species, concepts, definition. And what is that question? What are the natures of the particulars of our actual universe? We have come round to it in taking a closer look at Darwin's discussion of species. It is clear: there is no species-entity, mutable or immutable; all organisms differ, each is a variant, other and different from every other, modified in its descent and, if viewed over *time* (i.e., over the changes), the descents of organisms are lineages, discontinuous stages of relatedness and difference. The only handle taxonomic classification can grasp with regard to those genealogical productions is greater or lesser differences. Alleged similarities denote only lesser comparative differences, and cannot be used as principles of classification; nor can they make pluralities of organisms one or a kind. Underlying the assertion of similarity (i.e., lesser differences) may be a valuable homology (i.e., sameness) signifying relationship, but both expressions are metaphysical and have no actual reference. Suggesting relationship is a first step in determining if it is causal.

In other words, Darwin helped us to expose the actual natures of particulars, the fundamental issue which requires resolution before the problems of categorization, of universals, species, concepts, and definition can be solved.

We have shown how the natures of particulars bear not only on the problems of universals, species, concepts, and definition, but also on the general question of categorical thinking and its relation to logic, and its validity, in the scientific enterprise called rationalism. Rationalism uses the paraphernalia of realism in establishing scientific laws. Since metaphysical realism is false doctrine, the scientific framework that is rationalism is seriously put in question.

ENDNOTES

1 Richard Robinson, Definition. There are no complete works on definition. Richard Robinson's book is an exception. He asks: To what sort of entity does definition apply? Do we define things, or words, or concepts? In other words, are we realists, or nominalists, or conceptualists, about definition?" (p. 7) Robinson points out that for Socrates, Plato, and Aristotle (for the most part) "it was always RES or things that required definition, never nominal or words or concepts." (pp. 7-8). For Plato, the forms are the most "real" things there are, and to search for their definitions was the end of the process of knowing. For Aristotle, "definition" is giving "the account of the essence of the thing." Again, an "essence" is held to be the most "real" (i.e., unchanging) thing. For Kant, the "concept" is the thing that is defined, for to define is "to present the complete concept of a thing within its limits and in its primary character." What is never asked by Realists, Nominalists, or Conceptualists is the question of the legitimacy of pursing "definition." That is, can we ever obtain a "definition?" Aristotle was sure we could. He insisted that an individual, a particular thing, could. He insists that an individual, a particular thing, can NOT be defined (Metaph., Z 14 1040 a), only its essence. He made these remarks on definition: "A 'definition' is a phrase signifying a thing's essence." (Topics, I, 5,101b 38-39). "We conclude then that definition is (a) an indemonstrable statement of essential nature or (b) a syllogism of essential nature differing from demonstration in grammatical form, or (c) the conclusion of a demonstration giving essential nature." (An. Post. l, II 10,94a 11-14). As to "essential nature" Aristotle says, "What, then, you are by your very nature is your essence." (Metaph., Z 4 1029b 15) The essence makes us the kind of thing we are. For, nothing "Nothing…which is not a species of a genus will have an essence…" (Metaph., Z 4 1030a 11-12). And "only substance is definable." (Metaph., Z 4 1031a 1). And, "definition is of the universal and of the form." (Metaphy., Z11 1036a 29). He emphasizes, "clearly there can neither be definition nor demonstration about sensible individuals." (Metaph., Z 15 1040 a 1-2). Commenting on Aristotle, Copleston says: "Essential definitions are strict definitions by genus and difference, and Aristotle considered definition as involving a process of division down to the infama species. But it is important to remember that Aristotle, aware that we are by no means always able to attain an essential or real definition allows for nominal or descriptive definitions, even though he had no high opinion of them, regarding as he did essential definitions as the only type of definition really worthy of the name." (Hist., Vol. I, Pt. II, p.23). For Aristotle's remarks on definition by division, see Metaphy., Z 12). In contrast to "real definitions," which set us in pursuit of "real" entities, nominal definitions set us in pursuit of "meanings." "Meanings," if not simply sayings, are also incorrectly interpreted as "real" entities. Word-meanings which are claimed to be "the same" establish a definition. Synonymy therefore, is a crucial notion for Realists. Quine wrestled with this notion in his "Two Dogmas of Empiricism," in From a Logical Point of View. He says: "Just what it means to affirm synonymy, just what the interconnections may be which are necessary and sufficient in order that two linguistic forms be properly describable as synonymous, is far from clear, but, whatever these interconnections may be, ordinarily they are grounded in usage." (pp. 24-25). Looking for the "synonymy" of two words or of a definiens and definiendum is rather like looking for the "identity" of two things or, for that matter, the "resemblance" of two or more things. Neither sight nor usage is of much help here unless they put us in touch with an actual "synonymy" entity, an "identity" entity, or a "resemblance" entity connecting two or more things, including so-called "synonymous" words and phrases. It will be argued in this work that no such entity is ever seen.

2 A rather full overview of the problem of universals is A.D. Woozley's "Universals" in the Encyclopedia of Philosophy, 1972, Vol. 8, pp. 194-206, ed. Paul Edwards. Other worthwhile accounts are Fredrick Copleston's A History of Philosophy, Vols. I & II, M.H. Carre's Realists and Nominalists, R.I. Aaron's The Theory of Universals, H.H. Price's Thinking and Experience, The problem of Universals (ed. Charles Landesman). D.M Armstrong defends "universals." The notion of "universals can be traced to Plato's eide and Aristotle's ta katholou, that which is predicated of many. Woozley says, "Plato believed the existence of universals was required not only ontologically, to explain the nature of the world which as sentient and reflective beings we experience, but also epistemologically, to explain the nature of our experience of it...(and)...ever since, except for intervals of neglect, philosophers have been worrying about the nature and status of universals. No account has yet been propounded which has come near to receiving universal acceptance... ("Universals," p.194)." Woozley continues, "That in some sense or other there are universals, and that in some sense or other they are abstract objects, that is, objects of thought rather than of sense perception no philosopher would dispute." Aristotle says otherwise, as I will show. It is the claim that "abstract objects" called "universals" somehow exist, actually or metaphysically, that is Realism, a doctrine that I will dispute by pointing up the characters each and every actual particular thing and pluralities of them.

3 In the medieval period, Plato's theory of universalia ante rem (universals independent of particulars) and Aristotle's theory of universalia in rebus (universals in things) were discussed and two other views, nominalism and conceptualism, entered the debates. Roscelin was perhaps the first nominalist, claiming that universal names (i.e., common nouns) are nothing but breath of the voice (flatus vocis). His works have not survived, perhaps because he not only attacked the dominant realism of the day (the in re, or rebus, doctrine that general and species exist in things)., but also pushed his belief that all things are individual (i.e., are particulars). This belief leads, theologically, to tritheism: if only particulars exist, and if the persons of the trinity are particulars, they cannot be "one." The result is heresy. Roscelin was so charged. His doctrine of nominalism was advanced by others, including Hobbes and a long line of empiricist thinkers. Woozley is correct that "conceptualism should not be regarded strictly as a rival theory to realism [because if we start from an extreme Aristotelian position that everything which exists is particular, conceptualism concentrates on the fact that generality is an essential feature of both experience and language, and it seeks to answer the question n how mental concepts are formed, how they can be general if the data of experience from which they are formed are particular, ad how words are general in their significance (Woozley, Universals," p. 199). I will critique the notion that there are mental entities called "concepts" as well as claims regarding their formation. Nominalists would have us believe that there are no "abstractor "real" entities inside the head or outside it. However, they have the problem of explaining how general words apply to particulars. And, they inconsistently regard common nouns as "universals," but don't know how it is that they are. A contemporary view of "universals" was introduced by Hume, taken up by Wittgenstein in his theory of "family resemblance," advanced by his followers, and used by researchers in cognitive psychology (e.g., Rosch) and neurobiology (e.g., Edelman).

4 "Nothing" and "Nothingness" are much abused terms. The first abuse was Parmenides' claim that nothing cannot be thought. Of course he could not help mentioning and thinking about it, if only to deny its existence and then imaginatively fill it up with "Being." The Pythagoreans, along with the Atomists, held to a notion of empty space or void. To deny the void, as Aristotle did (in favor of a continuum of thingness however fine) is not to rid us of nothingness. Nothingness, for existentialists, was something to dread and therefore caused anxiety, a psychological reflection on the individual's ultimate non-existence. We do not possess the magical power to turn nothingness into something by reifying it into being. Heidegger did, adding that nothing is not a passive noun. It turns into an active verb by nothing. Attempts to reify nothingness must fail. On the other hand, attempts to use it as a material for ex nihilo creation must also fail. The step from imagination to reification is the step in creating a (metaphysical) "reality." This is exhibited in founding religion in a supernatural. Nothingness or Being are simply not very good candidates for theological musings. Zeller says of Parmenides' thinking: "The only perception which is true is that which shows us in everything an unchanging Being, namely Reason; the senses, on the other hand, which present to us a manifold of things, creation, destruction and change, that is a being of Not-Being, are the cause of all error." He concludes, "this extreme monist [Parmenides]…with his untenable rejection of the world of sense in favor of an abstract being only apprehended by thought, paved the way for the metaphysical dualism which found its most complete expression in the Platonic theory of ideas." (Outlines of the History of Greek Philosophy, p. 67) Parmenides holds an honored position in the history of philosophy, and not only because he persuaded philosophers to disbelieve their senses. His notion of Being has a long list of admirers besides Heidegger. (See also Anscombe's, From Parmenides to Wittgenstein.

BIBLIOGRAPHY

Aaron, R. I. (1952). *The theory of universals*. London: Oxford University Press.

Aristotle. (1941). *The basic works of Aristotle* (Ed. with an introduction by Richard McKeon). New York: Random House

Armstrong, D.M. (1978). *A theory of universals*. London: Cambridge University Press.

Atran, Scott. (1990). *Cognitive foundations of natural history*. Cambridge: Cambridge   University Press.

Bambrough, Renford. (1961). Universals and family resemblances. *Proceedings of the Aristotelian Society*, 61, pp.207-222.

Barnes, Jonathan. (1987). *Early Greek philosophy*. London: Penguin Books.

Berkeley, George. (1975). *Philosophical works* (Ed. with an introduction and notes by M.R. Ayers). London: Dent.

Berlin, Brent. (1978). Ethnobiological classification. In Rosch and Lloyd (Eds.), *Cognition and categorization*. Mahwah, NJ: Lawrence Erlbaum. Pp. 9-26.

Bury, R. G. (1933). *Sextus empiricus*. (Vol. 1, Outlines of Pyrrhonism, trans. R. G. Bury). New York: Harvard University Press. p. 137.

Cannon, Walter. (1972). John Herschel (Ed. by Paul

Edwards). *The Encyclopedia of Philosophy*, 3, pp.490-91.

Carre, M.H. (1946). *Realists and nominalists*. London: Oxford University Press.

Copelston, F. (1963). *A history of philosophy*. Garden City: Doubleday & Co., Inc.

Cornford, F.M. (1952). *Principium sapientiae: The origins of Greek philosophical thought*.   London: Cambridge.

Dantzig, Tobias. (1959). *Number the language of science*. New York: Charles Scribner's Sons.

Darwin, Charles. (1964). *On the origin of species* (facsimile of first edition). Ernst Mayr (Ed.). Cambridge: Harvard University Press.

De Beer, Gavin. (1964). *Charles Darwin*. Garden City: Doubleday & Co., Inc.

DeBlieu, Jan. (1992, June 14). Could the red wolf be a mutt? *New York Times Magazine*.

Descartes, René. (1927). *Descartes selections* (Ed. by Ralph M. Eaton). New York: Charles Scribner's Sons.

Dumanski, J.P. and C. Bruder. (2008). Genetic differences seen in identical twins. *American Journal of Human Genetics*, Feb, p. 26

Dupree, Hunter. (1968). *Asa Gray*. New York: Athenaeum.

Edelman, Gerald M. (1987). *Neural Darwinism*. New York: Basic Books, Inc.

Edwards, Paul (Ed.). (1972). *The encyclopedia of philosophy*. New York: Collier MacMillan Publishers.

Eldredge, N. (1985). *Unfinished synthesis: Biological hierarchies and modern evolutionary thought*. New York: Oxford University Press.

Ellegard, Alvar. (1957). The Darwinian theory and nineteenth century philosophies of science. *Journal of the History of Ideas*, 18, pp. 362-393.

Ghiselin, M. (1974). A radical solution to the species problem. *Systematic Biology*, 23, #4, pp. 536-44.

Ghiselin, M. (1981). Categories, life, and thinking. *The Behavioral and Brain Sciences*, 4, issue 2, pp. 269-283.

Goodman, Nelson. (1951). *The structure of appearance*. New York: The Bobbs-Merrill Co., Inc.

Goodman, Nelson. (1972). Seven strictures on similarity. *Problems and Projects*, pp. 22-32. New York: Bobbs-Merrill Co., Inc.

Goodman, Nelson. (1984). *Mind and Other Matters*. Cambridge: Harvard University Press.

Gould, Stephen Jay. (2002). *The structure of evolutionary theory*. Cambridge and London: The Belknap Press of Harvard University Press.

Hall, B.K. (Ed.). (1994). *The hierarchical basis off comparative biology*. San Diego: Academic Press.

Heidegger, Martin. (1975). *Early Greek thinking*. In Krell & Capuzzi (Trans.). New York: Harper & Row

Publishers.

Hobbes, Thomas. (1964). *Leviathan* (abridged and with an introduction by Francis B. Randall (Ed.). New York: Washington Square Press.

Hull, David. (1976). Are species really individuals? *Systematic Zoology*, 25, pp. 174-191.

Hull, David. (1988). *Science as process*. Chicago: The Chicago University Press.

Hume, David. (1969). *A treatise of human nature* (ed. by Ernest Mossner). Penguin Books.

Hume, David. (1962). *On human nature and understanding* (ed. with a new introduction by Anthony Flew). London: Collier-MacMillan Publishers.

Kant, Immanuel. (1881). *Critique of pure reason*. F. Max Muller (Trans.). London: MacMillan and Co.

Kant, Immanuel. (1974). *Logic* (ed. with introduction by R.S. Hartman and trans. W. Schwartz). New York: Dover Publications.

Kuhn, Thomas. (1997). Second thoughts on paradigms. In Frederick Suppe (Ed.), *The structure of scientific theories*. Urbana: University of Illinois Press.

Lakoff, George. (1987). *Women, fire, and dangerous things: What categories reveal about the mind*. Chicago: The University of Chicago Press.

Landesman, Charles (Ed.). (1971). *The problem of universals*. New York: Basic Books.

Leibniz, G.W. (1982). *New essays on human understanding.* P. Remnant and J. Bennett (Trans. and Ed.). London: Cambridge University Press.

Lewis, C.I. (1987). A pragmatic conception of the a priori. In Moser (ed.), *A priori knowledge.* London: Oxford University Press.

Lewis, David. (1991). *Parts of classes.* Cambridge: Basil Blackwell, Inc.

Lindley, David. (1993). *The end of physics.* New York: Basic Books, Inc.

Locke, John. (1974). *An essay concerning human understanding* (ed. with an introduction by A.D. Woozley). New York: Meridian.

Loux, Michael J., Ed. (1970). *Universals and particulars: Readings in ontology.* New York: Doubleday.

Loux, Michael J. (1974). *Ockham's theory of terms: Pt. I of the Summa Logicae.* Indiana: Notre Dame University Press.

Margolis, Joseph. (1978). Problems of Similarity. *The Monist, LXI.* Oxford: Oxford University Press.

Margolis, Joseph. (1982). Berkeley and others on the problem of universals. In Colin M. Turbane (Ed.), *Berkeley: Critical and Interpretative Essays.* Minneapolis, MN: University of Minnesota Press.

Mayr, Ernst. (1982). *The growth of biological thought: Diversity, evolution, inheritance.* Cambridge: Belknap Harvard

University Press.

McKeon, Richard. (1929). *Selections from medieval philosophers, vol. 1.* New York: Charles Scribner's Sons.

McKeon, Richard. (1930). *Selections from medieval philosophers, vol.2.* New York: Charles Scribner's Sons.

McKeon, Richard. (1941). *The basic works of Aristotle.* New York: Random House.

Montague, Ashley. (1964). *The concept of race.* New York: The Free Press.

Moser, Paul K. (Ed.). (1987). *A priori knowledge.* Oxford: Oxford University Press.

Nelson, Gareth and Norman Platnick. (1981). *Systematics and biogeoraphy: Cladistics and vicariance.* New York: Columbia University Press.

Nelson, Gareth. (1994). Homology and Systematics. In Hall, B.K. (Ed.), *The hierarchical basis of comparative biology.* San Diego: Academic Press.

Newell, R. (1986). *Objectivity, empiricism, and truth.* London: Routledge & Kegan Paul.

Pinker, Steven. (2007). *The stuff of thought.* New York: Viking, The Penguin Group

Plato. (1964). *The collected dialogues of Plato.* Hamilton and Cairns, (Eds.). New York: Bollinger Foundation and Pantheon Books.

Price, H.H. (1953). *Thinking and experience.* London.

Quine, W.V.O. (1953). Two dogmas of empiricism. *From a logical point of view*. New York: Harper & Rowe.

Quine, W.V.O. (1973). *Roots of reference*. Illinois: Open Court.

Quine. (1969). *Ontological relativity and other essays*. New York: Columbia University Press.

Randall, J.H., Jr. (1965). *The career of philosophy*. New York: Columbia University Press.

Ratner, Joseph. (1927). *The philosophy of Baruch Spinoza, selected from his chief works*. New York: Random House.

Ritvo, Harriet. (1997). *The platypus and the mermaid and other figments of the classifying imagination*. Cambridge: Harvard University Press.

Robinson, Richard. (1965). *Definition*. Oxford: Clarendon Press.

Rosch, Eleanor and B.B. Lloyd (Eds.). (1978). *Cognition and categorization*. Hillsdale, New Jersey: Lawrence Erlbaum Associates.

Smith, E.E. and D.L. Medin. (1981). *Concepts and categories*. Cambridge: Harvard University Press.

Smollen, Lee. (2006). *The trouble with physics*. New York: Houghton Mifflin.

Suppe, Frederick. (1997). *The structure of scientific theories*. Urbana: University of Illinois Press.

Thorpe, J.W. (1973). Whether the theory of family resemblances solves the problem of universals, *Mind*, pp. 567-70. Urbana: University of Illinois Press.

Tournay, Stephen. (1938). *Ockham: Studies and selections*. La Salle, Illinois: Open Court.

Tversky, Amos and I. Gati. (1978). Studies of Similarity. In Rosch and Lloyd, *Cognition and categorization* (pp. 79-98). Hillsdale, New Jersey: Lawrence Erlbaum Associates.

Weinberg, Steven. (1992). *Dreams of a final theory*. New York: Pantheon Books.

Windelband, W. (1956). *History of ancient philosophy*. New York: Dover Publications.

Wittgenstein, Ludwig. (1953). *Philosophical investigations*. New York: MacMillan.

Wittgenstein, Ludwig. (1965). *The blue and brown*. New York: Harper and Row.

Woozley, A.D. (1949). *Theory of knowledge*. London: Hutchinson's University Library.

Woozley, A.D. (1972). Universals. In Paul Edwards (Ed.), *The encyclopedia of philosophy*, vol. 8, pp. 194-206. New York: Macmillan/Collier.

Zeller, Eduard. (1955). *Outlines of the history of Greek philosophy*. New York: Meridian Books, Inc.

www.ingramcontent.com/pod-product-compliance
Lightning Source LLC
LaVergne TN
LVHW051540080426
835510LV00020B/2790